CW01572460

One Less Detective

**Red tape, blue lights,
and the trials of a
trainee police officer**

Olivia Gray

Please be aware that this memoir discusses suicide, sexual assault and other violence. Useful websites and places to get help can be found at the back of the book.

I dedicate this book to everyone who has, so far, been unable to tell their story. And to those who have had their story ignored, denied, or disrespected. I hear you.

Contents

Prologue

WE DESCEND THE STEEP slope into the hospital's underground car park; and pull into a bay reserved for emergency services.

As Stephen radios in our arrival, I listen carefully to his expert comms. I'm desperate to be able speak over the airwaves so confidently, with such ease.

I'm struggling so much with this important part of the job, especially when I'm on my own, which after just a few short weeks as a police constable, is most shifts.

Not today. Today I get to work with a colleague. And I'm so relieved.

How else can you learn crucial parts of such a risk-filled, and heavily scrutinised job? A job where getting it wrong can have devastating consequences.

As we wait for directions, I fidget in the passenger seat of our police car, dying to get out and stretch my legs. I don't do sitting down well, and we've been in the car for over an hour.

I like Stephen. I didn't at first. I thought he was difficult, and critical.

I realise now that he's an unintentionally awkward character, who is often misunderstood. Just like I felt, at police training school, just a few months ago.

Not fitting into such a dysfunctional environment, not always getting our words right, despite coming from a place of kindness, wanting to support others, do the right thing, and encourage others to do the same.

I realise we haven't worked together yet, as partners. Until this shift.

We're about to spend hours together, in a confined space, with a badly injured prisoner, as well as prison officers, doctors, nurses, and anyone else who may join us in a hospital room.

And we will have to ensure that they are all who they say they are.

Today, our job is to keep the prisoner alive, keep hospital staff safe, and ensure an effective investigation is possible.

Because someone tried to kill him today, inside The Oaks Prison.

And someone else may try to finish the job.

This is a hospital guard like no other that I do, during my six months as a police constable.

***

As Stephen and I walk into the hospital, people stop and stare. I'm used to this now. It used to be me when I saw uniformed police officers.

We find the room, and one of our colleagues opens the door to Stephen's knock.

We step into the crowded space, quickly assessing who is who, threats and risks.

There are too many people in here and I quickly feel suffocated.

In front, and to our right, there are three prison officers, and four police constables. To our left, the prisoner is lying on a hospital bed, propped up by pillows. He's handcuffed to the metal bed frame on his left and handcuffed to another prison officer on his right.

His head is tightly wrapped in white bandages, more to one side than the other, forcing one of his eyes and cheeks to be pushed down, his face is puffy. He doesn't have any other visible injuries that I can see.

Stephen and another police constable step out into the corridor, to do a handover briefing. It already feels a lot less claustrophobic. The rest of us do introductions.

I introduce myself to the prisoner, who for now is a patient: "Hi, I'm Olivia."

"Hi, I'm Harris," he replies with a smile.

My colleagues are desperate to get out of there, their shift ended half an hour ago, and rush hour has started. They've got to get out of the busy city, and back to Northcliffe in Oakshire, where we're based.

Handover briefing complete, our four colleagues leave. Shortly after, there's a changeover of prison officers too. We're now down to two of them, and two of us. Plus, Harris. The room feels the right size for this many people.

I feel the initial awkwardness subside and breathe a sigh of relief; we all have some personal space. Except for Harris, and the prison officer he's handcuffed to.

Everyone keeps offering me a seat, but I don't want to sit down. We're going to be here for ages, and that's before the long drive back, so I'll take any opportunity to be upright, and able to move. Not that I'm not grateful for the show of chivalry, something I encounter surprisingly often, during these challenging few months as a police constable.

I take the opportunity to chat to Harris, taking the couple of steps to his bedside.

"How are you feeling?"

"Yeah, not bad, considering."

Holding a hand up, and circling it around my own head I say: "I appreciate you've got all this going on, but are you comfortable?"

"Yeah," he replies. Adding, "thanks."

I feel a connection. I like him. I know he's done some seriously bad things in his life, but right now, this man is humble and polite. He's also interesting to talk with, as we build the conversation from the small talk that I find so uncomfortable and insignificant, into something deeper.

I believe people can change, if they can open up, learn, heal, and be heard; especially if they can change their circumstances. I'm also really interested to hear more about what has happened today. But I'm worryingly naïve about what kind of chat is allowed, in this kind of situation – what could constitute a victim interview. I wouldn't want to impact the investigation.

He seems a bit confused. I'm curious if it is the painkillers, or the disruption of all the people he's been sharing this room with. However hard this man is, it must be overwhelming.

But then he asks: "Why you being so nice to me? I'm not used to cops being nice to me."

My heart goes out to him.

"You're our responsibility and you're a victim right now, Harris," I reply.

He smiles a genuine smile and relaxes. As I smile back, I notice he has beautiful skin; and wonder what mess is under those bandages. Doctors and nurses come and go; and eventually the doctors responsible for deciding what surgery Harris will need arrive. They slowly unwrap the bandages, unwinding round, and round, until the wound is revealed.

I'm standing at the end of the bed, ensuring the safety of the doctors, should Harris react violently; recording the interaction with my body-worn camera. I doubt he will.

But then I see the gaping slice across his forehead.

It starts in the middle, and runs in an arc down one of his temples. It's over three inches long, one inch wide at its centre; and just one inch from one of his eyes.

My eyebrows involuntarily shoot up into my own forehead, and my eyes widen in shock.

Other prisoners at The Oaks had been involved in attempting to murder Harris. They'd created a makeshift weapon, out of toothbrushes and razor blades, and were aiming to slit his throat.

Harris, quick to react and flexible, had ducked; the blade slicing, and driving deep into his forehead, instead of his neck. He's lucky to be alive.

And his painkillers are clearly working.

Looking straight at me, and then at my body-worn camera, he asks: "Can I see?"

"Sure," I reply, unhooking it from my tac vest, and bringing it towards him.

The doctors lean away, as I lean in. Harris leans in too.

We all watch, as he sees his face reflected at him on the tiny screen, my camera recording.

And now he's in shock, but his eyebrows can't go up. His face can't move like that.

It's going to take some skilled surgery, to make sure he's not badly scarred for life.

***

In the four months I've been doing this job, I've learnt that the incidents we attend seem to come in batches, similar jobs all coming at once.

Last week was my first visit inside The Oaks Prison. Another prisoner had hanged himself in his cell, with his bed sheets. An elaborate and difficult to create noose, used seconds after one of the every 30-minute checks made on him by prison officers throughout the night.

He'd had mental health issues, many people who end up in prison do, that's why their lives become derailed. He only had a few weeks before he was getting out, going home. Maybe he knew he couldn't fit back into his life, it was too destructive for him, he'd probably be back in prison before long. The constant cycle for many people underserved by society.

A death in prison requires at least two police officers to guard the scene, until it's been viewed by a multitude of people, and before the body can be removed.

That day this rule seemed strange to me. It was early morning, around 6am, and all the other prisoners were still locked in their cells. Surely, we weren't needed to stand on a prison landing, outside a locked cell, with two prison officers, surrounded by other locked cells.

I'd gone to The Oaks with my colleague Max. He'd been a prison officer there before becoming a police officer, so knew the place inside out. We'd been sat in the office at Northcliffe police station, working on our investigations, when the call came in over the radio at 5.30am. Max volunteered to go, and our sergeant had asked me to go with him.

We still had an hour and a half left of our night shift, before the early shift arrived at 7am. The more experienced officers were kept free for major incidents, not the ones where you stand around doing very little – something I quickly learnt we do a lot of.

After signing in at the prison reception, and explaining that he knew the way, Max marched us through the buildings, and along what felt like never ending caged walkways.

I struggled to keep up with his long purposeful strides, only managing to grab chances as he slowed to say hello to ex-colleagues along the way. I'm old enough to be his mother, three decades apart in age, but there I was, trailing behind him like a child.

I was also distracted. I can't walk anywhere without taking it all in: the sights, sounds, smells, the way they were making me feel.

I was soaking up the eerie and claustrophobic feeling that the stone buildings, and giant walls, topped with industrial strength barbed wire, were giving me.

So much metal divided the prison into segregated areas. It was so quiet.

I imagined what it would be like later in the day, when the prisoners were allowed outside. How likely we'd have been closely watched, and probably cat called.

The sun hadn't made it high enough in the sky to bring any cheer to the place. Everything felt sombre – appropriate for what we were about to deal with.

I realised I felt safe. And it was another shift where I was so grateful, and relieved to be working with, and learning from a trusted colleague, from my awesome team at Northcliffe – a team I have so much respect for.

Max is a giant, a rugby player; and a good-looking young man – many of my colleagues fancy him. He's respectful, kind, empathetic, strong, decisive, he gets shit done; while avoiding conflict. He's already a brilliant police constable; and is less than two years into his policing career.

Like with Stephen, we only work together on a couple of shifts, but I really enjoy the dynamic.

They are amongst the rare occasions when I have fun doing this job; and the rare occasions I feel part of a team.

***

My name, for the purposes of this book, is Olivia Gray; and I was a trainee police constable and trainee detective constable, with Oakshire Constabulary, for 18 months – from January 2023 to July 2024.

All my stories are true, as well as I can remember them.

They are my experiences – others will, of course, see them differently.

I will give you as much detail as I can; while ensuring I maintain respect for the people involved, and the integrity of investigations that may still be ongoing, such is the slow process of the UK justice system.

I write with the full understanding, compassion and respect that everyone I talk about has their own personal struggle. We're all trying to do our best, with the experiences and circumstances life has given us.

This isn't a witch hunt. It's just me, telling my story, like all the other police officers who have done the same before me. Like them, I've changed the names of the people and places I talk about. I've blurred details of the organisation I worked for, and the timings of when things took place.

If you recognise me, or someone I talk about, including yourself, please think carefully about what you do next with that information.

In this mad world of social media obsession, a lot of damage can be done, very quickly.

Like I have learnt a lot about myself during this journey, accepting the decisions, and mistakes I have made, I implore you to do the same.

Face your fears, accept responsibility, don't blame others; use this as a learning. I promise you will grow as a person. If that's something you are prepared to do. And if you can find the empathy.

In the words of the wise and brilliant Gabor Maté in The Myth of Normal: "Whether we realise it or not, it is our woundedness, or how we cope with it, that dictates much of our behaviour, shapes our social habits, and informs our ways of thinking."

Part One: The beginning and the end

How I became a police officer

IT'S MAY 2022, AND I've made the decision to walk away from my 30-year career in the private sector, to embark on a new challenge. What that looks like for now is unclear.

What I do know is that I need to leave the commercial world, learn something new, stretch my brain, and do something useful in the community in which I live. I need to find a job that challenges me, and enables me to get fit again.

I'm done with the politics, unnecessary bureaucracy and admin; and being held back by people who don't have my experience, or skill set. I want freedom to base decisions on my life experience and gut instinct, as well as my listening skills, and strong understanding of people and behaviours.

During my career, I've spent too many years sitting at a desk, dedicating way too much time to work, and putting everything ahead of myself, my wellbeing, and my fitness. The job I'm doing now engaged and challenged me at first, but then it killed my passion for a career I've loved.

I have a three-month notice period and to be able to enjoy some of the summer, I need to resign asap. Despite having no plan, I know I'll have no problem filling my days while I take time out to figure out what I want to do next.

With the decision made, I reach out to friends to get inspiration for my next chapter. I ask what they do for work, and whether they love it or not. I discover that not many people truly enjoy their jobs.

My friend Suzanne sends me a message which sparks my interest: "Why don't you look at the Oakshire Constabulary website? They've got some interesting jobs."

***

By the end of June, I've made my decision. I've seen an advert for an Accelerated Detective Programme and it excites me.

The advert for the programme explains that the first year will equip you with the skills and knowledge required to be a police constable, through rigorous training and practical experience. During the second year you complete placements in different investigation teams, to meet the skills and knowledge required to be a detective constable.

There will be study and exams for investigative qualifications, including the Professional Investigation Programme (PIP1 and PIP2) and the National Investigators Exam (NIE).

Then, at the end of the two-year programme, you're posted into a detective role.

They are looking for people with integrity, strong interpersonal skills and inquisitive minds. It will be challenging but rewarding.

Apparently, no prior policing experience is necessary.

This is the job for me. This is the change I'm looking for. I want to be a detective, and I'm excited about having a few weeks being a police constable as part of the programme. What an incredible opportunity.

I've always had a Copper's nose, the ability to detect when something just doesn't feel right, and have often toyed with the idea of being a detective. I spot trouble before it happens, or when others can't see what's right in front of them – like drug deals taking place; I see it everywhere. I pick up on building tension, and identify dysfunction in any environment, long before others do.

I love watching crime related TV shows; identifying the dysfunctional behaviours, testing my instincts, by trying to suss out the story lines before they happen. It drives my husband mad. I can't sit quietly through any TV programme. I'm always drawn to new opportunities to learn about human behaviour, and talk about what's going on, what might happen next.

The starting salary is just over £26,500 per annum, and you get it from day one, at training school. This means more than halving my salary; but is more than if I'd started again in some other careers. It's a big sacrifice but should be worth it, according to the advert.

So, at the beginning of July 2022, I start the long and multi-faceted application process.

***

Two weeks in, and I've made it through the first stage, and while waiting to hear about the next stage, I apply for a Ride Along.

What better way to get a taste of what to expect, and either put me off the idea, or cement my decision. It's something you can do if you're interested in becoming a police officer.

I'm asked to provide dates I can do and email a long list of when I'm available over the coming weeks.

Two weeks later, I get an email. I'm going to be joining a Friday late shift in the middle of August, in Marsham. It's a date that wasn't on my list.

***

I'm now over a month into my application process, and I'm confused about what to expect and when; the process is disjointed and unclear at times. Sometimes emails come from the HR team, sometimes from the College of Policing, and sometimes from a separate recruitment team; and I'm not sure what they all do.

I reach out to someone, via one of the multiple email addresses I've now collected in my inbox and ask what the application process timescale is. I'm told it's anything between four and six months. I'm shocked. They are desperate to recruit, why so long?

Because of the lengthy process, there's promises of keep in touch (KIT) days, but it's not clear what these are, what their purpose is, or how to book onto one.

I've got a few more weeks until I finish my current job. Because no one is interested in engaging with me anymore, I'm already enjoying the summer at a much slower pace.

I'm spending as much time outside as possible walking and gardening; and loads of time with friends having coffee and lunch.

Despite being disappointed that I'm not going to start my new career any time soon, I'm going to have many more months to enjoy not working at all. I make peace with eating into my savings and having as much fun as I can, before my world completely changes.

Ride Along

The day of the Ride Along. My weekend plans lie in ruins – I've scrapped everything because I'll be awake for at least 21 hours straight, crawling into bed Saturday morning like some kind of shift-work zombie.

Decades since I've done this. The late-night drinking, the clubbing – all ancient history. My body rebels at the thought of sleeping through the day, then heading out again that evening. *What have I signed up for?*

4.45pm on the Friday evening comes round. The instructions are crystal clear about the time but maddeningly vague about everything else. No entry point specified. No phone number to call. Just show up at Marsham police station – a fortress of security passes I don't possess.

My knuckles rap against the nearest door, beside the parked police cars. Silence. Of course.

I circle to the council office entrance. Locked. But then – *buzz* – someone lets me in. *Thank God.* Police stations often share space with councils these days, cutting costs for taxpayers. The lovely receptionist picks up her phone, calls through to the station.

A young police constable appears minutes later, uniform crisp, face impossibly youthful. *They really are getting younger,* I think, then catch myself. *No, I'm getting older.*

"I'm here for a Ride Along," I tell him. "Tried the side door, but..."

"Yup, that's locked. We never answer it." He guides me through another security door, explaining as we walk. "You can only walk into three police stations in Oakshire – Southpine, Harrisville and Westrock. They have receptions, that's where the custodies are. All the others need appointments. Yellow phone outside, or ring 101 for the FCR."

"What's the FCR?"

"Force Control Room."

The station office hits me like a wave. *Massive.* Banks of desks stretch across the space, mostly empty. A few officers glance up from laptops as I enter. I mumble hellos to anyone who acknowledges me, completely lost – no idea what their shoulder epaulettes mean, what rank anyone holds.

Nervited. That's exactly what I am – nervous and excited rolled into one churning mess. *This is actually happening.* Ten hours, 5pm to 3am, shadowing real police officers. And if everything goes right, I'll be one of them in less than a year. Maybe even here.

"We didn't know you were coming." The sergeant's voice carries irritation or stress – hard to tell which. Three chevron stripes on his shoulder. *Mental note: remember that.*

My stomach drops. "Oh, sorry, I can show you the email. If it's a problem, I'm happy to..."

"No, it's fine. I just need to work out who to crew you with."

Awkward. Nobody knows what to do with me. I hover, unsure whether to sit or stand, while everyone half-listens. The heat presses down. It's one of the hottest days of the year. I try subtle deep breaths, then realize with horror that my trousers are cutting into my belly. *Oh God, hours in these things.*

"We're starting our shift briefing." The sergeant points toward a door. "Head in there."

***

Nerves obliterate excitement. *This is so weird.* I'm sitting around an oblong table with actual police officers. Out-of-body doesn't begin to cover it.

The team radiates kindness, everyone working to make me feel welcome. I know their job is difficult, but sitting here, I have zero comprehension of how insane a Marsham night can become. How incredible this tiny crew of mostly twenty-somethings really is.

The briefing intensity overwhelms – intelligence reports, people to watch for, vehicles to flag. Then everyone gets to speak. Including me.

What on earth am I supposed to say?

"Thanks for having me." The words tumble out.

The sergeant confirms, "I'm putting you with Amelia and Emma."

Knowing glances ping around the table. Unsubtle. Sympathetic. *They've been here before. It didn't go well.*

"Don't worry, you'll be fine," someone reassures me.

Later, Amelia introduces herself with a rueful smile. "We call it the curse of the Ride Along. Every time we have someone with us, the shift becomes a shit show."

***

Ten-hour Friday and Saturday shifts. No crossover between earlies and lates. The early team clocked out at 5pm just as we entered briefing, leaving Friday evening incidents already backing up. We're called out immediately.

Blue lights slash through the evening as we race toward a domestic. Fighting couple, seven-year-old in the house, worried neighbours.

Our sirens fade as we pull into the cul-de-sac. Two other police constables have beaten us here.

Amelia and Emma leap out. "I'll stay in the car," I call. I don't feel right standing around watching this.

Smart choice. The couple are drunk. Grandma's here too, supposedly minding their child, but she's also drinking. This is Marsham's hidden face, the one behind closed doors that many residents and visitors never see.

The four officers work magic, diffusing everything brilliantly. With domestic incidents involving mutual fighting, the goal is peacekeeping and child protection. Arrest everyone who fights with their partner and there'd be no time for serious crime.

They convince dad to walk away, sober up somewhere else for a few hours. He's agitated initially but knows these officers, respects them. He calms, follows instructions, walks away amicably.

I'm trapped. The realization hits as I watch from the car. *And I'm cooking.*

Back seats are usually for prisoners – no window or door controls. The engine's off, no air conditioning. No air, period. I try deep breathing, but my trousers feel even tighter sitting down. *Don't panic.* A taste of what prisoners experience.

Amelia appears at my window like she's reading my mind, sees my pink, worried face. "So sorry, you must be baking." Engine and air con roar to life.

"Really, it's fine. You've got more important things..."

"We should be going shortly. Just encouraging grandma to take the girl to hers while the parents sober up."

Radios crackle to life. Movement outside. Amelia dives into the driver's seat, Emma into the passenger.

We're moving. Another incident.

"You know," Emma says as we speed away, "as we were leaving, grandma asked if she could go back." Pause. "And get her bottle of wine."

She'd been told no.

"What happens to the little girl?" I ask.

"We'll do a referral to Social Services." Amelia's voice carries resignation.

***

Thirty minutes after leaving the police station, incident two. A young woman's gone missing from a mental health facility. Serious welfare concerns – she's slashed her arm, bleeding heavily.

Again, I stay put. Too many people searching, too dangerous. She has a knife. She's found nearby, persuaded to return.

Twenty-five minutes after that: another missing person. Potential suicide risk, known self-harmer.

This time I'm out, keeping watch while Amelia and Emma search houses after getting no answer at his address. I'm supposed to observe, not participate, but I'm already invested in helping these remarkable women.

Third incident in just over an hour.

While they search elsewhere, I spot someone matching the description slinking back into his house, hoping to go unnoticed. *Another missing person found.*

Just under an hour later we're across town at a nasty RTC (road traffic collision) – motorbike versus 4x4 at a busy town centre junction.

The selfishness staggers me. People mount pavements in their cars, squeezing dangerously past the ambulance, police cars, cones. Their convenience trumps the motorcyclist lying in the road.

More officers arrive, securing the scene. Marsham gridlocks during rush hour.

Uncertain prognosis means statements from everyone: car driver, passenger, witnesses – there are several in this busy area. CCTV calls go out. Roads policing officers assess the scene.

Every box must be ticked before reopening the road. It's done faster than expected – not that commuters appreciate this. They don't know that if this man dies, it becomes the offence of Causing Death by Careless or Inconsiderate Driving – maximum five years prison.

Despite multiple police cars and ambulances, people still ask: "How long is this going to take?"

I want to ask back: "How long would this exact situation take you to handle?"

The paramedics shout. They're blue lighting the motorcyclist to St Margaret's City Hospital. Now.

***

Five hours in, halfway through this insane shift, night shift officers arrive. We finally stop for a break.

Four police cars pull into spaces outside a row of fast-food joints. Chicken and kebab meals head back to the station. I eat my healthy packed food, wondering how officers maintain energy on processed food. *At my age, I can't.*

Meal breaks are rare luxuries. Most likely chance for sit-down eating is late shift around 10.30pm during crossover with nights. But even that's not guaranteed. These officers' lives are dictated by the misbehaving Oakshire public.

***

Less than 30 minutes later we're back out, multiple officers blue-lighting toward an 18-year-old's party. A 16-year-old is brandishing three knives. Seven police vehicles respond. I can't count the officers.

Forty-five minutes after that: public order rounds. Later than usual because of the party, the team is now covering Marsham and some quieter towns nearby, for pub closing time. The sergeant takes over driving from Amelia, who moves to passenger seat. The three of us head to the quieter towns.

Emma joins other officers on foot in Marsham. Police hats mandatory for public order rounds. Even though it's after 11pm, it's still baking outside and wearing hats is torture. Nobody's sweat-drenched hair looks good back at the station.

Our car rounds take forty-five minutes. As we head back into Marsham, a domestic violence call crackles over radio – the sergeant floors it, blue lights and sirens screaming. *Colleagues in trouble. Violent guy kicking off. They need help.*

12.30am, we arrive to find a bundle on the ground and four officers wrestling with a man who's not particularly big but possesses ridiculous strength.

His voice cuts through the night: "Facking cants, geroff me, you facking cants. Useless pieces of shit. Who are you? Who are you? Yeah, make sure your cameras are recording. You fink you're the big man. I've done nuffink wrong."

On and on and on. Exactly like TV as they handcuff and restrain him. He *has* done something wrong – badly beaten his girlfriend in her own home, not for the first time.

Arrest. Custody. Five vehicles, eight officers for this incident.

As he's loaded into the van, officers and cars peel away to other calls. The sergeant and Amelia remain at scene, I'm still safely in the car, then suddenly they leap in and we're moving bloody fast, blue lights blazing.

Someone's pressed their red button. *The* one that stops all radio chatter, gives ten seconds of clear airtime to relay what they can about their incident and, hopefully, their exact location. Radios are trackable, but that's backup.

Not a word in our car. We're all listening. I fight to stay calm as we fly over speed bumps at impossible speeds. The sergeant's driving skills amaze me. I don't feel scared at all.

Radio chaos now – loads of officers trying to speak. I have no idea what's happening, but it sounds serious. We hit wider roads; the sergeant drives faster.

We arrive at a four-vehicle RTC, and it feels like it took 30 seconds to cross the entire town.

We all leap out – the sergeant has strategically parked across a side street entrance. My head spins, no time for anyone to think about me. *Nor should they.* They run toward the scene other officers are containing. More cars arrive, shouting across the wide road.

I stand by our car, waiting for my adrenaline to slow. *Can't make decisions right now.* The scene's too big, too many people, don't know where to go. *Here is safe.*

Nothing prepares you for this. I start calming, taking it in.

1am. Two hours left, and I sense nobody's going home on time.

Two cars hit head-on, two others smashed in the collision and spin-out. The drama is still unravelling, drawing bigger crowds on both sides of the road and I think how strange it is that so many people are out and about in this location at 1am.

I walk closer, pick a spot among pavement onlookers.

Officers talk to the three drivers whose vehicles have been smashed into. The fourth driver – the one who caused this chaos overtaking other vehicles, driving into oncoming traffic – got out, but his girlfriend's still in their vehicle and now being detained.

She's shouting. He's clearly still on scene: "I've got the bag, Nathan."

A witness near me points and shouts: "He's over there, under that car." Officers run, dive to the ground, drag Nathan out, handcuff him.

Drug dealer. Barely twenty. I expect prison for the carnage he's caused, plus the large quantity of drugs in that bag. *Little do I know how much work goes into securing a conviction after something like this.*

***

Back at the station, 2.30am. The sergeant suggests I head home as they have mountains of paperwork after the predicted 'Ride Along curse' shit show. None are leaving on time at 3am. They don't need me hanging around.

I've seen and heard enough. More than I can process. *Knackered, brain whirring.* I don't know if I'll sleep.

Tonight I've travelled in four different police vehicles – they swap constantly depending on how incidents develop: the Volvo 'area car', police van, 'panda' car, BMW.

I didn't drive here. I knew I'd be too tired to get home safely. I'd planned a cab home. Amelia offers to drive me. I can't believe it. This woman has given me so much time during a seriously challenging shift and now risks leaving very late. It's not a short drive.

I'm blown away by her kindness, support, how engaging she is.

On the way home she talks about wanting sergeant rank soon. Four years in the job already it's now time to focus on career progression rather than training others. *No doubt she'll make a great leader.* I hope I work with her in future. I'd love a boss like Amelia.

Trying to unwind, getting ready for bed, I reflect on my biggest learnings: how long each incident takes; how under-resourced the team was for all the reported incidents (loads were never attended); how frequently jobs require all officers on duty and all available vehicles.

And ultimately how amazing police officers are. Their ability to switch between so many different people and distressing situations is remarkable. Something I'll always hold deep respect for.

Reflections

It's July 2024 and nearly two years on from that night, I'm watching the water lapping over the edges of a turquoise swimming pool. It's too busy for me to get in. I wait patiently, as one by one all the people get out, until there is calm; the pool settling into a mill pond stillness, glasslike, and inviting.

I stare at the water transfixed; disbelief that this is part of my new chapter. I am filled with gratitude, and take a moment to reflect on my life, how I got here, to this point, to this day, to this place.

***

I was the child of an alcoholic.

Never knowing what state my dad would be in when he came through the front door. Wondering whether he would be home before my mum left for her night shift at our local hospital. Or if he would bother to return from the pub, in time for our once-a-week family meal – a Sunday roast; the only day we would all sit down together.

My dad was the unwanted, undiagnosed neurodivergent child of an artist, and a World War II RAF Bomber Command pilot. Inevitably, he developed an insecure attachment style.

Developed in early childhood, due to inconsistent or un-available caregivers, insecure attachment styles can lead to difficulties in relationships, and emotional regulation as an adult.

My brother and I grew up with an underlying fear of aggres-sion, and on occasion violence, which made us feel unsafe.

Both my parents were war babies. Children that grew up during rations and make do and mend times. Mum's upbring-ing was equally challenging and complicated but filled with much more love.

My parents' relationship was volatile, to say the least. They met relatively late in life, for their generation, and were in a rush to get married, and have children.

They were hardworking, career minded, and ultimately ab-sent a lot of the time; for my brother and I, but also for each other.

You'd think the fact they had good careers meant we were comfortably off, but bailiffs came knocking at our door, on more than one occasion.

Dad forgot to insure our family car; the flimsy Renault 4 that we called the 'grey box on wheels'. And it wasn't serviced, becoming a potential death trap.

My brother and I were rarely allowed to complain about illnesses or injuries, because mum nursed seriously sick and damaged children, as a nurse on the paediatrics ward.

She'd also been a children's nurse during the Vietnam war; healing severely injured children, some damaged by the notorious Agent Orange. I only recently started to understand the traumatic impact this would have had on her, when I read a book about an American nurse: The Women by Kristin Hannah.

As a result of all this dysfunction, my brother and mine's psychological needs were rarely met; and we inherited trauma from both our parents.

Thanks to an awesome therapist during my 40s, I know these were adverse childhood experiences (ACEs). Something that 50% of us grow up having, and what impacts society, and policing so negatively.

An impact that I believe could be massively reduced through different societal attitudes, as well as different political and economic choices.

I also believe, most people would benefit from some form of therapy, or at least access to good expertise they can utilise, to build their understanding of their behaviour. And I don't mean the basic CBT, which can benefit some, but isn't the answer to dealing with childhood trauma.

I'm a massive fan of Dr Chatterjee, his Feel Better, Live More podcasts and books have transformed my understanding of so many health and wellbeing subjects. My gut, sleep, and fitness have never been so good.

My brother was the academic sibling. But as I've learned, having a high IQ is no match for having a high EQ when it comes to dealing with life's challenges. I'm grateful for being blessed with the latter.

It was instrumental in my success during my three-decade career in the private sector. I developed many transferable skills which, along with my life experiences, would stand me in good stead for being a police officer.

***

But that was all then, and this is now. And now is a great place, and a great time for me.

Although there are still some things I need to heal.

I put down my book, grab my goggles, and get up carefully from the sunbed; one of a number neatly arranged along the side of the pool. I've learnt over the past months to go slowly after getting up.

My Achilles are damaged from learning to run; one of the many sacrifices I made for what turned out to be my unexpectedly short policing career. Learning to run when you're in your late 40s, and one leg shorter than the other, is not ideal when you've never been a runner.

My ankles seize up when I'm not moving, and walking can be painful, and difficult when I first get up. Right now, I'm feeling a lot older than I am.

So, I take a few careful steps to the pool's edge, and then down the metal steps. The water is cool but not cold; a perfect temperature for swimming.

I gently push myself off the edge on my back; and look up at the blue reflective ceiling. I love watching myself floating, it's so relaxing, like an out of body experience. As I float, I stretch my body as far as it will go, in every direction, and enjoy the moment.

To calm my jumping mind, I focus on my breathing: deep breath in, long exhale.

I remember the quote from mindfulness guru Jon Kabat-Zin: "It is remarkable how liberating it feels to be able to see that your thoughts are just thoughts, and that they are not 'you' or 'reality.'"

Something I wish I had been able to remember during some of the dark times during the last 18 months, but my brain didn't have that capacity.

Swimming for me is like riding a bike. Only it's my version of this old terminology, that is meant to indicate that it's easy to get back on a bike, and ride like you could when you were a child.

This never was the case for me. I could get on and ride a bike, but to turn corners or be brave enough to breathe and take my hands off a handlebar to indicate left or right, was downright terrifying.

So, getting back into swimming is like riding a bike for me. I can do lots of lengths, but getting the breathing right, lifting my head out of the water, to take breaths at the right intervals, is like indicating left or right on a bike. Tricky to do without losing control.

As I swim, I challenge myself to alternate between my natural breathing side on the right, risking taking a breath to the left.

And just like that, swimming makes me feel just like policing did; out of control, and as if I'm drowning.

And then I'm reminded to be kind to myself; it's been four years since I last swam.

My short policing career taught me that I don't always have to achieve my goals, some are meant to be aspirations that teach us huge lessons along the way.

I've also learned how much I can teach myself; and now I have time to enjoy the learning experience.

Not like in policing, where learning was made so hard, so unnecessarily damn stressful.

Part Two: Police Training School

One of the 20,000

FILLED WITH EXPECTATIONS, AS I start 2023 and a new career in a disciplined organisation, I'm confident that police training will be organised, structured, and appropriate.

They've been doing this for years, they must know what they are doing, right?

So many new police officers have gone through this, provided their feedback, raised their concerns; this should be amongst the best training I have ever had.

After all, I'm on a programme, one that's carefully designed to accelerate my journey to become a detective; with all the training I need.

Oakshire Constabulary has a desperately under-resourced workforce, so should do everything they can to retain all the new police officers they are recruiting. *They need us, so, they'll want our journey to be positive; encouraging us every step of the way, to stay working here. Won't they?*

Particularly now, as the April 2023 deadline looms, set by the UK's Conservative government, as they seek to fill the giant gap left by their austerity policies of 2010. Their slash to police, and many other public sector budgets, led to the decimation of 20,000 officers: officers they've been trying to replace since September 2019.

So, I'm convinced this is going to be a great experience. And I'm excited for everything this opportunity will bring.

But I'm also apprehensive. It's been over 25 years since I was in a classroom.

Day one – January 2023

The first challenge is getting into the car park at Oakshire Constabulary's headquarters in Oakwood. Then where to park and how to get back out of the car park, on foot, and into the main reception. The signage is not helpful, or welcoming.

I take a deep breath as I ascend the concrete steps, push open the glass door into reception, and into a whole new world.

I walk to the window, and smiling, introduce myself to the receptionist behind. "Hi, I'm a new starter, Olivia Gray."

"Welcome, I'm Brenda, how are you?" she says, with a comforting smile back.

"I'm great thanks. How're you doing?"

Brenda points to some chairs: "If you just wait over there, someone will come and collect you, and the others shortly."

I thank her as I turn around to wait with the other new starters; and look for someone to chat to.

The four twenty-somethings are all on their phones, none look up to make eye-contact.

Maybe they're just nervous?

While I'm challenged with my own anxiety, I know many people find these first encounters difficult; so I'm brave when it comes to speaking to strangers.

In a moment like this I know how important it is to engage and connect. These people are going to be sitting in the same classroom as me for the next five months, and we need to be able to acknowledge each other.

"Hello, I'm Olivia. How're you doing? Are you starting today too?" I say to a friendly looking, and very tall young man.

He instantly puts down his phone, replying with enthusiasm: "Hi, yes, I'm Tariq, it's my first day too."

"Great to meet you."

"You too."

Like a first day at school, Tariq instantly becomes my work bestie.

The locked door that leads out of reception into the rest of HQ, clicks open; and a lady asks us to follow her.

***

We step into a courtyard and I take in the architecturally uninspiring buildings that surround us. To our right, in the centre of the courtyard is a grassy area, with a lone tree.

Around its edges are rose bushes, too many to count. I love roses, and I'm curious what this area will look like in spring. Now, in the cold of winter, they are pruned and look bare.

In front of us is the building in which we will spend the next five months learning.

The lady uses her security pass to open the door and let us in, telling us our classroom is the second door on the left. She leaves us to walk the narrow corridor on our own; there's barely enough room for two people to pass, without touching the walls.

One of the others opens the door, and we enter the classroom one by one.

I'm surprised at the size of it and how many desks and chairs there are. Considering the state of HQ, the walls look freshly painted – bright white.

The lighting is also bright white, as are the desks; half of which already have people sitting at them.

They all turn and stare. I can't make out faces at this stage, because I'm dazzled by the whiteness, the brightness of everything in here.

Thank goodness for the blue chairs. I'm relieved that they look new too as I expect we're going to be doing a lot of sitting.

I walk along the front of the classroom, between the front row of desks, and the giant screen, and find a seat at the far end, near the back. I always go for an end of row seat.

I hope the desk I've chosen will be less disruptive than those at the entrance to the room.

Tariq has followed me and takes the seat next to me.

Once settled, it's our turn to stare every time that door opens, and the rest of our new colleagues enter the room. More batches of newbies, entering the dazzling white space.

***

Two middle-aged white men, who've been circulating the room, make their way to the front. The first introduces himself as Scott, he's going to be our lead trainer. He then introduces Liam, who will be in support. They appear slightly awkward in each other's company.

As usual in these types of situations we all must introduce ourselves, to break the ice.

Scott explains: "We're going to go round the room, please say your name, how old you are, what you did before, why you joined the police, and something interesting about your-selves."

And so police training school starts, with 32 students and two trainers talking about themselves.

"Hi, I'm Reid and I'm 35. I was a sports centre manager. And this is my friend from school, Rory," one of my cohort says, pointing to the guy next to him.

"We had no idea we were both joining today. We just bumped into each other in the car park. Hadn't seen each other for years."

Next up is Rory: "Hi, my name is Rory, I'm 37. Last few years I've been a carpenter, and before that I was in the Met."

There are moans and groans from around the room, in particular from Scott, in reaction to Rory's mention of the Met. I don't get it.

There's a huge age range in our class: 18 to 57. We're about 50/50 male/female, most born in Britain, two in Hungary. There's only two non-white people: my new friend Tariq, and Anthony.

Then it's my turn: "I'm Olivia, I'm 48. I've spent 30 years in the private sector. I joined because I want to learn new things, stretch my brain, have new challenges, and stave off dementia. Oh, and I love sharks; they're super smart, and totally misunderstood."

The list of reasons I wanted to join is too long to mention them all here; you'll find them at the back of this book, along with why I stayed, and why I left. That first day I decide against saying that I've joined because I want to help people as it seems too obvious. *Shouldn't we all be here for that?*

Scott has also asked us to say if we're on the Accelerated Detective Programme (ADP), so I mention that.

It's nearly lunchtime by the time we finish this exercise, during which time I discover that only two others in this room of 32 student officers are on the ADP.

This seems odd.

Why would they put just three of us in such a big class, where the other 29 are taking a different entry route? How will they accommodate our learning needs? How will we experience our programme?

Week one

During week one Scott explains: "There will be three exams to test your knowledge of the law that you'll be learning during training school. They'll be in weeks 6, 13, and 20; with 60, 70, and 80 questions respectively. You need to get 80% right to pass."

Alongside, the three of us on the ADP must study for the notoriously difficult National Investigators Exam (NIE) at the same time.

During the week, several of us ask for a copy of the timetable but Scott is not prepared to share it with us. This also seems odd to me and causes me some anxiety.

About a decade ago, it was my brother who had suggested that our dad was neurodivergent. Not long after that I identified that my brother probably was too. The penny finally dropped a few years ago that I am also neurodivergent and I realised why I've had to work so damn hard to navigate social norms.

I don't always say things that society expects, and I don't find some things funny, like others do. And while I want to spend time connecting with people, I can't bear small talk. I need to connect on a deeper level; make close connections that matter. And time on my own is essential to recharge.

I've learnt that some neurodivergent people benefit from having lists, or a plan to assist in their everyday activities; and I'm one of those. It's what helps me hold my focus, and get stuff done.

Neurodivergent people can sometimes find it incredibly difficult to navigate a neurotypical world; and not having a plan in place, like a timetable, can be very overwhelming.

I know I'm not the only one who needs this in the class; and none of us need police training school to feel anymore overwhelming than it already is. A well-structured timetable can help reduce stress by providing a sense of control and predictability, helping our mental health, and reducing anxiety. Whether you're neurodivergent, or not. *What good reason is there not to simply give us the timetable?*

***

It's day three, and we're starting to make our way through the huge amount of law we've got to learn when we're sent off on a tangent, and asked to complete a learning style questionnaire.

I'm delighted. *Surely this means they are going to adapt their teaching style to our needs. Yes, this should help a lot, hopefully identifying my learning challenges, which are starting to become glaringly obvious to me. I hope this means we will get any support we need.*

***

In the afternoon, Scott says: "Right, you lot, I want you to come up, one by one, so I can take your photo."

Some of the image conscious in the class rush to find mirrors, do their hair, and try to make themselves look as gorgeous as possible. I don't wear makeup, and my hair is short, so only takes two minutes to dry, and four brush strokes to put into place.

In the noise of the room (where a lot of things don't get heard by all of us) if it was ever mentioned, I missed why Scott needs these photos.

One by one, we stand against the white painted brick wall at the front of the class, Scott aiming his mobile phone at us. It's been so long since someone took a photo of me like this, I have no idea where to look at his phone.

***

We've started the week in smart clothes, but as the week goes on our kit and uniform starts to arrive, in giant kit bags.

With a cohort this size, not everyone's bag has arrived for week one; but mine has.

We're not allowed to travel in our uniform, but we're not afforded the luxury of lockers at training school. The HQ car park is some distance from the classroom, and I realise we're going to have to lug our kit bags, and laptop bags, to and from the car park, every day.

These bags are not designed well – it's impossible to carry the load evenly, or in a way that reduces risk to our backs.

The irony of the online manual handling training, one of around 50 online courses we have to do in our own time, is not lost on me. It teaches you to carry heavy items evenly, with both hands and arms. These bags are designed to be carried on one side of your body.

I realise how weak I am, and how my back is not used to carrying this type of weight, or load, so I really struggle with it. I wonder if I'll ever be strong enough and how or where I'll be lugging this bag in the future.

People start to wear their uniforms to class, and we begin to look like a bunch of police officers.

I'm not one of them, because while my kit bag has arrived, my boots and trousers are too small; despite having spent ages giving precise body measurements before joining.

I've also been supplied with three short sleeve black shirts, and only one long. Summer is sorted, but I'm not sure what I'll do in the winter. *Do they expect us to wear the same shirt for four shifts in a row, or buy our own winter wear?*

Pledging our Allegiance

The final day of week one. Our training has only just begun, but here we are – Attestation Day. A Magistrate is coming to HQ to conduct our ceremony. Usually this happens at court, but our cohort's too big. Better use of her time to travel to us.

"Make sure you wear your uniforms and look tidy," Scott explains. "Jacket zips need to be pulled up to the line of the reflective strip." The blue and white striped strips circle our police jackets from chest height.

During morning break, I slip into Scott's office.

"I'm not sure what to do this afternoon – I don't have all my uniform."

"Don't worry, we'll figure out who's got what. You can borrow stuff off the others."

How's that going to work in time? My eyes drift to our photos on the wall. *Good God, mine's awful – I'm looking up in the air!* Heat creeps up my neck. *How embarrassing. I hope not too many people notice.*

***

Early afternoon. We're split into four groups by classroom row, filing into the empty room next door – awaiting another cohort in a couple of weeks.

My row goes third. We face the Magistrate to affirm our commitment to serve the Crown, uphold fundamental human rights, discharge our duties fairly and according to law.

I stand as straight as possible, horribly uncomfortable in this ill-fitting uniform cobbled together from borrowed pieces. I can hardly breathe. My boots are so small my feet feel crushed, making my hypermobile ankles even more unstable.

Oh no. Facing the Magistrate, I realise my jacket zip isn't done up enough. She watches us with stern expression. *Can I zip this up without her noticing?*

I carefully raise my hands, zip the final inch into place. She turns to look straight at me.

Perfect timing.

Every police officer takes the Oath of Attestation: "I PC NUMBER NAME of POLICE FORCE do solemnly and sincerely declare and affirm that I will well and truly serve the King in the office of constable, with fairness, integrity, diligence and impartiality, upholding fundamental human rights and according equal respect to all people; and that I will, to the best of my power, cause the peace to be kept and preserved and prevent all offences against people and property; and that while I continue to hold the said office I will, to the best of my skill and knowledge, discharge all the duties thereof faithfully according to law."

Someone gives us the nod. We're off, reciting words from paper. I look up from the page, making eye contact as I read. The Magistrate remains stern – no semblance of a smile.

Support for the neurodivergent

As a middle-aged woman, I haven't been officially diagnosed as neurodivergent; I'm from a generation where it wasn't widely recognised.

So, when asked the question about disabilities (neurodivergence being included) on the application form, I felt like an imposter ticking the box. So, I didn't. I thought I'd be fine.

But I'm finding the classroom environment incredibly overwhelming. 32 students in one room is too much. Putting this many people in one cohort feels like madness.

I'm starting to worry about how I'm going to learn in this room, let alone do exams.

It turns out that it's against the College of Policing guidelines to have this many in a cohort; the recommended classroom size is around 19.

I notice that some people are photographing the slides and once I start to do the same, I realise how much it helps to have the immediate visual reminder. I can re-read the content when I get home each evening.

I also take notes, constantly, and almost verbatim. It cements my learning and distracts me from the awkwardness of the classroom.

It turns out that nothing ever happened with the week one forms we completed about our learning styles. *What happened to them?*

However, during the next few weeks, I discover that the younger members of the class, those who have been diagnosed as neurodivergent and put it down on their application, are being given extra help. They get the slides ahead of class, so they have time to review them, or process them at their own speed during a class. And some are going to be doing their exams in a separate room, to reduce the overwhelm.

At the next opportunity, I ask Scott: "Please can I get the slides in advance? I hear other people are getting them."

He agrees and tells me: "They're all on a shared drive, " and explains where to find them.

Well, that would have been useful to know before now. I discover that all the syllabus content is available in one place. *I could have saved so much time and energy and life could have been so much easier – re-reading slides on my laptop, instead of photos on my phone!*

"Can I also do the exams in another room?"

This request is refused because I've not been diagnosed. So, I'm forced to crack on, as I always have.

Oakshire Constabulary has a commitment to supporting neurodivergent applicants, and officers, but what this type of support is and how we get it hasn't been made clear in training school.

What has become clear, as I chat with people on my cohort, is that some of them were invited to the keep in touch (KIT) days; I wasn't.

There seems to be a lot of inconsistencies with the support offered to new starters.

Enter Rob and the c-word

Just a few weeks into training school, and our trainer Liam is regularly absent. His mum is very ill and he needs to take care of her. As she deteriorates Liam makes the decision to take compassionate leave.

I'm sad because he's a decent guy, and I know what it's like to care for parents. But also because he manages to keep control of the class.

The entry into our classroom, by our new trainer Rob, is like a tornado. We go from relative calm to an atmosphere of unease and disruption within a week. My high sensitivity radar is on alert.

It becomes apparent, very quickly, that Rob has a disruptive personality. He is someone who enjoys creating a feeling of discomfort, anxiety, and unease in others.

He uses the c-word as frequently as possible, and sometimes in the most bizarre circumstances.

"What do you think of Rob?" I ask someone during a break one day, interested to understand if I'm being over-sensitive, and if others think it's an appropriate use of language, in a classroom.

"I like his teaching style, but his language is unnecessary," is the reply, and the consensus in the people I ask.

"I agree," I tell them. "He's super smart, and knows his stuff, but why that word? And have you noticed that he looks at certain people in the room when he uses it? He seems to be looking for a reaction."

Without the respectful influence of Liam, I'm also starting to notice a change in the language Scott uses, as well as his general attitude. He and Rob are clearly close friends. It turns out they used to work together.

It is also clear that our training experience from now on is going to be very different and probably chaotic.

Scott has started slagging off his wife, and Rob somehow manages to pepper his teaching with language like: "No foreplay, straight to the cum shot." And I start to ask myself: "Who is monitoring the trainers, and how they behave?"

This language has no place in a supposedly disciplined environment where respect is meant to be a key value. Hearing it from the people we will be dealing with as police officers is one thing, but from trainers? This is not what I signed up for.

Having respect for those who are teaching us is important, but I'm starting to struggle, and so are others in the class.

Unfortunately, some of the class laugh at Scott and Rob's comments, demonstrating acceptance, and encouraging it to continue. A clear divide is being created in this classroom; and I'm reminded of how often I've seen the devastating outcome one toxic person can have in a team.

The irony is not lost on me that when we're taught about Betari's box during the same week, this language and behaviour escalates.

The Betari Box model illustrates how our attitudes and behaviours directly affect the attitudes and behaviours of other people around us.

One day, when I manage to get a rare moment alone with Scott, I call out the use of bad language in our classroom, telling him, "Rob's language is pretty bad. I've never heard the c-word used so many times. Is he ok? He seems a bit wired."

Uncomfortable hearing my question, Scott finds something to distract him, and I don't get an answer. And sadly, this conversation comes back to bite me. The next time Rob uses the c-word, he turns and looks straight at me, for an uncomfortably long time.

From then on, I don't raise my concerns with my trainers. *I can't trust them.*

Until now, the c-word has brought back fond memories of my friend Kerrie, who used it all the time. Sadly, she died of leukaemia in 2017, in her mid-30s.

Before police training, whenever I heard the c-word, it reminded me of our time together. Our conversations going 1000 miles an hour, desperate to get our stories out, and constantly talking over each other. We'd hardly stop for breath, unless we were laughing, which we did all the time. She'd drop the c-word into conversation in the most random of places.

Sadly, hearing the word no longer makes me smile and remember Kerrie. It's so much more aggressive to hear it being used by a man. A man who is teaching us.

PST

Six weeks in, and we're starting two full weeks of Personal Safety Training, a key part of our training, at Oakwood Grange sports centre.

At the same time, I've started an intensive 12-week study timetable for the National Investigators Exam (NIE), so I'm listening to nothing else but Julianna Mitchell's audio revision course. There's around 25 hours of subject matter from all sections of the NIE syllabus, together with revision questions to help measure your progress.

I'm cramming in law knowledge every time I'm in the car, when I'm cleaning, or doing anything that doesn't require my focus elsewhere. And my weekends are taken up reading Blackstone's Police Manuals, a set of official study guides used by UK police officers for legal training and promotion exams which cover various aspects of policing, including crime, evidence, procedure, road policing, and general police duties. Each one is nearly 1ft long, 1.5 inches deep, and around 700 pages each. As I go, I make endless notecards which I stick to a giant whiteboard.

On the ADP we have two Blackstone's to read: the red Handbook for Policing Students, and the blue Police Investigators Manual. I read both books from beginning to end; some of my cohort don't even open one.

My world seems to have become all about the law, so while I have mixed feelings about what to expect over the next two weeks, I'm relieved to be doing something physical at last.

I've been looking forward to learning how to defend myself in a fight, or rather "manage situations involving conflict safely and effectively." We will learn how to diffuse situations, how to use handcuffs, a baton and PAVA spray, unarmed self-defence, using limb restraints, and for those that need it: listening and communication skills.

***

I've only ever hit one person in my life, and I need to learn to strike and kick effectively, to be able to take control of dangerous situations. If I hadn't joined the police, I would have signed up for some sort of self-defence training. I feel it's important for women, I'd just never made time for it before.

Like most women, aside from dealing with a general lack of respect, sexism, and misogyny, I've also experienced sexual assault.

Eighteen years old, walking to the toilet in a nightclub, I was grabbed from behind by a guy I didn't know and he took a tight hold of my breasts. My survival instinct kicked in and I spun around, and punched him in the face.

Initially shocked, his face then turned into a smirk. I was furious. And glad I'd hit it.

***

I park up, and lug my kit bag into the sports centre. We've had to bring everything with us, and once again there's nowhere to store it; so, we'll be lugging it in every day.

The sports centre houses a large hall where the bleep test is conducted. We're told we'll be doing it tomorrow, and must reach 6.0 before stopping, much higher than expected.

Many of us are dreading doing the bleep test. It's only a few months since we all had to pass it to get accepted into the police, reaching the standard 5.4. Since then, we've been sitting in a classroom day after day. Being hunched over desks and books is doing no good for my posture or my motivation to run.

There are rumours there's asbestos in this building, and there's also rumours it will be torn down soon. It doesn't take long to realise there's always rumours in the police. Most of which aren't true. But the asbestos one I can believe. This building has an uncomfortable feel to it. The total lack of natural light, the musty smells, the attempts to smarten it up in some places but not others.

Listening to rumours in the police is like consuming social media, so I zone out or walk away when these types of conversations start up. I find them exhausting; everyone gossiping and speculating on stuff that is entirely wrong. It's such a waste of energy, and I want to put everything I have into my learning.

Because our cohort is too big for one trainer to manage us all, we've been split into two teams, one led by Scott and the other by Rob. I'm extremely grateful to get Scott.

An hour or two into the day, and we discover there's no running water in the building. The toilets aren't flushing and there's well over 100 people using them. I won't describe the smell or mess.

With no taps running, we can't wash our hands. No one in charge thinks to put hand sanitiser by the sinks. And then I discover that some of the men's facilities are working.

My birthday gift – the bleep test

It's day two of PST, and it's my birthday. No one wishes me a Happy Birthday and some would have known. I say nothing. I appreciate that PST is overwhelming for everyone, but I'm gutted that not one person has said anything.

And today we must run the bleep test. Happy Birthday to me. What a gift.

I believe fitness can be measured in many ways. I don't believe doing the bleep test is a true reflection of everyone's fitness. If your VO2 max, a measure of your aerobic capacity, is good, then you can always break into a run if necessary.

Many officers lose their ability to run to the bleep test 5.4 standard in between each yearly test. And because women in the UK have nearly five hours a week less leisure time than men, many more female officers fail the test. It's not good for morale, causes injuries that result in lost work days and fewer police officers available to deal with crime.

The bleep test is one of the many things that are not adapted for women, even though it's scientifically proven that there are several reasons why running is different for men and women. We have different skills and fitness abilities, and these differences should be embraced, and supported. Like they are in sports, and major sporting events.

If Oakshire Constabulary was more strategic, they would ask some key questions like:

"What are our priorities?"

"What are our objectives?"

"Will the bleep test help us achieve them?"

"Or will it remove great officers from frontline duties?"

"Do we want older people working for us, with their life skills?"

"How do we support them to succeed?"

"How do we look after women, who spend around 10 years going through menopause, and the challenges that brings to their bodies?"

"What about mothers who suffer the indignity of pissing themselves when they run?"

But the conversation around the bleep test is controversial, and policing strategies are behind the times; like the NHS focusing on treating symptoms, not causes.

***

I won't bore you with the details of what happens; 32 people running up and down a hall is not interesting. What matters is that we all pass; job done for another year.

The two weeks at Oakwood Grange pass by in a flash, and we also all pass our Personal Safety Training.

It's an uncomfortable experience, with unusual training, and teaching styles. Everything feels rushed because there's so many of us. It doesn't feel like I've learnt what I need to, to feel safe on the streets.

Lots of us come out with a variety of injuries. I get a back injury when slammed against the padded wall during one exercise, winding me, and bruising some ribs.

We all go home with bruised wrists from handcuffing practice, and I'm not confident I can get it right. *I'm going to have to learn on the streets, in a live situation.*

Fortunately for us, it's been decided that new recruits don't have to experience having PAVA sprayed in our faces, so our practice is with water. Many people moan about this, saying that we all need to know what it's like.

PAVA is an incapacitant spray similar to pepper spray which is dispensed from a handheld canister, in a liquid stream. Aimed at the eyes, it usually has an instant reaction, giving police officers time to gain control of a violent person, or one trying to evade police.

I think I have enough empathy to understand what it's like to have this stuff sprayed in your eyes, but not everyone has empathy, or understanding. I'm beginning to learn that there's a few in my cohort like that.

Despite having looked forward to it, I'm now glad PST is over and that we're heading back to the classroom. At least we have daylight in there, it doesn't stink of old sweat, and I don't have to touch any of my colleagues or have them touch me. Six weeks was all too soon for that.

Unfortunately, but also no surprise, with the state of hygiene at Oakwood Grange, a few us end up with Covid; and we're not allowed back to the classroom until we test negative.

Weirdly, the following week, another of our cohort gets Covid; but she is allowed into the classroom, while continuing to test positive.

I'm pissed off because there's training I didn't want to miss, but wasn't given the choice.

When I question the apparent unfairness of this situation, I'm told it's because we have role-plays to do; and she can't miss out.

Inspector Thornton delivers a shock

We're recovering from PST, and some of us from Covid, when a female inspector comes in to speak to us.

It's becoming clear why Scott didn't want to share the timetable with us. What should be a simple training structure, repeated for all cohorts, is not that easy to manage.

With so many new cohorts, the pressure people like Inspector Thornton are under, to take time out of their busy day jobs to come and speak to us is immense. They don't always turn up when they are expected.

But she's an inspector, so she can turn up when she likes. I think it's great to see her. I know how important seeing leaders face to face is, for maintaining morale, as well as getting a better understanding of the organisation we work for.

"Stand up when she comes in," Scott tells us.

I have high hopes that this visit will set the scene for our future. *Maybe it will even reset some of the attitudes in the room?*

***

The way Scott and Rob are talking about Inspector Thornton – their eye rolls, their barely concealed irritation – is setting my teeth on edge and making my stomach tight. This is how they introduce her?

Maybe she's interrupting something important on the timetable, but still. The disrespect is palpable.

Chaos erupts as she walks in. I'm on my feet, but half the class is still sitting, heads swivelling in confusion, because clearly not everyone has noticed. "Why are people standing?" someone murmurs. The room's too big, voices don't carry.

Finally, everyone scrambles upright just as Inspector Thornton reaches the front.

"Good morning everyone, please sit down." Her voice cuts through the murmur. "I'm here to see how you're doing and give you a bit more information about what happens at the end of your training."

The words *bullying, racism, sexism, misogyny* hang heavy in the air. Come to her if we have concerns, she says. My mind flashes to faces around the room – some I trust, others I don't.

"This behaviour is not tolerated, so if you see it, report it. We need to stop offences by police officers like those committed by David Carrick and Wayne Couzens." The names hit like stones. "Their crimes are horrendous. They were well known by colleagues for behaving badly, and we don't want that happening here."

Some of us can spot the wrong 'uns easily enough. The thought surfaces. *It's what we do with that knowledge that matters.* But when you don't feel safe speaking up, nothing gets done. Bad behaviour festers, grows.

She's talking about email forms, choosing stations. My attention snaps back.

"When you get to your stations, you'll first spend four weeks with a tutor on a Neighbourhood Policing Team. This gives you time to get to grips with the basics and get to know the areas you will be policing, at a slower pace."

Four weeks of breathing room. The relief starts to settle in my chest.

"After that you'll join your Response teams and have a different tutor for the following 10 weeks. If all goes well, that's the team you will be part of long term."

Then: "Who in the room is on the Accelerated Detective Programme? I know there's a few of you."

My hand shoots up. Across the room, Rosie and James raise theirs too. We're scattered – them clustered together, me isolated on the other side. *Always on the outside,* I think, *missing the casual conversations that bind groups together.*

"You three won't be doing the four weeks with a Neighbourhood Policing Team. You will join your Response teams immediately, and spend your whole six months with them, before moving on to a Central Crime Investigation Team."

The words slam into me. *What?* My hand hovers in the air, forgotten. The relief I felt moments ago evaporates.

She keeps talking, but her voice becomes white noise. My brain is stuck, grinding through the implications: *No four weeks of gentle introduction. No time to learn the systems, the radio, the streets. Straight into high-octane emergency response, racing to urgent calls at breakneck speed. Only ten weeks with a tutor before I'm on my own.*

This is insane. We signed up to be detectives, not Response officers. The word "accelerated" suddenly feels like a threat.

"My wife isn't going to be happy." James's voice is tight during our break huddle. "I thought we just did 10 weeks in Response, then straight to detective training."

I stare at him. "No way James, are you serious?"

Rosie and I exchange glances. *When did we find out it was six months?* Not during the early stage of our applications, that's certain. Someone must have mentioned it in passing, just before training started. A throwaway comment that changed everything.

I almost didn't join when I learned this. But I'd already invested so much time. I assumed they knew what they were doing with this programme. Assumed there was logic behind it.

"Seriously," James continues, his voice cracking slightly. "I don't know how we'll manage with me doing night shifts for six months with the kids."

The weight of what we've signed up for settles over us like a heavy blanket.

More bad behaviour

During my previous career, I saw plenty of poor behaviour, lack of respect, and sexism in the workplace.

Considering it's an important part of the Code of Ethics, I'm surprised at the lack of respect I'm seeing in the classroom here. People don't seem to understand, or care about the impact they are having on others, with the attitude and tone in which they are delivering their words.

I'm also saddened by how much bitching goes on. It feels childish. And it's not just my classmates, it's our trainers too. It feels like no one is safe from criticism. I've heard the CPS, the firearms team, the Fire Service, the Ambulance Service, the HR team, and detectives, all under attack.

Personally, I don't find it very constructive to hear other teams, and agencies we will be working with, being slagged off. Imagine if they were all 'trained' to feel that way about us?

I'm also learning, that Oakshire has some entitled, and very judgemental young people. There's a stark contrast between the behaviour of the privileged and entitled, and those from other backgrounds, who are less so.

I have never been one to fit into the 'normal' crowd. I've always gravitated towards different people, who I can learn from, who I find interesting to listen to, and those with different backgrounds to me.

I was lucky on day one to find myself surrounded by exactly that. Even though there's been a couple of desk moves in the classroom, I've fought to keep a seat in the same area, with the same people.

Not only is it where I find the conversation more interesting, the chat is never bitchy, people seem kinder, more respectful of each other. That's when the guys are not play-fighting which brings us all some light relief.

I can also focus as there's less distractions where I sit. It's not an easy fight to stay here. I feel like I must regularly explain to Scott and Rob why I need to be at the end of a row, so I can focus and learn effectively.

***

About an hour after Inspector Thornton's visit, something happens in our classroom that I can't ignore. I'm busy scribbling notes as Rob teaches when Harvey's voice cuts through the room. Loud. Deliberate. Making sure the whole class can hear. He's talking about a female colleague he'd seen at Oakwood Grange during our PST training last week.

"She had orange skin and these eyelashes." His tone drips with bitchy disrespect as he demonstrates with his fingers how big our colleague's eyelashes are.

My stomach tightens. There are female officers in our cohort with similar appearance. *What are they thinking right now?*

So many women in my cohort have already stopped talking in class. In such a short time, we've been knocked down, disgusted by behaviour in this environment. We just don't engage anymore.

Quickly, others join in, commenting on colleagues' appearances from Oakwood Grange. Another female officer comes under attack.

I can't ignore this. These women need defending. Despite my experience so far, it's not in my nature to stay silent.

"Come on guys, we just had a presentation from the inspector where she talked about stuff like this, and it's been forgotten already." I direct my comment at no one in particular.

Harvey – short, twenty-something, radiating an attitude that he's something special – swings round in his chair, glaring. "What's the problem?"

His aggression hits me like a slap. *I'm not prepared for this.* His demeanour, his tone – he's clearly angry at me. *And now I'm furious. How dare he behave like that to me, or anyone? Who does he think he is?* How can this person, with these behaviours, be on track to become a police officer?

"You were commenting on women's appearance, and Inspector Thornton has just said this type of behaviour is not acceptable."

He has no idea there's a connection between the two things.

We're caught in a standoff. He stares at me, I stare back. Neither will back down. Both as angry as each other.

Some people really don't like being challenged – however kindly, politely, well-meaningly the challenge is delivered. It dents their ego, offends the version of themselves they've created in their minds.

My gut is screaming: this guy is a bad apple. Can he learn? Or will this behaviour just escalate over time?

Harvey sits next to Chloe, another twenty-something. She's also staring at me like I'm mad. *She'll learn, eventually, but not from me, not today.* She's only interested in backing Harvey right now. *I'm clearly the enemy.*

Our confrontation draws Rob's attention. "What's going on?"

My adrenaline pumps, heat floods my neck – a typical sign of any emotion for me – and I start shaking. Apart from being totally caught off guard that this is happening in a classroom, in what should be a professional and safe environment, I'm still not feeling 100% after getting over Covid.

The whole class goes quiet. Tension fills the air, everyone listening. Faintness whooshes over me.

"Harvey commented on a female colleague's appearance, talking about her orange skin and eyelashes. We've only just been spoken to earlier about this type of thing."

I look between Harvey and Rob. Blood pumps in my ears, drowning out Harvey's response. I look back at Rob – he doesn't seem to know what to do next. Doesn't say a word. The silence is palpable.

"I was just calling it out, something we've been told to do on a number of occasions in this classroom."

"Well, it's been said now." Rob's voice cuts through the pumping in my ears. He might say something else, but the words don't register. Some people look over at Harvey and me, others at Rob. Muttering starts.

"Right everyone, be quiet." Rob carries on teaching.

Just like that.

I try chatting to Harvey in our next break, smoothing things over. I listen carefully to what he has to say – it's important to understand other people's viewpoints. Naïvely, maybe hopefully, I expect him to show some level of respect to do the same for me.

Harvey tries excusing what he's said. *That speaks volumes.* He's implying that because Rob said something similar about female officers' appearance in class a few weeks back, what he's said is acceptable.

I remember Rob talking about how much makeup women should wear in the job. I'd thought at the time: *it's not your place, or your expertise, to comment about this.* This type of conversation should be discussed by senior female officers, not males, if at all. Women have the right to wear as much makeup as they like, whatever your opinion.

What's playing out right now just shows how impressionable people are, how easily they accept bad attitudes and repeat them.

"I don't think it's appropriate to talk about the appearance of women in that way."

"Well, I don't think it's a problem."

He's missed the point. This isn't just about words, but he's not likely to understand. Many men think they can objectify women if they find them attractive, or comment negatively about their appearance if they don't.

There's another young man in the cohort, still a teenager, who's even worse at this. He's extremely disrespectful in the way he speaks about girls he fancies.

To be fair to men, this has become more of an issue with women also slagging off other women – social media creating a more judgemental, nasty, negative society.

Calmly, I tackle the other issue: "You were quite aggressive in the way you spoke to me."

One last look of disdain from Harvey, and he turns to face the front. He's muttering under his breath, exchanging looks with Chloe, who gives me one final glare.

During our confrontation, he's demonstrated through his behaviour and words that he hasn't heard me. He seems totally disinterested in understanding another viewpoint.

I'm curious whether this has ever happened to him before, or if he's got to his twenties without being challenged, and therefore thinks I'm the problem.

I have no doubt that I'll be bitched about by people in this room. People inexperienced in life, still with a lot to learn about what is and isn't acceptable, respectful behaviour.

Young people who'll be going out into the world, meeting people like me, people my age, that they have to deal with as victims, witnesses, and suspects. *How will they manage? What kind of service will they deliver for the public?*

In the next break, I bump into Rob in the long thin corridor outside the classroom. Always awkward – we must come into very close contact. I fill the silence: "I've clearly annoyed Harvey, but his behaviour was aggressive and inappropriate."

Nothing in return except a look that says he doesn't know how to handle the situation.

I want to continue challenging poor behaviour – we've been encouraged to – but do I really want to put myself in this situation again?

***

Unfortunately, this isn't the first time Harvey has disrespected a colleague, and it won't be the last.

One of our two Hungarian colleagues, Eva, comes up to me later. "You know he told me to shut up the other day?"

"No way, when?"

"I was trying to ask Scott a question about something I didn't understand. He's just rude."

No more is needed. We give each other a knowing look.

***

I draft an email to Inspector Thornton.

I tell her about Harvey and Rob's behaviour, and how raising it with her makes me nervous, because of the potential repercussions.

I let her know about the lack of respect in our classroom, and my concerns that bad behaviours are being bred.

But I never send it.

It's not safe.

I learned that lesson early on.

It's one of my strongest learning lessons of police training school.

The uniform challenge

The following week, I'm one of the last to finally be able to wear a complete uniform, with every item fitting comfortably. To achieve this, I've had to resort to buying some items myself online, including boots and trousers.

We know by now, that getting trousers that fit is an issue for most of the ladies at Oakshire Constabulary.

In my giant kit bag during week one, I had found three pairs of male patrol trousers which only fit if your body is shaped like a man's. Mine is not. Others were lucky to get female trousers, although in varying sizes of too large or too small.

Trouser swapping went on most weeks as people received replacements. The uniform team is under significant pressure, with all the new officers starting; and don't reply to emails. There doesn't seem to be a system in place to solve what should be such a simple problem. Like having a rack of trousers for ladies to try on, so we can order the right size.

I'm delighted to have trousers I can sit down in and not feel like I'm being sliced in half.

Right now, we don't need them, but I've found out that we're not supplied with torches, so we must spend our own money on those too. It's a fundamental piece of kit, if you want police officers to be able to search for things in the dark.

In total, so far, along with the Juliana Mitchell audio tracks, and the Police Pass books and online Multiple-Choice Questions, to support my National Investigators Exam (NIE) studies, I have spent £332.32 to do this job. I've been here less than three months.

Honesty and integrity

One day in the classroom, while having a moment of gratitude, that I no longer have to extract my trousers from my crotch, I notice a couple of people have the online training packages open on their screens; the ones we're meant to be doing in our own time.

I realise that they're not actually reading the content. They are letting it play out on the screen, occasionally clicking a button to move on to the next section. To call it what it is, they are cheating their way through part of the police training curriculum.

I wonder how that fits with the first of the 10 standards of professional behaviour we've learnt about: honesty and integrity.

Unfortunately, I've already learned that following standard number 10 can have negative outcomes: challenging and re-porting improper conduct.

So, I say nothing, again.

Police suicide

One morning, Scott and Rob walk into the classroom, in an altogether different mood. They are dragging their feet, their heads are hanging low, and when they do look up it's with a heaviness that speaks sadness, and anxiety. These two are hurting.

Something serious has happened. And someone is going to be in the firing line if we don't behave today.

They don't say anything at first, they try to teach the class, but it is an uncomfortable experience; and people get snapped at.

Eventually Scott can't hold it in anymore: "There's something we need to say. Someone we worked closely with killed himself yesterday."

No one says a word. This is the second police suicide since training school started.

The story unfolds throughout the day, and I'm shocked by how much is being shared with us. I'm not going to reveal the details; it's a very personal story that is not mine to tell. And we should never have known as much as we did.

A court appearance

It's the Easter holidays, and we've been forced to take the week off. Quite frankly I'm relieved, I need time away from the chaos of training school. Plus, we've got our second exam soon, so it's good to have a few days to fully focus on revising the law we've learnt so far.

Surprisingly, I'm not doing badly at the exams, but I'm studying really hard. There was an extra one during PST that we weren't told about at the beginning of training school. *If only we had that timetable to manage our expectations.*

I decide to make use of the time and visit one of Oakshire's four Magistrates' Courts which are in Southpine, Marsham, Westrock and Harrisville.

I want to see what it's like, and what the process is; so I'll be comfortable when I have to attend a hearing, as a police constable or detective.

Apparently, court visits used to be part of the training school experience.

All criminal cases start in a Magistrates' court. Cases are heard by either two or three Magistrates, or a District Judge. They decide if the defendant is guilty or not, and what sentence to give.

A Magistrates' Court normally handles cases known as 'summary offences' such as motoring offences, minor criminal damage, common assault. It can also deal with some of the more serious offences such as burglary or drugs offences. These are called 'either way' offences and can be heard either in a Magistrates' Court, or a Crown Court.

Magistrates' Courts always pass the most serious crimes to the Crown Court, known as 'indictable offences' which include: murder, rape, robbery, and grievous bodily harm.

A Crown Court normally has a jury which decides if the defendant is guilty or not, and a judge who decides on the sentence.

The court staff are all helpful, one of the court clerks shows me around, and suggests a drink drive case for me to watch. As I head for the courtroom door, I see a nervous looking lady in the waiting area; and think she could be the defendant's wife.

The hearing is about to start, so I let myself in, make a subtle acknowledgement to the people already inside, who smile back, and I settle myself into the public seats at the back.

The Judicial Assistant calls "all rise" and in walk the three Magistrates, who take their high seats at the other end of the large, high-ceilinged room.

I recognise the Magistrate from Attestation; she looks at me as if she recognises me too. Or maybe she is just checking out who is in her courtroom. The public seats are rarely taken in small hearings like this.

A few days later, on the bank holiday Monday, my husband and I visit Southpine Magistrates Court together. He has a friend who is a Magistrate, who knows about my new career, and let us know he's going to be doing the hearings that day.

I didn't realise Magistrates Courts open on bank holiday Mondays. It's necessary to deal with those arrested, interviewed, charged and remanded at the beginning of the bank holiday weekend. It's a long wait until Tuesday to appear at court, and custodies need to free up space.

Harvey's at it again

The British are generally lazy when it comes to speaking other languages, partly because English is a language spoken across the globe. I'm always impressed by people for whom English is not their first language, and their ability to speak it so well, or try hard to understand and be understood.

We have two Hungarians in our cohort: Eva and Janos.

The day after our second classroom exam, I hear Harvey and Chloe laughing at Janos, behind their hands, like children, as he tries to ask Rob a question.

His Hungarian accent is strong, as is his voice which projects well into the room. It's a real skill to have a voice that projects well, but doesn't dominate.

Rob looks at Janos, with confusion on his face. It's clear he hasn't heard or understood Janos. And once again, he doesn't know how to handle an uncomfortable situation.

The awkwardness is palpable. I'm screaming in my head: "Just ask him what he said, don't make a big deal of it. If you didn't understand, just ask him what he said."

Janos is embarrassed, he can sense that he hasn't been understood and tries to ask the question again.

Harvey and Chloe are now talking about him. I can't hear what they are saying, but it is obvious there's bitching going on. Rob pulls all our attention back to his lesson, and we carry on as if nothing has happened. There is unresolved tension in the air.

Janos has clearly picked up on Harvey and Chloe's behaviour and when he gets home that day, sends a WhatsApp message on the group chat, citing what he thinks is racist behaviour. It sends shockwaves around the group.

Tariq jumps into the debate, deciding to get involved in resolving it. He's got ambitions to be Prime Minister one day, so great politics practise.

I'm in the waiting room of my local vets, when I get a message from Tariq: "Janos said you heard what went on today, what are your thoughts?"

This evening is not a great time for me to get caught up in this situation. My cat is seriously ill, close to death after one of my neighbour's cats attacked her, on our garden patio. I brought her here yesterday after our exam and I haven't seen her since.

During the heavy and drama filled day at training school, I'm about to drive her, in her incredibly delicate state, to a specialist animal hospital I've never been to, and which is over an hour away. It's her only chance of survival. She needs to go now and it's quicker if I take her, than wait for a vet ambulance.

When the vet brings her out to me, the poor little thing, who usually has boundless energy, looks like she could take her last breath at any moment. She can't move. She just looks up at me with big sad eyes.

I call Tariq from the car, "Hiya, you ok?"

"Yes mate, you?"

"I'm not great, my cat's really sick and I'm driving her to a specialist vets."

"Oh sorry."

"Don't worry, I just wanted to let you know I didn't hear what Harvey and Chloe said. I just saw their behaviour. They were clearly bitching about Janos. And it's not the first time."

There's so much more I would normally have been able to explain, the things I pick up in the classroom, but my head is just not in the right place. The conversation is short, and Tariq decides what happened isn't racism.

After handing my precious cargo over to the specialist vet, fighting back the tears, and wondering if I'll see her alive again, I head back home. I'm knackered.

During the drive, I remember seeing the kind of behaviour I'd witnessed during meetings in the private sector. People who are not as clear, articulate, or loud as others, have their contributions laughed at, shot down or talked over, or just plain ignored.

As someone who struggles to project my voice, I often swallow my words, resulting in not being heard. As well as seeing this happening to others, it's happened to me.

A couple of years earlier, I'd read a fascinating BBC Work-life article about linguistic racism by Christine Ro. In it she talks about "seeing an Asian face makes some Americans consider that speaker's English to be hard to understand, regardless of how they actually speak or where they were born."

She then goes on to say: "These perceptions feed into linguistic racism, or racism based on accent, dialect and speech patterns."

"The overt form of linguistic racism can involve deliberate belittling or shaming, such as 'ethnic-accent bullying' that occurs despite someone's actual English proficiency. Or it can be more covert, like the unwitting social exclusion of people with foreign-accented English."

Janos is made to apologise to the group, and we are told, in no uncertain terms by Scott, not to say that people are being racist, or misogynistic.

Wow. There it is. In police training school. Those who are behaving badly, have just been given the go ahead to continue treating others with no respect. Behaviours we've been warned about, and that I do not believe to be acceptable, are being brushed under the carpet.

Unless their behaviour changes between now and June, I don't want to work with some of these people. I'm also not comfortable knowing they will be out in public before long. What if they behave in the way I see them behave in the class?

This is not what I, or some others in this room, expected of training school. I am so disappointed.

This is not setting the scene for a positive future at Oakshire Constabulary.

My gut is screaming at me. And my head is pounding.

***

As the weeks at training school go on, I feel like I am becoming more and more isolated. As we are regularly forced to swap desks, something I find disruptive, Tariq moves further away to a desk at the centre of the room, with the cool crowd. He starts to become louder, more confrontational, and more disrespectful; I realise he's no longer my work bestie.

This dysfunctional environment is starting to strip away the well-rounded, respectful human I met on day one. *I'm really sad about that.*

Choosing our police stations

While my cat fights for her life at the specialist vets, I distract myself with my studies; and keep to myself at training school.

One day, Scott announces: "There should be an email about choosing which police station you want to be based at. Make sure you reply quickly."

We must complete a form with our preferences, with the option to say why.

From what I'm hearing, from the chatter in the classroom, many people know which station they want; some where their friends are, some near to home, or some other reason. I know nothing about any of the stations, and no one is telling us anything useful that will help me make the choice.

I know I don't want to do my six months of Response policing near my hometown; or drive a long distance, at either end of the nine or 10-hour shifts.

So, I pick the five I think I'd be happy travelling to, police stations not too far, but far enough.

I think it would be useful to be where there are large teams of detectives, where the three custodies are, so put Southpine down as one of my top choices.

***

A couple of days later, I get an email.

From: inspector.thornton@oakshire.police.uk
To: olivia.gray@oakshire.police.uk
Date: April2023
Subject: Northcliffe

Dear Olivia
To support operational demand, we need to send additional officers from your cohort to Northcliffe, as they are low on resources.
Please let me know if you would be happy to be posted there.
Kind regards
Inspector Thornton

Always flexible, wanting to do the right thing I reply:

From: olivia.gray@oakshire.police.uk
To: inspector.thornton@oakshire.police.uk
Date: TheNextDayApril2023
Subject: Northcliffe

Dear Inspector Thornton
Thank you for your email.

I am very happy to support the organisation and be based at Northcliffe.
I had thought being at Southpine would be good for building relationships for my future career, but I am sure I will have other opportunities to do that.
Kind regards
Olivia

It turns out that my ADP colleague James has also been asked to be based at Northcliffe.

Neither of us understand how it makes sense "to meet operational demands," by putting two officers on the ADP into an area struggling for resources.

We'll only be there for six months.

The first time I nearly quit

Three and a half months since I started police training, and I'm already thinking about quitting.

The sacrifices pile up around me. Way less joy in my life. Gone are my nature walks, time in the garden, coffee, lunch or wine with friends. I'm working my socks off studying seven days a week. *My gut is screaming: there's something very wrong with this organisation.*

The training school environment crushes me daily. My mental and physical health crumble under the weight. Anxiety claws at me constantly, making it difficult to learn, to remember. *This just isn't a safe space.*

I don't think the way my brain works aligns with how training school operates. When we hear about lockdown training – all online – I know I would have thrived. A quiet, calm learning environment. Time to reflect, go at my own pace, circle back to refresh on bits I need.

That would beat having to re-read and re-learn everything taught in the classroom, which is what I'm doing now. In my own time, on top of my NIE learning which – thank God – turns out to be very similar content.

Maybe I'm just not right for this?

One evening, I talk to my husband.

"I'm just so tired of the dysfunction." The words spill over a large glass of wine. "I'm not sure I want to make any more sacrifices for this job. And I'm nowhere near ready to go out as a Response officer. I'm just totally unprepared for the practical side."

It's hard for him to hear all of this – the sacrifices impact him too.

"I don't really know how to help." He doesn't have answers. But his listening enables me to get it out of my system. *I'm so grateful for that.*

My rant continues: "We see so little practical stuff, what it's really like to do the job. Like body-worn footage of officers in action. All we have is nonstop law which I could learn so much better at home.

"And the role-plays." My voice hardens. "I hate doing those role-plays. It's mostly people from our class playing the stooges, but a few of them are out to get others. I'm so uncomfortable having my capabilities judged by them."

Frustration bubbles up. *I know I can do this.* Life has been full of challenges I've overcome. This is just one more to work through. Training school is just a short part of what will hopefully be at least a ten-year career in policing.

I need to find a way to get more time – to learn, prepare, absorb content before feeling confident to perform in role-play scenarios. *Maybe I just need longer to get to grips with the practical side.*

This is strange to me. I'm a practical person, I normally pick things up quickly. Learning from others, then cracking on myself. But learning from others doesn't seem to be the approach here. I'm left wondering why – to me it seems the most practical way to learn a practical job.

The fact that we were only told halfway through training school that we don't get four weeks on NPT like everyone else gnaws at me. Having a significant impact on how I feel.

There are some things you can accelerate. But learning the basics? *You just can't.*

Being highly sensitive

I remind myself that I'm highly sensitive, and no wonder this experience is overwhelming.

It was only in my late 30s that I discovered that I'm highly sensitive, when a friend recommended that I read a book called The Highly Sensitive Person by Dr Elaine Aron. It was at the end of a trip to Australia, and I devoured the whole book on the flight home, in floods of tears.

That book changed my life, how I viewed myself, my experiences, and my understanding of my reactions to things. Dr Aron explains that individuals with highly sensitive temperaments possess what she terms emotional leadership. According to her research, highly sensitive people tend to experience emotional responses more quickly and intensely than others – they may cry or become angry before those around them and are generally more emotionally affected by situations. She notes that approximately 20% of both human and animal populations exhibit this trait of high sensitivity. Highly sensitive people are easily overstimulated in social situations; and overwhelmed by things like strong smells, loud noises, bright lights, and coarse fabrics.

We make a point of avoiding violent movies and TV shows; we need to withdraw during busy days, into bed or a darkened room or some other place where we can have privacy and relief from the situation; we notice or enjoy delicate or fine scents, tastes, sounds, or works of art; we have rich and complex inner lives; and it is likely that others saw us as sensitive or shy when we were children.

Highly sensitive people also usually make it a high priority to arrange their lives to avoid upsetting or overwhelming situations. However, my integrity and sense of fairness, and justice, mean I've always stood up for what is right, and I often get myself into these types of situations.

They have been hard to deal with, but I always thought I could deal with them and always found ways to decompress after being stuck in them.

That's why I believe I can be a highly sensitive person and still be a good police officer.

What I'm realising now is just how much being highly sensitive makes me nervous, unable to perform in front of others, during things like role-plays.

Learning about domestic abuse

Violence against women and girls is a priority for Oakshire Constabulary, and the CPS, but our training doesn't give this impression or reflect the enormity of the problem in Oak-shire.

Today, Rob is teaching us about domestic abuse, domestic violence, and crimes like Controlling and Coercive Behaviour.

Domestic abuse isn't always physical. Coercive control is an act or a pattern of acts of assault, threats, humiliation, and intimidation, or other abuse that is used to harm, punish, or frighten a victim.

Coercive and controlling behaviour is at the heart of domestic abuse. This behaviour is designed to make a person dependent by isolating them from support, exploiting them, depriving them of independence, and regulating their everyday behaviour.

I overhear people in the classroom saying: "Why do they stay, why don't they just leave?"

I wonder why is it always the victim that is blamed, still. *Surely over time we've learned enough to teach this subject in a compelling way to drill it into people?*

Why don't people ask: "Why does the perpetrator do it?"

Why can't people interpret, from the list of behaviour on the big screen at the front of the room, why it would be so hard for a victim to leave? It's clear that they are broken.

You try walking away from a dysfunctional situation, when you're broken.

There doesn't seem to be any input in this lesson as to why; just the stats that tell us it takes seven attempts for a victim to be able to leave their abuser.

I sense that Rob is about to wrap up the lesson. Surely, we can't move on, leaving this subject with such a small input, and lack of understanding.

A lot of people in this room have lived easy privileged lives and have no idea how to talk to a domestic abuse victim, especially one decades older than them.

So, I dare to speak out again: "Is there a script to help us engage with victims of domestic abuse?"

Rob looks at me blankly.

Bravely, I continue: "Like a set of words we can use to ensure these victims are engaged in the right way, feel supported, heard and pointed in the right direction?"

Rob stares at me in disbelief, almost disdain: "No, there isn't."

I don't know why asking this question is such a problem. I see people in the room looking at me like I'm mad. Again. But for me it's a simple solution.

Sadly, the content of this lesson doesn't go anywhere near enough preparing people to deal with domestic abuse incidents. I speculate whether it's because the person teaching it isn't right for the subject. I think back to school, and how I found subjects boring, or lacking somehow, because of how they were taught and who by.

I'm perplexed. If this is a key priority for us, and we're learning about it right now, how come there isn't a structured, clear, unambiguous way for us to learn how to deal with it.

I know every situation is different, but there really should be a basic template approach to start us off with. A victim focused approach?

The dawn of the reality of the ADP

Many people dislike the Accelerated Detective Programme. We hear it right from the start at training school. And colleagues constantly slag off the fact that we don't do a minimum of two years of Response policing.

During our 20 weeks of police training school, there is only one hour of input on training to become a detective, presented to the entire cohort. Nothing in training school is adapted to the ADP.

While there are people theoretically overseeing the programme, it has become very clear that they are not interested in our experience. We've been lost in this huge cohort of people on a totally different entry route into Oakshire Constabulary.

With no one guiding us on how to navigate the programme; Rosie, James, and I begin to doubt our choice.

While we were told about the multiple resources to tap into, which we've had to pay for ourselves, we've not had suggestions of people to speak to about what might work for us, and our learning styles.

A few weeks in, we asked Scott if we could speak to people already on the ADP; an obvious thing that could have formed part of the programme. This request was ignored.

But finally, we see an opportunity, when a really engaging sergeant who has moved from Response to head up the recruitment team (I still don't really know what they do) comes in to talk to us.

He's chilled, and personable; and, as with other guest speakers we see during training school, he's also interested to know who is on the ADP.

He talks passionately about a lady from his Response team who is also on the ADP. He's so complimentary about her abilities; and she's just moved to her first detective placement.

During the break immediately after, the three of us pounce on him. Rosie asks: "Can we meet her? We'd really like to hear from someone on the ADP."

He agrees to put us in touch, and when we meet her, it gives us a much better insight into what to expect. It's not going to be easy, but none of us expected that.

She tells us, "You will have very high highs, and incredibly low lows. I've spent a lot of time crying. But you'll get through."

And then she shares a warning: "Once you're out of training school, and you're working in Response you don't have any time to study. One of the guys on my cohort still hasn't passed the NIE. He's about to do it for the third time."

He'll be taking it at the same time as us, in just a few weeks' time. I do not want to be in that situation. This gives me the motivation to continue sacrificing my life outside Oakshire Constabulary, I must pass the NIE first time.

***

The lack of interest in those of us on the ADP becomes even more obvious two weeks before our crucial NIE exam. We're scheduled to get a week of study leave to fully focus on our detective syllabus. The one we're doing in our own time.

Other than the extra Blackstone's book, the force has signed us up for a four-day intensive online crammer course which runs until 1pm every day. A brilliant way to recap on our learning so far, and cram anything we haven't remembered, or learned.

I'm really looking forward to it and have planned how I'm going to use the afternoons to reflect on each of the day's topics, reading over my notes, and making any additional notecards that might be helpful.

I plan to use the Friday to consolidate all the learning. Followed by a big walk, to give my brain a rest from all the cramming. To let it all settle in my mind, and fall into place while out in nature which has been seriously lacking recently, due to the intensity of studying.

The week before the crammer, the three of us are told we must be back in class on the Friday.

And then just a few days before it starts, we're asked to come back to the class straight after day four ends at 1pm on the Thursday. So, no time to get our thoughts in order, after four highly intense days.

Once again, I'm left wondering who makes these decisions, and if anyone cares about our experience.

NIE crammer

It's day one of the NIE crammer, and I've opted to do it from home where I can focus, and learn more effectively. Unfortunately, it means I'll miss the final section to make sure I'm back in the classroom on Thursday.

The rest of our cohort has their crime management system training this week.

The crime management system is used to record investigations and cases. It has the smallest font, and multiple sections that can be enlarged and shrunk, so you can read it, but that are occasionally lost.

As the NIE crammer presenters talk 1000 miles an hour, and slides whizz across the screen, out of the corner of my eye I can see my phone flashing.

A series of WhatsApp messages has started on the cohort group chat. It seems that they don't like the trainer, or his teaching style. Then some serious bitching starts, taking the piss out of him.

I'm surprised at the frantic level of messaging that's going on during their training, and put my phone in another room.

Managing our cohort, with the huge age-range, abilities and behaviours is a hard job. It takes a certain kind of person to manage that. Maybe this trainer doesn't have that skill set.

Throwing out the revision schedule

While it is a huge amount of work, revising for police training school and the detective exams at the same time means I can have a combined schedule.

The initial stress that I'd had about having to do both at the same time reduced, as I got into the swing of cramming law into my unpractised brain.

I feel confident that the work I've been putting in is as much as I could possibly do.

But I'm finding the lack of connection with my friends – there's now no time for a walk and catch up – is impacting my mental health and wonder again if this is worth all the sacrifice.

Then I remember how close I am to the end of this part of my policing journey. We've only got two weeks until the end of police training school.

Scott announces: "We're bringing forward your final exam to Thursday this week."

There's shock in the room, and it quickly descends into chaotic chatter.

In three days' time we're expected to be ready for our final exam. We've just lost two weekends of study time. My revision schedule goes out the window.

"What the fuck," I hear one of the guys say from the other side of the room.

"I can't believe it," I hear another say.

I mutter: "That's just ridiculous."

I can't count the number of times I've thought this during my training.

I don't think whoever oversees this decision has any idea what an impact this is going to have. I doubt they care. The bad feeling about this organisation just keeps building.

Our final policing exam

Rob's been out of the picture for a few weeks. His behaviour got so out of control on three separate occasions, that he's not been allowed back to teach us.

The last straw was when he stormed into the classroom one day while we were all working on writing witness statements. Everyone was scattered around the room, or other areas of HQ, and I'd been talking to Scott at the front of the classroom.

Rob stomped past us so fast you could feel the wind. As he rounded some desks a few feet away, we stood and watched as he bent down and started shouting right into a student's face. Rob is a large man; this student was sitting down, and this was intimidating behaviour.

Thinking that this guy must have done something seriously wrong, to warrant this outburst from a trainer, I'm shocked as I listen to Rob berate him on how he'd written his statement.

I could see, from the resigned expression on Scott's face, that he knew he had no choice but to deal with Rob's behaviour once and for all.

***

Post Rob's departure, and with no one able to step in to help train us in those final weeks, Scott has been struggling to keep on top of the admin of a class of 32; and the escalating bad behaviour that has been allowed to play out. It's clear to me he is burned out. I really feel for him.

I'm starting to understand the impact working at Oakshire Constabulary has on people. Maybe Rob's behaviour is because he's been broken by the job?

I hold no grudges against any of these people, it's tough here, and for all the wrong reasons.

Alarmingly, the number of police officers in Oakshire that have taken their own lives through suicide since I started training school, is now three.

According to the Office for National Statistics (ONS), between 2011 and 2020, in England: 13 senior police officers, 160 police officers (sergeant and below), and six police community support officers, took their own lives.

In a decade, 179 people, whose job it is to keep the British public safe, have killed themselves.

***

Today is our final exam and one of the other trainers, Keith, steps in to invigilate. This throws everyone.

It was bad enough bringing the exam forward, but without Scott and Rob there to give us the thumbs up or thumbs down, to let us know if we've passed, before we hit the submit button, we're running the risk of failing, and having to redo the exam another day.

There are some nervous people in the room, me included.

It didn't seem right, but it also didn't seem like cheating. Until now, Scott and Rob would just check the system to see if we'd passed. Thumbs up if we had. If not, we got the thumbs down. We'd re-check our answers until we passed.

We were told not to tell anyone that they do this, but it became very clear that everyone knew it was happening. It became a bone of contention amongst other cohorts training at the same time as us. Obviously being unfair to other students, many of whom were failing first time, in all their exams.

Without them to do this today, we're going to have to trust in ourselves, and hit the submit button blind.

I decide to go very slowly, taking as much time as we are allowed, while one by one the rest of the class files out and heads to the canteen.

I hate it in there after exams; all the chat about the questions, going over and over. Some people crying, others sitting back with an air of arrogance. It's just not my scene. I need to reflect on my own and not absorb others' dramas. So, I'm in no rush to finish and join them.

I get to the point where I can't do anymore, and I hit submit. Keith wanders over to me, and says I've failed by one question. I walk out through the side door, leaving only Eva in the room.

I find Rosie outside, having a walk. Her face tells me she's as frustrated as me.

She asks: "How did you do?"

"I failed by one mark. I'm so pissed off," I reply.

"Me too, it's ridiculous. And all that extra unnecessary stress and now we've now got to do it again; for one mark, when we could have passed if Scott had been there. It's not as if he gives us the answers."

I reply: "It's a shitshow, just really unfair. And bringing the exam forward was a bad idea. What did they think was going to happen?"

Keith comes out through the side door: "Can you get the others to come back in please?"

Rosie wanders back over to the canteen, and I go back into the classroom to see Eva.

"How did you do?" I ask her.

"I failed by four questions," her eyes filled with tears.

Everyone bundles back into the classroom, and we discover that half the class have failed, and about a third by only one question.

Will anyone realise the negative impact that moving the exam last minute has had?

What a waste of time and energy for so many.

***

Because of the pressures of the upcoming NIE, Scott allows Rosie and I to do the re-sit in his office, ahead of everyone else. James had passed it, so doesn't need to join us.

So, the following week, with another weekend of study crammed into our brains, we try to get comfortable in the chaotic and distracting room. It's filled with policing paraphernalia, paperwork, and a multitude of stuff adorning the walls, including the photos Scott took weeks ago, to distract us.

There's barely enough space to fit our laptops on the desks, and the chairs are bloody uncomfortable. But we take this small victory, being able to get this out of the way now, so we can focus on the NIE.

Rosie and I look at each other, wish each other good luck, get our heads down, and hit the start button.

Scott leaves us to it, knowing he can trust us to be professional, and not cheat. We battle once again, through a new set of 80 questions.

I must work hard to stop myself from looking up from my laptop, knowing there are so many things to draw my attention away from the question set before me.

Voices outside raise and lower, as HQ employees, and our cohort pass by the open window. It's warm outside, and I think of all the school students taking exams too.

In what feels like no time, Scott comes back in, confirms we've both easily passed, and we hit submit.

We're done, thank goodness.

Only one more exam to go; the one that really matters to us.

The National Investigators' Exam

Rosie, James and I are sitting the NIE.

I've never worked so hard for an exam in my life, and I'm confident I couldn't have done any more.

I'm less confident about the exam itself, my stomach is in knots; and I can feel an adrenaline rush, as I get myself set up.

Good news is that we get to sit it alone, at home, on our laptops. No pressure of having other people, or distractions around us. It's my perfect exam conditions.

It's also open book exam, which means we can be surrounded by our books and notecards; even have web pages open.

We have two hours to complete the 80-question multiple-choice examination and can take it anytime between 8am and 8pm. We all take it in the morning because we want it over and done with.

The two hours fly by; with one and a half minutes to read, digest, and answer each question, the open book concept doesn't help much.

Some of the questions and answer options are so long I end up with seconds to pick one of the four possible answers.

Noticing the countdown clock keeps the adrenaline rush going. And then it's over, there's nothing more I can do.

Graduation Day

Graduation Day. We're asked to be in for 9am, although the ceremony doesn't start until 12pm.

This is the last day we'll all be together, the last day in this classroom. I feel no sadness about this. I'm excited to get out of this environment – into what I hope will be a more grown-up place of work.

It's also, thankfully, the last day lugging all our stuff what feels like half a mile from car to classroom.

Stuff everywhere. Ironed white shirts hang from every safe place people can find, avoiding creases. Hats perch on desks. Boots get their final shine, also on desks.

Rob is back. People are asking why. *Is it appropriate?* For some it's downright disconcerting.

***

Twenty degrees Celsius, but feels way hotter because the sun blazes and we're in multiple layers: black boots, socks, black trousers, the smarter white shirt ironed to within an inch of its life, black tie, and topping it all off – black blouson jacket. *This time my zip is in the right place.*

We're all dressed, ready to go. Our guests start arriving, everyone getting messages, getting distracted.

"Alright, go meet your families and friends, and be back here at 11.45pm." Scott's voice manages to cut through the chatter.

People rush out of both exits, meeting guests in various locations around HQ grounds.

I find my husband – who's taken a rare afternoon off work – and my friend Suzanne, who couldn't miss this momentous occasion. It's her that kick-started my journey to this place.

"I'm so proud of you, I can't believe it. You look great in your uniform." She beams at me.

I'm chuffed. Today feels like a much bigger deal now. A real sense of achievement washes over me. And relief.

"Let me take a photo of you two." She gets her phone out, points me towards my husband.

As I walk over, he gives me a smile, puts his arm around me. He's not one for words, but I can tell he's proud of me.

***

Back in the classroom, Scott gives instructions: "You won't be marching to the lineup. Just make your way to the grass area in front of the main building. And line up as we've practised."

I look at James. *He's going to be annoyed.* His face shows it.

Over the last month we've been sent out to the HQ car park to learn marching. James, with his military background, and Harvey, with his police cadet experience, had led one half of our cohort each – trying to teach us to march so we could look disciplined on Graduation Day.

It hadn't been easy for them. People took the piss, didn't take it seriously. Some of us aren't that coordinated. I'd found it fun – being outside in late spring sunshine, an opportunity to move.

We'd organised ourselves into four rows: tallest at the left, smallest at the right of each row. All we had to do was re-member which row to stand in, who was to our left and right, ensure we have an arm's length between each of us.

Now, while we haven't had to march into place, we have managed to walk over and get ourselves tidily lined up.

It's a miracle. People are finally taking this seriously. I look around, proud of this rabble and how we've all scrubbed up.

It feels like forever – standing in these rows, waiting for the Deputy Chief Constable in the summer sun. Usually his responsibility to host these events, the Chief Constable is busy elsewhere today.

Standing still for this long challenges most people, but with our arms behind our backs, dressed head to toe in black, facing into glaring sunshine, all our friends and family staring at us – I'm concerned whether anyone is struggling.

We get through it without anyone fainting. And lots of handshaking later, we're all packed into a stiflingly hot room with our friends and relatives. Not big enough for our cohort and all our guests, some of them are now standing in the heat.

We hear speeches from the Deputy Chief Constable and our trainers. Then we're called up, one by one, to receive our graduation certificates.

It takes time, but it's a proud moment for everyone. *We've made it.*

Just like that, nearly five months at training school is over.

NIE results are in

I've decided that the best way to get through the ADP is to have a holiday between each of the different elements of the programme, to clear my head, and start afresh each time I move. I know I'll have to be lucky because booking holiday is notoriously difficult.

My husband and I have managed to get a few days away, in Greece.

We spent time reconnecting, soaking up the sunshine, swimming, and watching the ocean ebb and flow; totally re-laxing. While we spent our days resting by the pool and on the beach, I read a fascinating book that had just been published.

No Comment was written by Jess McDonald, one of the first people to gain a place on the Metropolitan Police's accelerated detective programme.

Naïvely, as I read the eye-opening, and often shocking account, exploring the reality of being a trainee detective in the Met, and written by a woman with the same ambitions as me, I think things must have changed in the four years since her experience. *They must have...*

I brush aside an uncomfortable, nagging feeling.

With police training school washed from my system, I feel more than ready to start Response, and mentally prepared for starting night shifts. It's time to use all the law knowledge; and get out there.

I'm still full of the promise of the recruiting teams at Oakshire Constabulary; things will be different here, things will be different for me, surely?

***

I'm out for a now rare walk and coffee with Suzanne, when I see a message from Rosie on our ADP WhatsApp group: "Results are in."

I relay the news to Suzanne: "Wow. The NIE results are out."

Neither of us can believe they've come through while we're together.

Suzanne says: "Oh my God, have you passed?"

"I have no idea. I have to access the results through my work emails. I'll have to wait until I'm home."

"Shall we leave now?" she asks.

"Oh no, let's enjoy this moment. But do you want to come round, and be with me when I find out?"

"Yes, I'd love to, how exciting. I'm sure you'll have done brilliantly."

Suzanne is so kind, and incredibly supportive during my policing journey, even if I do lovingly describe her as, "the one that got me into this mess."

I try hard not to look at my phone when I'm with friends but today is an exception and Suzanne is as invested as I am.

I see another message appear from Rosie: "Failed."

Closely followed by one from James: "Me too."

Now I'm really nervous. And I really feel for them; what a disappointment.

I reply: "I'm so sorry guys. I'm out at the mo, so can't check mine."

The walk back home seems to take so much longer than the walk there, and Suzanne and I rush into my house.

I'm apprehensive about logging on to my work laptop, it seems to take forever.

And finally, there it is, the email.

I double click to open it, and discover there's more clicks, and new windows to open, before seeing the results.

I've passed! My hard work, and sacrifices have paid off. I'm so proud of myself.

And Suzanne is so proud of me, she's beaming, as she throws her arms around me in congratulations: "Olivia, that's amazing, well done. I knew you'd do it."

And better still I got 68%. I'm blown away. I never expected that.

I let the others know; feeling bad for them as I hit send on the WhatsApp message.

In this sitting, 20 out of 38 at Oakshire Constabulary pass, with 55.7% or above.

Exams at school weren't great for me, my parents' dysfunctional marriage and the tensions at home impacted my ability to focus. I start to think that, despite having my confidence shattered, and my brain fried, by training school, *maybe I can really do this, now I'm out of there.*

Part Three: Response

Day one

STRAP YOURSELF IN, IT'S going to be a wild ride.

I'm a middle-aged probationer police constable, on her first day at Northcliffe police station. It's one of the busiest policing areas of Oakshire and I'm here for six months.

Drugs and domestics are a big issue in Northcliffe, along with theft – usually to fund drug habits that stem from mental health issues that stem from adverse childhood experiences.

I'm not daunted by what seems to others as too big a change of job, working hours, and environment.

While I've been office based my whole life, I've also spent time in factories and warehouses, warm and cold, during the day and night; depending on what projects I was working on at the time.

And no one really knows all the details of my previous work experience.

They'd be surprised to hear that I had to deal with employees who committed various criminal offences: rape, dangerous driving in HGVs, and assisting a murderer, by transporting the victim's body parts, in a work vehicle.

***

I count myself lucky, because I'd had a welcome email from an acting sergeant a few weeks earlier. I'd arranged to come in to meet my new team one Sunday morning and sat in during their 7am briefing.

It had been a slightly awkward experience because it was early, and people were tired. Even so, I was glad I'd done it, because it means I know some of the faces I see when I arrive today.

I'd also met Dom, one of the nicest people I've met at Oakshire Constabulary; so kind and well mannered. He'd really looked after me that morning, showing me around the station.

We've been messaging in the run up to today, so my nerves are in check, and I have a healthy amount of adrenaline.

As luck would have it, he's the first person I bump into as I use my warrant card (complete with hideous photo from training school) and which doubles as a security pass, to get into the police station.

As we head into the kitchen, where the all-important tea making is underway, ready for the shift briefing, Dom tells me the news I'd been hoping for: "I'm going to be your tutor."

I beam: "Oh that's brilliant. I'm so pleased."

I know working with him is going to put me at ease, and my learning journey will be so much less stressful than training school.

I really needed a break like this, if I'm going to stick with this new career choice.

It's day one at Northcliffe police station, and things are looking up.

***

My first day is the beginning of a set of four late public order shifts. Start time is 3pm, and we are meant to finish at midnight.

3pm is when we get paid from, when shift briefing starts. But we must get there way before that, to get into our kit and ready for briefing.

If you're on tea duty, you've got to factor time in for that too.

I sit through my first shift briefing as a police constable; this is real now. And now I must try and remember the huge amount of information that is fired at us via the briefing slides.

After briefing, I get five minutes with the sergeants.

Already acutely aware of some people's dubious reactions to me, as if they have already decided my fate in this organisation, I get the same sense today.

Week one

It's day two, and another member of our team, Larissa, has heard that a woman has been arrested by officers on the Neighbourhood Policing Team (NPT), brought to the station, and needs searching.

"Do you want a search for your OneFile? We need a female officer to search a suspect, as the arresting officers are both male," she asks me.

"Uh, yes," I reply, hesitantly, not feeling ready for this opportunity.

OneFile is the software platform we use to track and complete examples of work we've done, so we can move onto each next stage of our policing careers. The first stage must be completed during our time with a tutor, before we become fit for independent patrol (FIP).

Larissa sticks her head into the sergeants' office: "Sarge, are you OK for Olivia to do this search for NPT?"

"Yeah, good idea." I hear him yell back to her.

This definitely feels too soon. I've not seen anyone else do this on the job yet, and panic that I won't remember all the words from training school which is still a blur.

But the thing with policing is that you just have to get on with it, and I'm used to that. So, Larissa and I wander out to the car park, chat to our NPT colleagues, and I ask if there's anything I need to inform the suspect of, before starting the search.

One says: "Nah, we just need the search doing before we take her to custody."

If a police officer does a Stop Search, they must tell the person why they've been stopped, and that they will be searched. We use the mnemonic 'GOWISELY,' to remind us of everything we need to say.

Each letter in the acronym represents a piece of information we must communicate: Grounds for suspicion, Object of the search, Warrant card (if not in uniform), our Identity, the

Station we're from, their Entitlement to a search record, and the Legal power we're using.

The Y represents: You are detained for the purposes of a search which is obviously important to say first, not last.

Today, this woman has been arrested, although it's unclear what for, so I don't need to use GOWISELY.

I just have to search her entire body, to make sure she's got nothing harmful on her.

"Hi, I'm PC Gray, I'm going to search you now. I'm going to start at your head and work my way down. Let me know if there are any issues."

It's a boiling hot day, and she's not wearing much so there's nowhere to hide anything in her clothes. Checking around the bra area is important, but she's not wearing one. I still have to run my hand around the area, to ensure nothing is taped there.

She's been through this before. She's not bothered by what I'm doing. I think this is an easy first search. I find nothing on her.

Larissa and I wander back inside and she says: "That was a really thorough search, well done."

I'm pleased, I have always prided myself on doing a good job, and it's such a relief to hear I've done well. I realise I've had no encouraging feedback on my progress at Oakshire Constabulary; not even when I passed the NIE.

As we go back inside, passing the sergeant's office, Larissa sticks her head through the door.

"Olivia did really well," she tells the sergeant.

Then I hear him shout: "What powers did you use?"

I stop suddenly in the corridor outside the office and freeze, realising he's speaking to me. I'm stumped. I didn't get the full story before doing the search, it all seemed rushed. And I'm not someone who performs well when put on the spot like this.

I don't answer his question quickly enough, hesitating a moment too long, I can't get my currently overstimulated brain to function, and pull the information from where it is stored.

We must have a police power to do anything. This refers to the inherent authority of the state to regulate behaviour and maintain order within its territory to ensure public welfare, health, safety, and morals.

This power encompasses a wide range of actions, including the ability to arrest individuals, stop and search people and vehicles, enter private property, and seize items. It's rooted in the concept of the government's responsibility to protect its citizens and uphold the law.

"Always know your powers, Olivia. Always know your powers," he shouts again.

I'm gutted. I feel like a total twat.

Hot sweaty summer

I've started Response policing during a heatwave.

Usually, I'd be wearing shorts at the weekend, and light-weight dresses to work, but I'm now doing a job which involves wearing the most ridiculous number of layers, and mostly black synthetic fibres.

My first couple of weeks at Northcliffe police station are made so much more challenging by the constant feeling that I may pass out.

Once kitted up in the kit room on the first floor, I lug my oversized backpack, filled with more kit (hats, high vis traffic jackets, that we might need while out and about), and my laptop bag, down to the main office, known as the report writing room, where I try to find a seat.

The room is a large wide rectangle, with a bank of cupboards that runs almost to the far end, separating the detectives from the Response and NPT teams.

Walls, and sides of cupboards, are adorned with posters that have become wallpaper, because there's little time to consume their content.

A large television sits high on each of the side walls and are switched on for major events. The sound coming from them slightly out of sync. Being highly sensitive, the noise makes learning, focusing, or concentrating difficult.

The report writing room is generally a welcoming environment. But those at the end of our nine or 10-hour shifts are usually so knackered from the multitude of incidents they've dealt with, that sometimes they can hardly speak. They can't get their brains to function.

That will be me soon.

While they try to smile as we arrive fresh for the start of our shift, the faces of those we are taking over from show the dread of the ever-looming paperwork, that I'm quickly learning, remains untouched from shift to shift.

Sometimes, they'll chat about incidents they've dealt with, fights, chases, take downs, who got PAVAd, and an array of unbelievable stuff that's happened to them for the first time.

They also process the evidence bags that must be completed before they can go home. This means bagging stuff up, labelling it and taking it to SOCO (scenes of crime officers).

I see young people, decades younger than me, who should be full of life and energy, but who are exhausted, and broken.

I wonder if the two large fridges, full of ultra-processed, sugary, caffeinated food and drink, are partly to blame. Nearly a year after my Ride Along, I wonder again how young people doing this job survive on this stuff which is partly to blame for the UK's obesity crisis.

The rushes and crashes they are putting their bodies through; and the lack of nutrition is shocking to me. This stuff is not food.

***

At shift changeover, finding a seat in the report writing room isn't always possible, so I go straight to the briefing room. Pocket notebook at the ready and laptop out, I quickly check emails before not having time to look at them again until the next shift.

Anything past midday, and temperatures in the briefing room reach over 40 degrees Celsius – the sun shines on it all day, and if no one has closed the blinds it gets even hotter.

The debate is always whether to open the windows, and let in more heat and car fumes from the busy and noisy road outside, or keep them shut to try to maintain a very slightly lower temperature.

Rush hour traffic in Northcliffe is busy and tempers fray in the heat. Frustrated and angry drivers beep their horns at the roundabout nearby. This sudden and jolting sound constantly interrupts the flow of our briefings as we review photos of local criminals who are wanted, missing people who need to be found, and areas that are being targeted for crime.

The long rectangular table has plenty of uncomfortable chairs to seat the whole team. Chair backs angled in a way that make your pelvis tilt awkwardly, compressing the spine with the weight of our kit.

Any spare chairs are going to be filled in the coming months – I've heard there's loads more probationers joining the team.

Tea duty

Someone must make the tea for our briefings, and that falls to whoever most recently became fit for independent patrol (FIP). It's a rite of passage in policing. Currently that's Paul's responsibility.

Paul is also on the ADP; and has been on the team for seven months already. He's taking a lifetime to get enough of his second stage OneFile done so that he can move to his first detective placement which should have happened by now.

With no one else becoming FIP for at least 10 weeks, Kim and I muck in.

Kim and I met in the ladies changing room at HQ one day during training school. We'd been chatting about the female trouser fitting debacle and realised we'd be on the same team. She was five weeks ahead of me on her journey.

She's just finished her four weeks on NPT, so we're starting in Response just one set of shifts apart. I'm so grateful for our connection, as we bond over the challenges of learning this job.

10 weeks with a tutor

Every new police officer gets a minimum of 10 weeks with a tutor in Response. Those who spend time on NPT get a tutor for those four weeks too.

I'm so lucky that my team is currently really experienced, as many teams are already full of officers with less than two years' experience. We have six with over five years, and that makes a big difference: attitudes, ability to learn from, and ability to deal with certain types of jobs.

Having put the years in, these experienced officers will all be tested over the coming months with all the new probationers joining, all of whom need a tutor.

Sadly, most don't want to be tutors, and some actively avoid doing the role. Tristan is one of those. He's insistent that if he gets a tutee, he's not having a workload as well.

Workload refers to the investigations that we input to the crime management system after each incident we attend. It's also incidents we haven't attended but reports that the FCR have dealt with, added to the crime management system, and allocated out for investigation.

I think how lucky I've been to get Dom as my tutor. I am confident these short 10 weeks will get me on the right track, before I go out policing on my own.

Being tutored – first three weeks

I've got so much to learn, but spending my days with Dom is an experience I will always cherish and be so grateful for.

Dom is tall, muscular and in his late 20s. He's been doing the job for six years. He makes me feel safe and feeling safe is something I haven't experienced in this organisation so far.

I think he is brilliant; everyone thinks he's brilliant. He has time for everyone. Well, he doesn't, but he tries his hardest to make time. He arrives early and leaves late because he invests time in engaging with people.

I see a vulnerability there, lying under the kind human, and excellent police constable. He is the kind of police constable I want to be and he is the kind of leader I love to work for.

Dom is a response driver, highly trained to operate police vehicles under emergency conditions and equipped to navigate traffic at high speeds, so we can respond quickly to incidents.

So, we mostly spend our shifts travelling fast, blue lights and sirens on, going from one incident to another.

In the rare moments we're not at an incident, we drive around looking for suspicious behaviour and being a presence on the streets of Northcliffe.

Dom tries hard to build my confidence in using the radio and tests my police powers and law knowledge. I feel comfortable with his approach and rarely freeze when questioned by him.

I discover early on that my tendency to be brief when answering questions, and delivering information doesn't always work when relaying information to the Force Control Room (FCR).

The radio makes me anxious. I never get the hang of it. And I certainly never get a love for using it.

I feel like an idiot trying to work out which buttons to press, how long for, when is the right or best time to radio in. I avoid it as much as I can, finding other ways to update without my voice flying across the airways, for all to hear and judge.

Dom and I have deep and meaningful conversations about life. These are my favourite kinds of conversations.

In all interactions, I try to keep the high level "how are you" and "I'm fine" to a minimum, before trying to find a deeper connection with people, to have conversations around. We're able to do this, so I feel a real connection build with Dom.

This is what I was looking for in a team environment.

Ghosts in Alderhorn

Northcliffe covers around 100 square miles, and each shift there are incidents across the whole area. We spend a lot of time policing dangerous A roads, trying to manage traffic at a high risk to our own lives.

There are regular disputes about jobs on our borders with other constabularies. Add into the mix our colleagues in the Roads Policing Unit, and it's a constant battle of who gets to deal with the incident.

Only when a job is 'juicy', potentially involving a serious conviction, chasing a drug dealer or a death, does everyone want to turn up and deal with it.

***

Amongst our responsibilities of areas to patrol regularly, is the Alderhorn estate, one of Dom's favourite places to go. Especially on a night shift. We can cover a lot of ground travelling there and back, ensuring large sections of Northcliffe have a police presence, and particularly the many estates of huge houses that are burglary risks.

We're on one of our trips there one night when Dom asks: "Did you know it's haunted around here?"

"What, the house?"

"No, the area just down the road. I'll take you there."

"No thanks. I have a sixth sense, and I'm not sure I'm ready for that."

I really don't need any distractions while I'm trying to learn this job.

Dom pulls into a parking space outside Alderhorn House, a historic stately home built in the mid 1800s. We maintain relationships, and patrols, at several strategic locations across Northcliffe, so pop in to say hello to the security team.

We're warmly greeted at the door, our arrival having been spotted on the CCTV: "Good evening," the head of security says, inviting us in for a coffee.

I'm still getting used to working night shifts, drinking caffeine after 1pm, and eating in the middle of the night. Science has proved that it is incredibly unhealthy to eat at night, when you're meant to be sleeping. As night shift workers, we have no choice, and we're constantly trying to adjust our body and digestion clocks.

I work hard to try and maintain a fasting window of a maximum of 12 hours, ideally 10; but some nights it's hard because we use up so much energy and must eat. I am managing to stick to my strict rules about how many hours between my last coffee, and going to bed; whatever time of day or night that might be.

We enter Alderhorn House via the door to the right of the vast building. Despite visiting the estate so many times for walks with friends, and going for coffee at the pretty cafe, I've never been into the main building or gardens.

Not far in through the door, you step into the main hall which boasts a large stone floating staircase. The engineering blows my mind.

What feels like 100 feet above us, is an impressive ceiling. Giant scallops surround a centre circle and sit neatly above arched windows. Lighting illuminates a multitude of features. The colours are bright in this space, and the effect is spectacular.

We're shown into a beautiful wood panelled room where we find the coffee and biscuits, I take one, knowing it will do me no good, before being shown around parts of the building that aren't locked up for the night.

For a moment, it makes me sad as to how many of the world's historic buildings have been wiped out due to wars and terrorism. Sociopaths fighting for what is not theirs. I long for a world where women have a fairer share of power and are enabled to be themselves, so this madness can be reduced.

As we get back in the police car and make our way out of the vast estate, we find ourselves on an empty winding road, eerie in the pitch black, huge trees surrounding us. We can only see what the police car lights illuminate in front of us.

I wind the window down to listen to the night; and hear an owl in the distance. My vivid imagination hears screaming.

It creeps me out, and I don't want to drive down this road again, especially alone.

I stink

Never in my life do I stink as much as I do this summer.

I am not a sweaty person; it takes a lot for me to sweat. I normally just go very red in the face, and my neck becomes blotchy. It's not a great look. I've spent most of my life trying hard not to feel self-conscious about it, particularly when people just can't stop themselves from looking.

Daytime temperatures of at least 25 degrees Celsius have lasted for over a fortnight, and with high humidity, the nights are providing little respite. The briefing and kit rooms don't cool down for weeks.

I've adapted well to shiftwork, and sleeping during the day. Not having children helps, although my cats do ensure that sleep is never continuous.

My poorly cat has made a remarkable recovery and is back to her old self, if not a little clingier than before. I often wake up asking myself why my back or legs are in pain, and realise I have a cat lying on top of me.

But I can't resist them, they bring so much joy to my life, their unconditional love has got me through some dark days. Always a happy welcome whenever I get home, whatever time of day or night. Their soft grey fur clings to everything I wear, especially my black uniform, and lands on every surface in our home. Lint rollers are a permanent feature.

But this heat is making daytime sleeping a real challenge.

***

Today is the hottest day of the year so far, and as I put on all my kit in preparation for a late shift, it's 36 degrees Celsius. With temperatures at their highest, I put on black boots and socks, black trousers and a black polyester polo shirt (apparently breathable), as well as a stab vest with multiple layers to save our lives.

And to top it all off, a tac vest holding various gadgets: a radio, a torch, handcuffs, a baton, a body-worn camera, leg restraints, PAVA, a pocket notebook, pens, and several pairs of blue nitrile gloves.

I start to sweat before I've left the kit room. By the time I lug my bags down the stairs, I'm horribly uncomfortable, and feeling woozy. All I can think about is the nine and a half hours ahead of me; and that's only if I'm lucky to get off shift on time.

I just can't believe the heat that has already built up inside all those layers; and that I'm sweating. These uniforms create an ecosystem of their own; trapping air, until you can bear it no longer.

***

Several hours into the shift, exhausted from the heat, I slump into a chair in the report writing room.

There's meant to be air conditioning in here, but it doesn't work. Unable to bear it any longer, I unzip my tac vest, then my stab vest, pulling the uncomfortable weight away from my body.

I'm met with a stench I've never experienced from my own body before.

"Oh my God, I can't believe how much I stink," I say out loud at the shock.

One of the team gives me some great advice, that's sadly too late for today: "Never remove your uniform until the end of shift. It's so much worse when you have to put it back on."

My first sudden death

I experienced the loss of several relatives and friends, relatively early in my life.

In my late 20s, over a period of two years, six people I loved died, including my mum. I'd looked after her for the five short weeks that she lived, following her cancer diagnosis.

She was 63 and I was 29. I watched her die, an honoured experience, but one that seemed to go on for hours, after the sound of the death rattle that I'd always thought death immediately followed.

My brother had been in New Zealand and was half way back on a plane when she took her last breath. I had to pick him up from the airport the next day and break the news.

I'd been close to mum's parents, and was involved in their care, spending a lot of time with both at the end of their lives. I was there for their final days too.

The days related to the death of a loved one, are days you never forget.

So, I'd seen a few dead bodies before joining the police; and wasn't concerned about seeing my first 'on the job.'

Dom and I have just collected some CCTV from Sainsbury's, and as we head across the car park back to the police car I say: "I probably should've gone for a wee."

"Do you want to go?"

"Nah, I can't be bothered."

I've learnt that when you're new, any time spent eating, using the toilet, or talking to colleagues has consequences. The workload mounts fast.

Before we've settled back into the police car; we're assigned a 'concern for welfare' job.

Theresa is in her mid-50s, not much older than me and we know from the details relayed to us, from the FCR, that she's been very unwell, and recently come out of hospital.

She lives in a lovely community, where neighbours look out for each other. A couple of them had reported their concerns to the police when they hadn't seen her for a few days.

Theresa's shower is still running when we get there. Her first-floor flat front door is also unlocked. I wonder if she knew how ill she was, and thought it would be easier for people to get in to help her. Or if she was so unwell that she simply forgot.

We find her dead body, yellow and naked, face-down on the floor, half in the hallway and half in the living room. It's such an awkward position we have to step over her multiple times.

Not sure what else to do, and always looking for something practical, I asked Dom: "Can I switch the shower off?"

"Yes."

The same answer is not given when, regretting my decision not to go for a wee at Sainsbury's, I ask him if I can use Theresa's toilet which hasn't been flushed. I'm not sure why I'm not allowed to use it.

If it had been the week before, the week I stank, this experience would have been much, much more challenging; but today while it's still late 20s, it feels much cooler.

Even so, we open the lovely big windows of Theresa's flat, as the place needs ventilating.

Dom's chatting on his radio and when he gets off says: "We're going to be here for a few hours. The undertakers are at a funeral miles away. They're meant to get here within an hour, but that's not going to happen."

Then he tries explaining the sudden death process to me, showing me the online forms that we can complete offline. But I am now so desperate for a wee that I can't concentrate. I'm jumping from foot to foot, trying to focus on what he's saying.

We're in Theresa's tiny kitchen, separated from the sparsely furnished, but decent sized lounge, by an arch. It's the only place we have a surface to complete our paperwork on.

"I have to find a toilet, sorry," I say as I race out of the property, and round the corner to a supermarket nearby.

What a relief; and what a big learning lesson. I expect I'll be drinking a lot less water from now on. And sacrificing my hydration for the job.

One of the neighbours has spotted me going back into Theresa's flat, and a few minutes later we hear a quiet female voice. And then see a head peering around the edge of the front door which she has opened; fortunately, not wide enough for her to see Theresa's body.

"Hello," I say to her.

She replies: "Hello, sorry, we've been so worried about her. We haven't seen her for days. One of my neighbours heard her shower running for ages; and then we realised it was still running the next day. Is she ok?"

This is such a difficult question to handle; and the first time I must break the news of someone's death in this job.

"I'm really sorry but she's died. We're waiting for the undertakers."

After she's gone, Dom says: "We need to turn the body to check the other side."

We need to make sure she doesn't have any injuries that could make her a victim of a crime. It's why police attend sudden deaths, to ensure there's no suspicious circumstances.

I look at Dom and realise he means me. I bend down, trying not to kneel on the body which is taking up most of the floorspace. I try to shift the heavy cold weight by her shoulder. I can barely move her, but manage just enough to see her bloodied face, where she's broken her nose as she hit the floor.

Nothing else gives us the impression that this is a suspicious death. It's just a sad and lonely end to a broken human's life.

I will never unsee her naked yellow body; a woman who has no one to organise her funeral.

The undertakers don't reach us for four hours; a long time to spend with a naked dead body, in a three-room home.

Being tutored – the next seven weeks

Tristan has made it very clear that he doesn't want to be a tutor.

But at the end of my first three weeks, with most of the team in the report writing room at the end of a set of three late shifts, Dom announces:

"I'm going to be tutoring Kim from the next set of shifts. Tristan is going to be tutoring you, Olivia."

Tristan, who is standing nearby, is clearly unhappy about this decision. And for obvious reasons, so am I. In fact, I'm downright disappointed and gutted.

I'm making progress with Dom, and enjoying my time as a police constable. It's a safe learning environment, and has some structure to it. Dom makes such an effort to develop me and my skills. And he is an awesome human.

I feel our conversations are mutually beneficial. He learns from my middle-aged woman wisdom, while teaching me to be a well-rounded and confident officer.

He also guides me with the mounting investigations that have already landed on my workload, seven so far. These are mainly shop thefts, a criminal damage, and a domestic abuse investigation; we get out and about, trying to tackle the necessary enquiries to progress them.

I gather CCTV and take witness statements; something I need to learn to do well, before I'm on my own. I also get time to call the victims, and speak to Dom to build my understanding of where I can take each investigation next.

Each investigation requires such a wide range of different actions, there is so much us probationers need to learn, that can only be learnt alongside experienced officers.

If not, we'll be making it up as we go along.

I'm not sure why this change in tutors hasn't been announced by a sergeant; but then I remember how absent they seem to be.

I haven't seen the one who I thought was my line manager since the first week. He was whisked off to CCID (the Central Crime Investigation Department) for 10 weeks; where I'm heading after Response.

Those few minutes I got with the sergeants on day one is the only time I've had with a senior officer.

***

The next shift I'm with Tristan, and everything changes; seeding more doubts about the organisation, and my policing career.

I'm going to start with the positives. There are things about Tristan that I really like, and moments during our time together that I really enjoy.

When we're out and about dealing with incidents, he really can be a great police officer. Unfortunately, while I am his tutee, the bad outweigh the good; and my seven weeks with him are painful.

I'm just amazed at how someone can be so good at the job, and overall professional, but at the same time so critical of everyone we encounter. He bitches about people all day long.

To start, I challenge his unjustified negative thinking about others, but it doesn't go down well. He struggles to understand that other people don't have his experience or expertise, so can't see things as he does.

Tristan is a poor communicator, he dictates rather than having a conversation, he doesn't ask or listen, and he doesn't know how to coach people. He simply doesn't like to hear others' opinions; he just wants to share his own.

And he's one of those people who manages to change most conversations around, so they become all about him.

I'm not sure how he finds the time, but he monitors what other colleagues are doing, by tracking their locations on the radio software, and then bitches about why they haven't gone to certain jobs.

It is disconcerting when you walk into the report writing room, and find Tristan whispering. You feel paranoid that you're his target.

More investigations have landed on my workload that I haven't been involved with, have no idea what to do with, and am now not getting support with. I'm not sure how the sergeants are deciding who gets what, but I seem to be getting more than my fair share.

One is a theft that has now been reclassified by a faceless person I don't know, as a robbery. Tristan's only contribution is: "That shouldn't be with you, it should go to LCID."

LCID is the Local Crime Investigation Department, the detectives on the other side of the report writing room.

It's overwhelming and unsettling, even before you feel like you're bitched about by colleagues who you thought you could trust.

I recommend to anyone that, unless you've had a conversation with the person you're bitching about, just remember that you don't have the whole picture. Try speaking to people, learn, and understand.

The world could be a much nicer place.

***

Today a few of us are in the report writing room, with some rare time to deal with our workloads.

Unusually, we've even got time to chat, and bond as a team; and our acting sergeant has joined us. I feel my shoulders drop and my breathing slow down, for what feels like the first time in ages.

Tristan has clearly been tracking one of our colleague's movements; and I hear him telling the sergeant: "She doesn't go to jobs that she should."

I'm shocked. I thought they were friends. And I thought we were a team. I thought we were meant to have each other's backs. This is policing, we need to be able to trust each other.

***

Tristan regularly reminds everyone that he's been told that tutors don't have workloads, as they spend their time helping their tutees with theirs. He is still very vocal about it.

It's not clear what percentage of a tutor's time is meant to be spent helping their tutees with their workload, but Tristan doesn't help me with mine. He'd say he does, but that's because on occasion, when I'm trying to decompress, and quietly looking at my workload on the crime management system, he will shout at me from across the banks of desks, and make suggestions on what I should do.

I'm never in the investigation that he's referring to, sometimes I don't even remember the details of the crime he's talking about because I've already got so many.

"Olivia, you need to call the manager at the Spar, get a victim statement done."

"Which investigation?"

I manage to get two words out before he starts with the next piece of advice. "And have you got the CCTV yet at Tesco? Make sure you get that asap."

"I don't know which investigations you're talking about. I'm in the domestic abuse one now, trying to find the number of the victim so I can call her."

"Have you invited Carl in for his suspect interview?"

"No, I need to speak to the victim first. You told me that the other day, but I haven't had time to do it yet."

He rarely gives me time to process what he's saying. And most of the time he talks so fast, I don't get the chance to write down what he's saying.

So, the result is that I don't take in much of what he tells me. And I make no progress, because when I ask for advice about a particular element of an investigation, he gets frustrated, because apparently, he's already told me what to do.

Just not working for me

Having Tristan as my tutor isn't working for me, and I'm feeling the stress and anxiety building; working with him gets more and more frustrating.

He doesn't understand how to train, coach or mentor people. I find him draining to be around.

He doesn't think of the things that are important for my police learning. Like talking me through different types of investigations that he's been involved in; and how I could manage similar ones in the future.

He works on things on his own that could be valuable for us to do together – like creating prisoner handover documents, wanted files, or adding details of suspects that need to be arrested by the next shift to the briefing content; even how to search for a vehicle using the ANPR system.

I'm just not getting the bigger policing picture.

What he does do, is regularly repeat instructions about the most basic things, things that I already know, and that I'm doing such as getting CCTV and completing sudden death paperwork.

I don't think I'm getting quality training, so I worry that I'm never going to be able to do the quality job I want to do.

I'm really proud about how I've managed to learn the law and pass exams. It's an area that I thought I wouldn't excel in. But Tristan belittles my achievement of passing the NIE first time, making it clear that the sergeants' exam, the one he has taken, is so much harder than the NIE.

Rather than recognising that important, and positive part of my policing journey, he makes his achievement of passing the sergeants' exam more important. He's still not a sergeant though.

When we're on the way to a job, he refuses my offers to use my phone to navigate our way there; he knows the way.

And then he gets shitty with me, when I'm not able to provide directions, getting frustrated when I can't input the information into my phone quickly enough.

Our work phones are notoriously bad, failing to connect to the Internet frequently, so after being on the receiving end of this behaviour, I give up using it; and use my personal mobile as sat nav. I also start putting the incident address into my maps every time, just in case.

It would help if all police cars had sat nav, it would save a huge amount of stress and delays. Few do.

Tristan also ignores many things I say to him, resulting in information not being passed on to others. Things that are important while we're in the middle of an incident, like some-thing a witness has said that could lead to a line of enquiry.

Sometimes he ends up driving us to the wrong place. This happens so many times that each time we're on a blue light response, I speculate about how far away from where we're meant to be that we'll end up. One shift we end up in completely the wrong town.

He shuts down a lot of what I say without discussion. Often, I just give up trying to engage with him, because it's a constant battle, so demotivating, and quite frankly exhausting. All the stress of training school is back, in yet another dysfunctional learning environment.

By the end of each shift, I often don't remember what we've done, only remembering the first, and last incidents. Everything in between becomes a mish mash of memories, or just nothing, because my brain is fried.

Job health risks

I know, from listening to countless Dr Chatterjee Feel Better, Live More podcasts, that ever-changing sleep times, stress and long-term shift work can cause chronic inflammation, and chronic disease; and I think my mum's cancer was a result of that lifestyle.

As far back as 2007, The International Agency for Research into Cancer (IARC) categorised shift-working as a "probable" cause of human cancer, because of the impact night-time light has on melatonin.

Light at night is relatively recent in human history and electric lights illuminate our cities 24/7. There are lights in our workplaces, cars, TVs, screens and mobile phones; even advertising billboards are no longer paper posters – they too are illuminated.

It's hard to get away from light and all this extra exposure to it has the potential to mess up the natural sleep-wake cycle, our circadian rhythm. As does night shift work.

The disruption can interfere with melatonin production, our motivation and our willingness to do the things required of us. Our drive is impacted. We lose focus, passion and can't resist temptation. Inevitably we consume more caffeine and sugar.

The more stable our sleep-wake timing, the higher levels of psychological functioning and more positive psychological functioning we have. It impacts our cardiorespiratory fitness.

It also affects our parasympathetic activity, part of the autonomic nervous system. This is what's often described as the "rest and digest" or "feed and breed" response, opposite to the "fight or flight" response of the sympathetic nervous system.

Essentially, it's the system that helps the body conserve energy, slow down bodily functions, and promote relaxation when it's not under stress. We need it to kick in to recover and avoid chronic stress.

Chronic stress can cause the body to produce hormones like cortisol, adrenaline, and noradrenaline. These hormones can weaken the immune system, which can lead to inflammation which can contribute to cancer development and progression.

Unfortunately, chronic stress can also lead to other health problems, like high blood pressure and depression. These problems can make it harder to maintain healthy habits, which can increase the risk of cancer.

I am becoming acutely aware that my "fight or flight" mode is on constantly and that being a police officer comes with massive health risks.

With the approach to training so bad, I'm questioning again whether I really want this. But despite everything, I love the actual job; and I really believe I could be good at it, with the right training and support.

Extra leg room please

BMWs were found unsafe as police vehicles – risk of engine failure and fire from the high speeds and constant idling. They're being replaced by Peugeots, mainly 308s.

These vehicles don't have enough boot room for all our equipment. Worse, Tristan is very tall with very long legs. To make himself comfortable, he has the seat as far back as it will go.

This isn't a problem – until we arrest someone.

I never arrested anyone with Dom, so I haven't sat in the back of a police car yet. Only in vans during public order shifts. Uncomfortable in there – kit taking up floorspace where feet should go. Worse if you're travelling backwards, often facing a drunk in the cage.

Tristan and I are in a Northcliffe park, following reports that a teenager's been threatened.

We're scanning for the suspect when a young lad – no older than fifteen – approaches, rolling a cigarette. "What you up to?"

I respond as vaguely as possible. In case he's our suspect. "We're looking for someone."

Seeing the lad as an irritant, Tristan snaps: "What's it got to do with you?"

"I'm only asking. You don't gotta be so rude."

I see a curious young man who can engage with adults. Polite to police officers. A young man who, given the right support and role models, could have a chance.

But he's also got a grinder. And it appears he's rolling a joint, not a cigarette.

"What's that?" Tristan's voice hardens.

"Nothing."

"You're rolling a joint right in front of us."

The lad looks up, stops rolling as Tristan pulls handcuffs from his tac vest. "I'm arresting you for possession of cannabis. You do not have to say anything, but it may harm your defence if you do not mention when questioned something you later rely on in court. Anything you do say may be given in evidence."

"What, man, I were being nice." His protest cuts through the afternoon air.

I really feel for him. And I'm irritated that we have to arrest him. *Massive waste of police time.* The cost is enormous – police constables, custody teams, detectives, the court system. All for a tiny bit of cannabis.

The situation escalates. Tristan and this lad have clashed, and Tristan can't de-escalate. The boy seems happy to talk to me – *I'm probably the same age as his nan* – but refuses to engage with Tristan beyond sniping.

Standing in handcuffs now, his only defence is silence. Won't give us his name. Any details.

So now we're trapped. No choice but custody. Without his details we can't deal with him at scene – the preferred option, because nobody likes taking kids to custody. We don't know who he is, how old, if he's wanted. *Can't do any usual checks.*

***

Off to custody. My first time. And I have to sit in the back behind Tristan and his long legs.

For everyone's safety, you always put prisoners behind the front passenger seat and avoid having someone in that seat. An officer always travels beside the prisoner.

We get the lad into the car – still sniping at Tristan. I make my way round to the other side, open the door. *There is no leg room.*

"Tristan, can you move your seat forward please?" I plead, showing him the impossible space.

"I won't be able to drive." He huffs and puffs, reluctantly moving his seat forward a tiny amount.

Ridiculous.

I squeeze one leg into the car, try navigating the rest of my body into the cramped space. My knees and shins crush against Tristan's chair back. My spine twists into an awkward position. I have to sit with my legs wide apart.

***

On the uncomfortable drive to custody, danger prickles at my awareness. *How unsafe is this?* If he's going to be this inconsiderate each time we transport prisoners, *this will become a physical problem.*

Also, if a prisoner next to me decided to kick off, there'd be nothing I could do. I'm trapped, unable to move my body to defend myself.

You must be fully aware of the risk – being a foot away from someone who knows they're about to spend hours locked in a cell.

Right now, I'm not concerned. This lad's way smaller than me. My gut tells me he's not going to cause problems.

But still. The vulnerability sits heavy in my chest.

***

On our way to custody, I reflect on the ridiculous situation we're in. Instead of continuing our search for the suspect of a more serious incident, we have been drawn away, because of the UK laws on drugs.

It's a controversial subject, and I'm no expert, but I believe these laws and our approach to drugs needs an overhaul.

Too much time and money are wasted dealing with the problem of drugs. We will never win the war on drugs. Drugs won't go away. There are too many people making too much money from them. There are too many people taking them out of choice. And there are too many damaged people reliant on them to escape their lives.

With all the brilliant minds in the UK, could society and the justice system work better if we decriminalised the taking of all drugs? Some argue that what people do in private, when it harms no one other than themselves, is not criminal.

Could it even be possible to commercialise the production and supply of drugs, run by non profit organisations. Tax the sale of them. Take the power and money from the drug gangs.

The money could be used to invest in solving the mental health problems that lead many people to drugs (and all the other things people become addicted to) in the first place.

We'd have many more resources to invest in prioritising and protecting the vulnerable, as well as dealing with crime that hurts others.

Young people wouldn't get sucked into a life of drug crime. We could even provide safe places for addicts who need somewhere to take their drugs, rather than on our streets, and in our parks, where children play.

With this approach, the drugs produced would be less harmful.

We could remove so many people, abused as children, from unsuitable and depressing accommodation, where they are sent to rot away. Where their drug addictions become so much worse, because there is endless temptation and desperation.

It's a vicious cycle that is negatively impacting society, because there's an attitude that some people don't matter, and that their lives can be thrown away.

In the words of Gabor Maté in one of his other brilliant books In the Realm of Hungry Ghosts: "No one chooses to be an addict." He says: "The question is never why the addiction; it is why the pain?"

People experience unimaginable pain and abuse, particularly as children and once scared they're now scarred.

If we'd lived their lives, we too would be addicts.

Gabor explains: "Drugs do not make anyone into an addict, any more than food makes a person into a compulsive eater. There has to be a pre-existing vulnerability. There has to also be significant stress."

There's also scientific evidence now, that the use of Psychedelics, such as LSD and MDMA, when used as part of Psychedelic therapy, can reverse debilitating effects of depression, anxiety, eating disorders and PTSD. These drugs have been linked to deep emotional processing, which allows the patient to explore trauma, fear, and anxiety in new ways.

Now why wouldn't we want to focus on that? Treat the causes, not the symptoms.

Although I say all of this with the caveat: there's also scientific evidence that alcohol and drugs are bad for our brains, especially young developing brains.

So it's usually best not to consume them, especially without medical expert advice.

St Margaret's public order

Everyone must do St Margaret's public order shifts; and tonight is my first.

It's still week one of being tutored by Tristan. He's not impressed. Because, like Dom, he's a response driver, and would rather be racing around Northcliffe at high speeds, than standing on the streets of St Margaret's, dealing with drunk people and being responsible for me.

I quickly discover that I love it.

I get to meet and learn from other officers and it's fun. I see a different side of policing. Plus it's an opportunity to be in a different environment and be outside in the fresh air – all night.

It's good for us to be out in the elements. Humans are becoming more and more incapable of dealing with the cold, and we're getting sicker as a result, then taking medication to combat the sickness. Experiencing the cold is essential for our health; and why would you want to medicate, when you can get outside instead.

The main objectives for this Friday and Saturday night role are to keep the peace, identify and protect vulnerable women, and stop the fights, as people exit the large club which can hold around 2000 people, and the multiple bars in the town.

We need to get people out of St Margaret's, safely and with minimum disruption to residents.

These are the same objectives for public order in all the towns across Oakshire, on Friday and Saturdays; and the responsibility falls to the team on the late shift.

To accommodate the nighttime economy activity, this shift is 10 hours and starts at 5pm. If we're lucky we finish at 3am, but that depends on arrests, and trips to custody, where you can get stuck for hours.

During St Margaret's public order, for seven hours, we work in tandem with the night shift from St Margaret's police station – they pick up the non-public order incidents. These are the other incidents and crimes that happen outside the town centre. And they take those arrested during public order to custody so we can stay in the town centre.

And this is when I get to see Tariq, for the first time since training school. I'm like a child when I see him: "Oh my God, it's so good to see you."

"Hey, how's it going? You enjoying it?"

"Well, mostly," I reply, hating the fact that we can't get into a deep conversation about our experiences so far right now – and probably won't ever. We're likely to only get snatched chats as our paths cross in this job.

"It's just so good to see you." And then we're drawn away, to deal with incidents.

It's brilliant to see that he's shed the temporary training school bad attitude and is back to his old self, now he's out of that dysfunctional environment. He looks like he's thriving in this job.

Our time on public order shifts is spent engaging with the nighttime economy customers. From teenagers learning how much drink or drugs they can tolerate, to the middle-aged who are shaking off the stresses of working life.

It can be a fun environment, but there's a very dark side. Most towns and cities have one if you look close enough, even in Oakshire.

As someone with a sixth sense, who notices everything, it is always amazing to me at what others find surprising.

Like my neighbours being surprised that there's thieves and burglars in our street. They'd be completely shocked if they had any idea about the level of sexual offences that happen in our town, or the level of domestic violence.

Much of society is blind to what doesn't affect them; until it does. Coming from a broken home this was never a possibility for me; and being hyper aware is part of who I am, and helps with this job.

Predators

The most concerning people we are on the lookout for are the predatory males; we identify and then monitor them. There's a surprising number, and they are often easy to spot. Even the ones who think they are being surreptitious.

Predators sometimes lurk in the shadows, but they also stand proud; and they grow in numbers towards closing time. Ready to pounce on the vulnerable. Ready to pretend they are taxi drivers or simply try and work their charm to get into women's knickers.

In training school, we'd been told about a documentary where journalist Ellie Flynn went undercover to expose the grim extent of sexual harassment women and girls face, both online and in person.

It had been suggested that we watch it in our own time, rather than using class time to watch it. I wonder how many bothered. They should have; it was eye-opening and would have taught some people a lot.

The Channel 4 documentary, Undercover: Sexual Harassment – The Truth, shows how Ellie was followed back to her hotel room by a man, despite repeatedly telling him she was fine on her own.

To most women, the overarching message of the documentary isn't surprising, we've all experienced it, to differing degrees. But the lengths men go to, to get what they want, from someone who is totally unable to consent is truly disturbing.

Women are at risk; intoxicated women are at significant risk. When we are there, this risk is removed. We ensure their safety, we guide them to licensed taxis or the Ubers they've actually booked but can't get to without our help.

For those of you who think women should be more careful, there are many reasons we become intoxicated beyond our control from time to time. Sometimes it's hormones, it could be food, it could be stress, and sometimes, on a night out it's because our drinks are spiked, by predators.

But there are also times when we just want to go out and get really drunk. We should be as free as men are to do this, and not be at risk from predators.

All of this is playing out here, in St Margaret's, right under our noses.

We've identified our suspects, and people are starting to spill out of the club. Now we're identifying the vulnerable. They are as easy to spot as the predators. Then we match the two. We watch the game begin, like watching big cats stalking their prey, the prey completely unaware of the predator's presence.

There's a subtle moment when you know a crime is starting to take shape, and you know it's time to step in. Police come under such scrutiny, and criticism that deciding that moment is crucial.

We're there to keep the peace and keep the public safe, but we must do it within unbelievably difficult parameters. Otherwise, we have people screaming at us, sticking cameras in our faces, or making suggestions about what we should have done; when those judging have no clue about what really took place.

Guiding vulnerable females to their cabs, or back to the safety of the group of friends that they've been separated from, is one of the things that makes me feel like I'm doing a good job. Keeping women and girls safe gives me a strong sense of purpose.

In these circumstances, I don't need anyone to tell me: "Well done." Removing someone from a potentially dangerous situation, where their lives could be changed forever, and they are oblivious to the fact, is one of the things I relish about public order shifts.

***

Aside from predators, there's the drug dealers, who are also easy to spot. And their minions, who are sent into the crowd to create distractions.

These people have no respect for the police, they think they are smarter than us. They think we don't notice. But we're watching, building a picture, building CCTV evidence, creating intelligence.

We also deal with the inevitable fights that break out. Tensions rise within the club and bars, and spill out onto the streets of St Margaret's, where the fresh air hits people, and whatever they've consumed becomes more potent. They think they are superhuman, their senses heightened, and they lose control.

A lot of police time is wasted dealing with men fighting each other for ridiculous pride-driven reasons.

Just trying to do my job

Because Tristan rarely enables me to do my investigations, and no sergeant seems interested in discussing my workload, I decide to be proactive. Once a month we have a training day, which is shorter than normal shifts and we're usually finished by mid-afternoon. Sometimes it's group training on a particular subject matter, but it usually ends up being a day to deal with workload, which is a godsend.

I decide to use some of my own time to do some enquiries on my own.

I need to progress two investigations that are going nowhere, because I haven't been able to speak to, or meet the victims, and encourage them to support police action. For this same reason, I also can't close them, a never-ending challenge in the police.

Face to face interactions are key, making all the difference in building relationships, and getting support. Being 'victim focused' is a priority for Oakshire Constabulary; but you wouldn't think it, based on how we're forced to work, due to sometimes ridiculous demands, and countless inefficiencies.

I call one victim, she runs a business which is a cafe by day, and wine bar by night, and has been the victim of criminal damage. I decide that even if she can't meet today, at least I can make an appointment to see her another day; and that's progress.

Amazingly she answers the phone and explains: "We're closed at the moment, but I'm very happy for you to come over."

This is great news, because we'll get to talk in private, she won't be distracted by customers, and it will be entirely safe. She's a woman in her early 40s, who runs a middle-class business, in a middle-class town.

I'm dressed in civvies, and don't have PPE (personal protection equipment), exactly like I will be when I become a detective and meet with suspects, victims, and witnesses.

I've assessed the risks and don't believe there are any. Unless I'm unlucky, and there's an aggressor who figures out I'm a plain clothed police officer and decides to attack me. I'm not sure how that would happen. I just look like a middle-aged woman going for a chat with another middle-aged woman. We generally get ignored by most of society.

Unfortunately, I don't realise I should have let the Force Control Room know where I was going. This hasn't been drummed into me yet, and it's not something I've noticed others doing.

"Would you like a drink?" she offers, as she shows me to a table by the window.

I politely decline, knowing I want to be as efficient as possible with my time: "No, but thanks so much. It's very kind of you."

As I sit, I say hello to a tradesman who is decorating the window nearby.

I listen to her frustrations about the police: "You're the only officer following up on several incidents I've reported."

I realise I've not had time, or even thought to do a background check which would have identified the incidents and the officers involved. A good learning lesson for next time.

"I'm sorry to hear that," I tell her. I'm frustrated that my colleagues' workload pressures have impacted my ability to get her support, until now.

"I'm happy to support this investigation, now we've met, and now I know it will go somewhere. Thank you for taking it seriously."

"No worries, thank you for your time and support."

We say goodbye and as I leave, stepping out into the cloudy July day, I'm delighted to have made this progress.

This is why face to face is so important.

On the way back, I pop into a shop that has been the victim of a burglary. I have a chat with the manager to give him an update. There's been confusion over his contact details, and I haven't been able to get hold of him on the phone.

I'm careful about who is around, ensure no one else knows who I am, and we talk in the office. It's risk free.

He's very grateful for my visit. I know from my limited experience so far that this investigation is going nowhere and now we've had this conversation, I can finalise the notes on the crime management system and send it for closure. I need to reduce my investigations which now stand at 12, and are full of things I don't know what to do with.

This progress has really motivated me.

***

There's been a lot of chat about what's happened with the tutoring situation in our team and the pressure everyone is going to be under when several more trainees join soon. There is some unrest, and politics playing out that I have no control over, and don't want to get involved in.

However, I need to vent because I've been frustrated that I haven't had the ability to work on my investigations during our shifts.

I mention to a couple of the team how pleased I am with the progress I made on my own on training day.

Towards the end of the set of shifts, always four lates after a training day, the acting sergeant calls me into the sergeants' office.

I have a sinking feeling, as I step into the office: "Hi sarge."

"Hi Olivia, I wanted to talk to you about you doing workload enquiries on your own."

"Ah, is it a problem?" I ask, already feeling like it is a problem, with a mix of embarrassment and irritation at the same time.

I'm told in no uncertain terms that this is not on. "Because you're being tutored and not fit for independent patrol yet, it's too risky."

I feel like an idiot being told off like this, replying: "OK, sorry."

The auditors

People love to film the police.

I'd heard about the self-proclaimed 'auditors' from one of my cohort at training school – a Special Constable who'd encountered them a few times while working in Northcliffe.

Somehow, I'd ended up with an image of professionals who were unofficially there to assess whether the police are doing a good job. But that's probably because I'm middle-aged and don't spend hours on social media watching videos. I like to see and experience the world that is actually happening directly around me.

What I didn't expect to see, the first time I met them, was a pair of 20-something, unkempt men, chatting shit into their phones, while filming the police station, police cars, and any police officers they can get in shot.

Unfortunately, today the car park entrance gates are not working. They're wide open, and a tempting invitation to the auditors. With unrestricted access, they have free reign to wander in.

In the UK, trespassing is generally a civil wrong, but certain types of trespassing are covered by criminal law. These two men know they don't have permission to be on the police station premises, because they've already been told, so they will commit a criminal offence if they step back in.

The problem with the auditors, and anyone else who thinks it's OK to film police doing their jobs, is that they can also inadvertently capture, and publish images of victims and witnesses. They don't care. They would if they were a victim, or someone in the witness protection programme, or a domestic abuse victim trying to hide from their abusive partner.

The obsession to film everything is one of the worst bits of policing for me. The thought of someone you don't know having footage of you, footage that you did not give permission for them to have, and them using it anyway they like, does not sit well with me.

This selfish, and childish behaviour, driven by the need for external validation, is another thing that makes me question whether I want to do this job.

I hate social media for that. It has given society permission to disrespect others, to such an extent that it makes me glad I've had the excuse of joining the police to come off it totally. Not that we're told to, we're just given advice to be careful about the content we publish.

I avoid people's phones at all costs and I've learnt to move fast when they are aimed at me. I will not have someone film me without my permission. In my private sector career, using people's image without their permission was not allowed; we always had to gain permission first.

Most of the time, filming and publishing content of the police does little to help the justice system, it only makes it harder to do our jobs properly and safely.

Tristan and I are pulling up to the station gates when we see the auditors.

"Oh God, here we go," he says as we get closer to them; and they turn to face us.

It takes some time for their brains to connect to their hands, their mobile phones are then lifted and pointed at us. They are blocking our entrance through the gates. I don't think that's their intention; they're just not smart enough to realise.

I often wonder, if people stopped to think about what they were trying to achieve, what their ultimate objective is, whether they'd realise what utter knobs they are being. And maybe they'd stop?

On his podcasts, Dr Chatterjee has often talked about what we would think when we're on our deathbeds, looking back at our lives, on what we've done, haven't done, and what we've achieved.

Would these people be proud of all this footage they've got? Would they be proud of the disruption, and anxiety they caused? Would they be proud that they impacted people's courage to come forward as victims and witnesses?

Social life on hold

As well as worrying that this job might kill me, I also have terrible guilt about not seeing my friends as much as I want to. There are many people I just can't find time to see now I'm working shifts; and I must focus on my closest friends.

I make a promise to myself, and my two best friends, that we will get together once a month.

I get much better at planning these get-togethers well in advance, around my days off at weekends and during the school holidays. I'm working three out of five weekends now, so it's not easy to coordinate.

Sometimes it will be just two of us, sometimes all three of us, sometimes with their kids.

I love these days. They are my favourite days. These are the days that bring me joy and remind me how precious life is. These are the days that give me strength and remind me what is important.

The other thing I've been sacrificing is my love of the theatre.

Usually, by this time of year, I've had a trip to London to see a play at Regents Park Open Air theatre; one of my favourite places. It's an important part of my summer; it reminds me of my mum, as we used to go together.

Now I go with my husband. We have the best day out, picking up delicious food from M&S and picnicking, usually in the summer sunshine, before watching a matinee performance.

I couldn't go during training school because I was studying in the evenings and weekends. Then I couldn't book for the rest of the summer because I had no idea what shifts I was going to be working from July onwards.

Planning anything is hard in this job.

20 years since mum died

It's the first week of August, and 20 years ago that I began five weeks of caring for my mum. Ferrying her in and out of hospital while she was diagnosed with, deteriorating from, and dying of cancer.

I realised what a challenging time of year it is for the NHS. You think winter is bad because it's the time of year when the British media repeat the same old narrative year in year out: creating unnecessary drama, and fear about waiting times, and stopping people who really need help from going to hospital. But there's little focus on what happens in the summer.

At the beginning of August, most junior doctors rotate to different wards to begin new roles, and newly qualified doctors enter their first postgraduate positions. It's when many mistakes are made.

These fresh-faced doctors must go on the same massively steep learning curve that we do as police officers – nothing is as it seems, and no training fully prepares you for the reality of the job.

While the NHS does an incredible job, sadly, often the focus is on treating symptoms, not causes. Treatments can be outdated, not keeping up with new science in all areas.

There isn't enough focus on the importance of stress reduction, or truly getting to the heart of why some people are prone to stress, or the importance of therapy alongside, or before, medication.

Because of the focus on medication, much of the UK, and US, population are naïve to the impact that their diet and lifestyles (including stress) are having the catastrophic effect on the massive spike in chronic diseases such as diabetes, cardiovascular disease, fibromyalgia, arthritis, Crohn's, IBS, and cancer; misunderstanding the smaller role genes play.

We're also duped by giant food companies that repress the science that clearly shows the impact that ultra-processed food is having on humans.

Changing what we put into our bodies, can often have far better results, without the side effects, than medication. Changing how we move our bodies, can have far better results than cutting off bits of our bodies.

Mum's death was inevitable; it turned out that she was riddled with cancer by the time she was diagnosed. It had metastasized and spread into multiple organs – she was going to die. But not as quickly as they predicted. We'd been given a three-to-six-month prognosis, always understanding that these things are difficult to measure.

She died within five weeks of her diagnosis. The acceleration was a result of a miscalculation of the dosage of her blood thinning drug by a junior doctor. Resources were low that day, it was holiday season.

I hold no grudges, it's one of the most difficult jobs in the world; for which I have even more respect now than I did then. This way, mum avoided unnecessary treatments that would have just prolonged her life for a few more months – a life that would have been full of hospital trips.

Instead, we had calmer, precious time together.

Guarding my first mental health detainee

This year in August is when I discover just how broken our mental health service is, the impact that has on the police; and the job I'm trying so hard to learn to do.

After extremely high temperatures in June, it's now been raining for what feels like weeks – impacting people's mental health. I've observed that people act out when the weather is crazy. Two days ago, there were more police in St Margaret's City Hospital's A&E department guarding mental health patients than there were doctors.

Today there's just Tristan and I, with another mental health patient to add to the huge number, who are no longer under police custody, but still here, living in this hospital. They are all waiting to get a space in a mental health facility, or for someone to figure out what else to do with them.

They gather outside the front of A&E, rolling cigarettes, smoking, and chatting, supporting each other in the best way they can. I see people who need community, a sense of purpose, and therapy. Someone to help unravel and then learn to live with memories of their adverse childhood experiences.

We're guarding Pete, who is in a bad way. He clearly needs urgent mental health help. He's head-banged something, and has a giant egg on his forehead, and blackening eyes. He did it again shortly after we arrived, catching us off guard before we learned how best to protect him from himself, and stop him from doing it again.

Other than that, he's pretty chilled; he's been in this situation before. But that doesn't detract from the sorry mess he's in, and how we must carefully manage his care while he's meant to be in the care of the NHS. We're not trained for this.

Pete was detained under Section 136 of the Mental Health Act yesterday; he has been here for 24 hours, and the whole time he's had a police guard. We took over at 9am, two hours into an early shift.

The poor officers we relieved, were already two hours into overtime from a night shift by then.

Tristan is less than impressed. Once again, if he didn't have me to tutor, he wouldn't be here.

These types of jobs are given to probationers, those with less than two years' service, and not completed their second stage OneFile yet, but also tutors with tutees, like Tristan and I. This frees up experienced officers to deal with crimes in action.

As well as not wanting to be here, being trapped in a small windowless space with a man who hasn't showered for a while, and no natural daylight is also playing havoc with Tristan's mood. And mine to be honest. I expect it also doesn't help any of the mental health patients trapped in here for hours on end.

Tristan is trying so hard to be professional. But it doesn't last. He openly talks in front of Pete about the broken system. I cringe and my heart breaks, knowing this talk can only make Pete feel worse.

Tristan isn't happy because he can't leave me alone with Pete. So, he can't take a break. I can't either. We are not meant to leave each other alone.

But today we are lucky. The nursing staff bring us food, and we're able to eat, without incident. This is unusual; usually we do this without food or toilet breaks.

We also manage to figure out a way to all go to the toilet, by going together. It's weird. Weeing while a colleague, and a mental health patient are right outside the door. And then vice versa. We take it in turns. Tristan only needs to go once the entire shift. I go each time he and Pete go. After the sudden death incident, I never miss an opportunity to go for a wee.

Of all the mental health patients I interact with during my time in Response, Pete is one of three I must protect from themselves.

He is not handcuffed, and while this is a risk, Pete's already done enough damage to his head and face, through head banging things, and he's been here so long it isn't justified to keep him restrained.

Section 136 of the Mental Health Act

Section 136 allows the police to take a person, or keep them at a place of safety, without a warrant, if they appear to have a mental disorder, AND if they are in any place other than a house, flat or room where the person is living, or a garden or garage that only one household has access to AND if they are 'in need of immediate care or control'; meaning we think it is necessary to keep them or others safe.

Before using Section 136, the police must consult a registered medical practitioner, a registered nurse, or an AMHP (approved mental health practitioner), occupational therapist or paramedic. So often they are arrested first and taken to custody. If their health is clearly an issue, then they go straight to one of Oakshire's A&Es.

The police can keep a person at the place of safety for up to 24 hours, which can be extended for another 12 hours if it was not possible to assess them in that time. The time starts on arrival at the place of safety, or whenever the police arrive, if they are not taken somewhere else.

If a police station is used as a place of safety the following rules apply:

- The police must check on the person's welfare every 30 minutes.
- A healthcare professional should be available throughout.
- The police must review at least hourly, or every three hours if asleep, whether the person

still needs to be kept at a police station rather than some other place of safety. If the person no longer needs to be at a police station they should be transferred to another place.

- Police stations must never be used as a place of safety for anyone under the age of 18.

Once detained under Section 136, patients must be guarded by two police officers, until the NHS takes over responsibility.

In my first months with Oakshire Constabulary, guarding a patient for up to 36 hours is commonplace. This means that if someone is sectioned at the beginning of a shift, and the NHS don't take responsibility for them until the end of those 36 hours, this can involve two police officers, from each of five shifts, guarding one person.

That's 10 police officers in total, taken away from dealing with new emergency incidents, and not investigating existing crimes, not policing the streets.

In between each of these shifts, is a journey from and to a police station, and a handover at the hospital. The amount of police time taken up is staggering. Officers can be drafted in from anywhere across the county, spending even more time travelling to A&E.

**

We're at St Margaret's City Hospital for nearly a full shift; lucky that we are relieved at 3.30pm by late shift officers. We're only a bit late off shift, not getting back to Northcliffe until after 4pm.

I don't think I've mentioned that for the first 30 minutes of overtime we work, we don't get paid.

I call it the free time we give the King, who is ultimately our boss, as we're not seen as employees of an organisation. Maybe that's why things are so shit here; the King isn't keeping an eye on his charges. We need his presence as our leader to be more visible.

Who's my line manager?

Even though there is a defined hierarchy in the police, and a desperation by many to ascend that hierarchy, in search of the increase in salary and pension, it's becoming clear that encouraging and supporting effective line managing is not a thing.

I don't seem to have a line manager, and I don't feel that I'm being looked after as a trainee.

The acting sergeant on our team is going through the painfully long, and laborious process of trying to become a substantive sergeant.

He isn't taking too well to being a leader; being responsible for others seems awkward for him. But, I'm grateful that, unlike the other sergeant, he does bother to ask me how I am a few times.

However, when I ask him for help on an investigation, by submitting a supervisor query through the crime management system, he rejects it with the click of a button, and I never get the help I need.

The investigation, the robbery at a supermarket, sits on my workload so long, with no guidance, that we miss the opportunity to prosecute. It gets closed with no further action.

I hadn't got a clue what I was doing, and no one was keeping a proper eye on my work.

My first head injury

Eight weeks as a police constable. Five weeks into my tutor period with Tristan.

A beautiful sunny August day. We're on early shift and it gets hot from mid-morning. *Like an oven inside the three layers already sticking to our bodies.*

The Marsham team has been struggling for resources – one of my Northcliffe team is already over there, covering the full shift. As sister stations, we always support each other with incidents. We share a radio channel too.

Today we find ourselves blue lighting between Northcliffe and Marsham multiple times. Most incidents are a total waste of police time.

Reporting persons have either exaggerated or lied about what's happened. Or situations have resolved themselves before we arrive. People have realised they can be grown-ups without our involvement.

On one run, our colleague Max decides to jump in with us. He's currently without a police car – not enough to go around. Several are at the garage having maintenance work. This happens a lot.

Max dives into the front seat, so I head for the rear door behind him. Tristan's and my bags cover the back seats, along with our traffic jackets. I step my left foot into the footwell, leaving my right on the ground, lean into the rear of the car. *Need to clear the backseat so I can get in.*

148

Half in, half out, my body suddenly slams into the door-frame. Then my head as I bounce in the opposite direction. The police car is moving. *What the fuck?*

Realising what he's done, Tristan suddenly stops. I bounce off the doorframe again. He doesn't say a word.

"Olivia, are you OK?" Max's voice cuts through my shock.

I can't tell you what my response is. I don't remember. I've just had a head injury.

What I know is that I don't want to make a fuss. We need to get going. *Need to get to Marsham as quickly as possible to support our colleagues.* So, because this is what I do, I pretend everything's OK and put the job ahead of myself.

I finish clearing the seat, climb in. We're off – blue lights on, siren going, heading back to Marsham for the third time today.

Max kindly continues checking on my welfare throughout the journey. He sounds genuinely concerned.

I'm not feeling good. Confused. We're going very fast. I'm in the back. Feel a bit sick now. I have no idea how I'm going to behave like a police officer when we get to this job. My head throbs. Still in shock. I just want to go home and curl up in a dark space with paracetamol.

Ten minutes later, the call's cancelled. Blue lights and sirens off, we're heading back to Northcliffe police station. *I can't believe I sustained a head injury for absolutely nothing.*

Back at the station. Still nothing from Tristan. No mention of the incident. No mention of what to do when something like this happens.

I think this is serious enough to require reporting – but it's not even mentioned to the sergeant.

I don't know if I'm meant to, or Tristan is. Surely there's a process? When you're new, you take the lead from those more experienced, more senior.

It becomes the elephant in the room. Because the issue's being ignored, I feel like I can't escalate it.

My experience of reporting issues at Oakshire Constabulary hasn't been good. I'm getting the sense that issues are brushed under the carpet. Those who raise concerns are made to feel like they're the problem.

Concealer

Soon we're heading back to Marsham again – an arrest enquiry. After lots of walking in the wrong direction, having my suggestions ignored, we successfully find the property we're looking for. Just as two other colleagues arrive to join us.

The wanted male is inside. I arrest him for Failing to Appear at Court. We head to custody – me squashed behind Tristan's seat again, unable to move.

I try making conversation with the prisoner, but he's not interested, staring straight ahead. So, I try getting my head around the wording I'll need at the custody desk, scribbling furiously in my pocket notebook, trying to ignore the awkward silence. And my banging head.

This man's known for concealing, and he's fidgeting a lot. As he's male, Tristan's done an initial search at arrest. I know he'll be strip–searched in custody.

Despite this being only my second arrest, custody's already become my least favourite place. *Overwhelming and unwelcoming.*

I wonder if it's because I'm not getting the support I need to feel comfortable and confident in what I'm doing. I feel like I'm not getting the information I need to deliver details to the custody sergeant. The questions I need answered, so I can build my narrative, are shot down. I'm told it's easy, no big deal.

Trust me, as a trainee, it really is a very big deal going to custody those first few times. What you need is someone to help build your confidence.

You need support from your tutor – not have them roll their eyes at the custody sergeant as you get your words wrong. What you need is guidance on how you could have done it better – not have someone take the piss out of you.

The male's shown to his cell, but because a strip-search is needed, the door's left open. Tristan stands in the doorway. I'm in the corridor. We're chatting about what needs to happen next.

"To do the strip-search, we're going to need three other male officers to help, can you go and find people?"

I'm sent off to search around Harrisville police station.

I don't know my way, where I'm going. I race around, trying to find people in the many isolated rooms separating different teams. Eventually I'm successful – finding three guys who say they'll come and join us in five minutes.

I get back to custody to see three other officers walking away from the cells.

"I've found some people, they'll be here in five minutes." Slightly out of breath.

"We've done the search."

"Right." *Why didn't he bother calling me on the radio?* Now I've got to find my way back to the other officers, let them know they're not needed.

Today has left me exhausted.

I want to hide from the world, so I'm quiet on the way back to Northcliffe. *I don't think I can do this job if it's going to be like this. I don't get why it must be made so difficult.*

Tristan finally asks: "Are you ok?"

"Not really, I feel terrible. With the bump to the head, and the raging eye infection I've been trying to fight for the last few days, I'm wiped out."

I've been doing a great job pretending I'm fine, but my eyelid bulges with infection. A sign of stress and fatigue.

"Sorry you feel so rough." Finally, a sign of care.

***

I wake up the next day at 5am and decide I can't go in. *I need to rest, to recover.*

I take one day off sick, then I'm back to work for the next two early shifts.

***

Over the coming days my body struggles. A large bump on the left back of my head makes it uncomfortable to sleep and very uncomfortable to put my head against any car headrest.

The left side of my neck and hip are painful. My pelvis is stiff and painful, travelling to my mid-back. It's from the car incident but not helped by the heavy kit, cramped cars, terrible chairs and stress. *I've even got pins and needles around one ankle.*

My body is screaming at me. But it doesn't feel like I can be off sick again – my workload's already large; the team's low on numbers.

So, I go to my trusted osteopath to help me get back on track. *She starts to unravel my damaged spine.*

6 in a hot tub

Despite not having the best tutoring experience, and now suffering from a head injury, the summer isn't all bad, there's also fun to be had.

A few weeks back, I'd heard Dom chatting about needing a venue for the team's yearly summer BBQ. It was a no-brainer, our home with plenty of garden space and a large BBQ area is perfect for it. So, I volunteered to host.

It's a gorgeous weekday. My husband has taken the day off work and is about to meet the people that make up my new world when our garden is invaded by 15 police officers.

He's usually in charge of the BBQ, but today my colleagues are taking over.

People arrive in dribs and drabs, dropped off by girlfriends, mums and Ubers.

Dan has bought the most enormous amount of food, and gets straight to work, doing a cracking job on the BBQ.

I'm nervited and a little bit overwhelmed. My partying days are long behind me and I'm not used to being in large groups anymore. I love a small but perfectly formed group, or one to one chats. I'm a bit out of my depth in this kind of situation unless I have a purpose, things to do.

And I want to make sure everyone is having a fab time. So, I spend so much time making sure everyone else has what they need, that I hardly chat to anyone for any length of time, flitting between everyone. They all seem to be relaxed and enjoying themselves; and that's what matters.

Dan's doing more cooking and drinking than eating, so the rest of us devour his delicious food, and watch in amusement as he continues to cook and get shitfaced.

Finally, the booze kicks in to my system; and I start to relax.

I love this team. They're awesome, and so funny, I laugh so much. I'll really miss them in a few months when I'm no longer part of this team. I'm so impressed every day at their respect for others, for each other, and for the attempts to work as a team.

I'm so grateful for how they want to help when I ask for their support. Sadly because of the policing demands in Northcliffe, getting time with them is often very hard. Having everyone over is a fantastic opportunity to properly catch up and show my appreciation.

It's even great to spend time with Tristan, seeing him in a different environment, because I get to see a decent guy – we're just not well matched for tutoring.

When we moved to our house we inherited an ageing hot tub from the previous owners. Not something we'd buy ourselves; it's been an awesome treat.

My favourite time to slip into the warm water is winter, when it's cold outside, and so much more challenging to get out at the end, the cold taking a grip, as it hits your wet body.

I've told everyone to bring their swimming trunks, and Jason is the first in. Before long, the hot tub is full, cocktails spilling in, and water spilling out.

The evening is messy, but the most fun I've had all year. I've not had an evening like this for a long time.

I'm so grateful for having these people in my life right now; it finally feels like the team environment I was longing for.

Fatal RTC

I've been a police constable in Response for two exhausting months; and I'm under pressure to be fit for independent patrol (FIP) by next weekend, because Tristan is going on holiday the following week.

Everyone is keen to get us trainees out there and off the hands of our tutors. The allocation of trainees in need of a tutor into teams seems to be horribly disorganised, with some teams like ours getting way more than is practical or manageable. It's draining for the experienced officers to have non-stop tutoring responsibilities.

There's three of us already on the team who are with tutors, and another two coming in the next couple of weeks. Soon there will be five of us with four or less months experience on our team.

One of the final things I've got to get done for OneFile, before becoming FIP, is an injury RTC (road traffic collision). We're meant to supply a completed yellow accident book to demonstrate our ability to record the accident and injury details.

This is one of many things those of us on the ADP wonder why we must do. We'll never be completing one of these books again and being measured on it is a waste of everyone's time.

***

It's the last of a set of three night shifts. I'm looking forward to getting off on time, having a short sleep, before trying to get my body clock back into normal hours, and spending some time with my husband.

With just a couple of hours left of the shift, outside the huge windows at Northcliffe police station, the sky is starting to get lighter, ahead of the sun rising in an hour or so.

Watching the sun rise, so early on summer days, is one of my favourite things about working at night. Some mornings are just spectacular, when you have the roads to yourself and the sky is throwing out an array of colours.

Our radios spark into life, there's reports of a car having left the carriageway on an A road.

Tristan leaps up: "We're going."

I grab my laptop, shove it, and whatever else I can quickly grab from the desk (just in case), into my laptop bag, and run to catch up with Tristan.

He's conscious to make sure I'm in the police car before driving out of the space.

Blue lights are on, but sirens are off for now because it's 5.30am, and we don't want to wake our sleeping neighbours in the flats next door to the police station.

Flying across the empty Northcliffe roads, we arrive first on scene 10 minutes later, closely followed by two colleagues in another police car. We come to a stop behind two other cars parked on the hard shoulder. They must be the RPs (reporting persons) who phoned it in.

They point to the location, and my colleagues run towards it, hurling themselves down the steep overgrown embankment. They spread in every direction.

I stop at the edge, take it all in, and await instructions from Tristan; at the bottom of the embankment is a row of huge trees, running alongside a farmer's field.

I see a single car which has clearly hit and felled one of the trees. The impact has split the car in two, the front half facing in one direction, the back half facing in the opposite direction.

It's a shocking scene.

Everything is happening in a matter of seconds.

I'm deciding whether to join my colleagues, or stay and talk to the RPs, to get more details. They've waited for us, but I don't know if they might leave, now we're here; and I'm the only one that could speak to them right now.

Still getting used to everything that happens when you're speeding to an incident, I haven't heard the details over the radio, and don't know exactly what my colleagues are looking for.

It turns out, what I'd missed is that there might have been five people in the vehicle.

I'm not going to get instructions from anyone, because they are fully stuck into the search, so I start to head down the embankment to join them. But then I hear a voice from behind me, and look up to see one of the RPs, holding his phone towards me. "The ambulance people want to speak to you."

I drag myself back up the steep embankment by my hands and reach up to take the phone off him; I introduce myself to the lady on the phone and answer her questions.

While I'm on the phone, more colleagues arrive on scene, and head for the car. They are fighting to get the doors open.

A police helicopter arrives, circling above, and confirms there's no other bodies in the surrounding area.

As the Ambulance Control Centre lady asks me questions, I shout them down to the guys at the car. She wants to know about the people in the car. How many? What condition? They confirm only one, the driver, who is trapped inside.

They are relaying information to me which I'm relaying over the phone. I feel useless. I can't answer the questions because the guys are still struggling to get the doors open.

And then somehow, they break them off, managing to get far enough into the vehicle, to feel for a pulse.

The driver is dead.

**

The speedometer is stuck at 125 miles an hour. There's a short set of tyre marks on the 70 mile-an-hour road.

The driver is so young. They didn't stand a chance. So many people are going to be utterly devastated by what's happened here today.

I suddenly realise there's loads of people on scene, all the emergency services, and teams from Northcliffe, Marsham, and the Roads Policing Unit.

Now the search is complete, and the state of the driver assessed, everything falls into a weird calm; there's a sense of peace.

It's just past 6am, and the sun is rising over the far end of the field. It's shining brightly into our faces, and directly onto the broken car, as it makes its way into the sky.

There's a very slight mist hovering over the ground. It feels surreal.

And it feels to me, like a spirit is being lifted away, towards the light.

I'm so grateful we have two rest days now. Although it will only be one and a half, after getting a few hours sleep this morning.

I'm FIP

It's the end of summer and we're working the dreaded set of Wednesday training day, followed by four late shifts, Thursday to Sunday. During the first shift I'm told I'm fit for independent patrol.

I'm about to be policing on my own, after just 10 weeks in the job; and this is my final shift with Tristan.

It's been agreed, probably to get me out there asap, that the recording and reporting of the fatal RTC can be used for my OneFile. This does not sit comfortably with me. It feels wrong that my career is progressing because of paperwork I did in relation to someone's death.

Everyone tells me "It's fine, it's best to get out there," and "you'll learn so much more when you're doing the job on your own." But I'd rather learn a lot more before I start making it up as I go along.

I'm not ready, and I have told people I am not ready. 10 weeks is not enough. My knowledge of the basics is not established. I feel horribly out of control, and anxious. But I have no choice.

I reach out to Rosie and James, to find out where they are on their FIP journey. Our ADP training school WhatsApp group still going strong, comparing notes on our experiences.

"Are you on track for FIP?"

Rosie replies: "Ha ha, nowhere near. I've had no tutor last set and looking like none for nights either. They are all away off sick. There were four of us on Monday and Tuesday, me and another degree student plus two who had just over a year in the force."

While I've been hammering through this first stage OneFile at breakneck speed, poor Rosie has not had a consistent tutor, often being left in the office on her own. No one thinks to let her jump in with them; to enable her to get exposure to the job.

James says: "I think we may have the smallest team and have one more trainee coming next week. Although the majority are still within their two years."

Two years is our probation period within which all police officers are meant to complete their second stage OneFile.

James has been much luckier than Rosie and I. His tutor, like Dom, is incredibly conscientious, and he's getting an A-star experience.

Rosie replies: "It's all sent to try us team ADP."

James replies: "Once we're FIP it's going to be absolutely mental."

Rosie: "Even more mental."

James: "100%."

Me: "It's pretty scary. Too much too soon. There's so much we don't know."

On top of mounting workload, and pressure to be FIP, James and Rosie both must re-sit the NIE soon. Neither have had time to revise, with the pressures of the job, and parenting during the summer holiday.

First FIP shift

No longer a tutee, my first FIP shift is Friday public order. I'm relieved not to have been made to police on my own for this first one. I'm partnered with Paul, who is still on the team, still trying to get his OneFile done, still waiting to get to his first detective placement. I'm relieved he's still here.

People take the piss out of Paul.

He and I are very similar, we're both very serious about learning this job, and have a need to focus hard to get through our workload. He teaches me that there are places around the police station to find peace and quiet to do that.

He's got a reputation for taking a long time to write statements; and it's not long before I realise I do too. He's often working overtime, I expect he never claims for it, conscious that he is slower than others.

It's the time you need to do the job properly, but sadly we are not afforded that time, constantly under pressure to work faster, move onto the next job; and therefore, not get every detail we need, to properly record or evidence crimes.

I write a statement with a victim late one night, and because I'm interrupted so many times to see if I'm finished, I lose my flow and forget to include details of his injuries. One of the key points to prove and essential for a statement.

This job is like a sand timer; time always slipping away too fast, and constant distractions.

***

Paul and I have a car, and as probationers we're getting all the shit jobs. That's fine with me. It's an important part of the learning process, and where you can cut your teeth as a police constable.

But this evening there's also a missing person to be found, he's 15. We don't get assigned any work on this incident, but when there's a 'Misper' we all keep an eye out.

In the last few weeks, I've got to know about some of the local kids who regularly go missing. They are kids whose homelife is chaotic, who can't get the peace they need, kids who don't fit into mainstream school, kids who are neurodivergent, kids who are different, whose difference the world needs to embrace, cultivate, and support.

I see a lot of myself in these kids at their age. From broken homes, with a lack of safety and security and absent parents, these kids join whatever group they can find solace in.

I've had dealings with the missing lad before. He and his friends had been causing havoc in the town centre one evening and had an altercation with an employee in the casino.

It was a fascinating dynamic when we arrived that evening. I could feel the tension, and thought it could go either way, depending on how my colleagues and I handled the situation.

The lads thought the casino guy was in the wrong, he'd come at them, they didn't understand that he was protecting the property, and that they were in the wrong to start with. Actions have consequences.

That night, one of the lads was hanging back from the group. I could see the sadness in his eyes, and the hunch in his shoulders. Dressed in drab dark clothes that weren't as trendy as his friends, he was trying to hide underneath his coat hood.

And then he came forward to us. Fired up by his friends, it was his turn to confront us.

But from the things he was saying, he clearly wasn't a risk. I could see he wanted to be heard, to be seen, to engage, and be respected. I stepped towards him and started to engage. His demeanour calmed and we talked, almost like adults.

***

As this evening heads into pub trouble time, we join the wider team who are in the public order vans.

We're walking from the car towards the pubs, when we spot a couple of lads sitting on some steps, eating chips.

I recognise them: "Paul, isn't that the missing lad, and one of his friends?"

Paul heads over to them, with me trying to catch up with his quick steps. I always seem to be lagging behind my colleagues.

As I catch up, he's asking them what they are up to, and what their names are. They are not rude, but their response has an edge that says they don't want to be challenged by police officers.

I turn to face the two lads, and I know for sure one is the missing lad.

"Hi, how are you doing?" I ask him and his friend, who are both shovelling chips into their mouths.

"Alright," the missing lad replies with a mouthful.

"We've met before, outside the casino."

"Oh yeah." His facial expression, and demeanour are like that night; my heart goes out to him.

"You've been reported missing; there's people looking for you."

"I don't want to go home. My dad's violent. We had an argument; I had to get out."

I hear Paul radioing our inspector, and one side of the conversation: "Hi guv, I think we've found the missing lad." "Yes." "OK thanks guv."

Paul addresses the lad: "We need to take you home."

I know we must try but also know it's not the right thing for this lad and if we force the issue, it's not going to go well for any of us. I don't want to send him home; he needs the safety and support of his friends right now.

"No way. I can't go back there. I want to stay with my friend," he pleads.

Paul gets back on the radio; this time he walks away so he can't be heard. He takes a few minutes and when he's back explains: "OK mate, we've had the OK from our inspector that you can stay out; she's spoken to your dad, and he's agreed."

I'm so relieved we've been able to make a sensible policing decision this evening. We know where this lad is, who he is with, and we've put his dad's mind at rest.

I'm sure it won't be the last time we're out looking for him.

On my own in the 'diary car'

The realisation that I'd spend much of my time working on my own, sets in less than three months in the job.

On my second day being FIP I get the 'diary car'. This is where you get a schedule of appointments to meet with victims, whose reports are serious enough to be seen within a couple of days, but have not met the requirements for immediate attendance on the day of their call.

I've never done the diary car before; we were never allocated it during my 10 weeks with my tutors. So, I have no idea what I'm doing.

I don't even know how to find, or use the system, which is different to all the other systems we use.

We've finished our shift briefing, and I'm sitting in the report writing room, the temperature is cooler now it's September. Still warm, but not uniform-sticking-to-your-body-warm.

I've found myself a desk at the end of a row, my preferred spot. Less going on around me to distract me.

"Can someone show me where I access the diary car appointments, please?" I ask out loud to the members of the team who haven't already been allocated an incident to deal with and are still in the station. Ed shouts over, "It's Storm."

"Isn't that what we use to access the ISRs logs? I'm confused. I thought it was a different system for diary car?"

"Yes, that's WebStorm, you want Storm." So, until now everyone has referred to WebStorm as Storm, and now I need the separate, Storm system.

"Go to the ICT portal, you'll find it there."

"OK thanks." More time is wasted while I dig around trying to find the software, then click on multiple buttons within it and finally get to the page I need to find the diary car appointments for this shift. It takes way longer than it should.

I'm in, and there's four. In an average shift, four would usually be manageable, but I'm on a public order shift from 5pm until 3am. So, realistically, once I get going at 5.30pm, I have less than five hours, because most people don't want to be speaking to police officers late at night.

Plus, I don't really know what I'm doing, so it's going to take me ages.

Fortunately, my first two come to the police station for their appointments.

First is Eric, the victim of a Common Assault, by a nasty neighbour. He's a sweet, cheery man in his early 70s. He's clearly incredibly fit as he'd been building a shed when the assault took place.

I'll have to log a new investigation on the crime management system, with all the details. But I don't have time before my second appointment arrives at the station and I must hurry Eric up, without appearing rude.

***

Rachel has arrived a few minutes early, and a colleague has come into the interview room to let me know.

I never get the hang of having my radio turned up while engaging with victims. It feels rude to be distracted, and I can't listen to two things at once. I'm always asking my husband to turn the TV down if he starts talking to me. It fries my brain trying to hear two sources of noise. I can't bear it when I'm somewhere where two different music sounds are being played in the same area.

So, frequently I miss people trying to contact me over the radio. This is not ideal in the police, and I don't feel good about it, but I'm not the only one and I'm new, so I'm not going to beat myself up about it. I just hope I'll get there, as my confidence grows.

Also, with our 'victim focus' approach, I do believe that fully focusing on the victim is what I'm meant to do. The radio is a source of safety, so in many situations not being available via it causes concern.

However, when you're sitting in an office, in the police station, and everyone knows where you are, it shouldn't be something we get in trouble about. I do feel judged about my radio handling ability.

Rachel is expecting to have a disclosure under Clare's Law.

Under Clare's Law you can apply for information about your current, or ex-partner, if you're worried they may have a history of abuse and are therefore a risk to you. You can do the same about the current or ex-partner of a friend or relative if you're worried they might be at risk.

Rachel's expectations were not managed when this appointment was set up. I'm already having to carefully navigate the horror of her domestic abuse situation, as she explains what has happened to her during the toxic relationship she's still stuck in.

I try so hard not to disappoint her when I must explain that, because she has made us aware of criminal offences against her during her Clare's Law application, we have a duty to discuss them with her, and that's why she was given this appointment, with me – not for me to disclose information about her abusive partner, but to deal with the offences.

Aside from Rachel being my first really serious domestic abuse victim, and the fact that I'm on my own, I've never had any training on handling a Clare's Law situation. So, I'm making this up as I go along. I certainly had no time to research her, or her violent boyfriend ahead of our meeting.

"I'm really sorry if this wasn't explained, but it won't be me giving you any disclosure."

Someone else will deal with the Clare's Law disclosure.

Rachel is a dowdy looking lady who appears way older than she is. Through our conversation I can see the beautiful woman behind the pain; behind the plain clothes she has been forced to wear by her abusive partner; because he is jealous if she wears anything he hasn't deemed appropriate.

I imagine that, in her life before him, she had been stylish, making an impact wherever she went.

While she isn't supportive of police action in relation to the historic offences, I give Rachel my email, and ask if she would be happy to send the photos of her injuries, so we have a record. My gut is telling me that this evidence will be important at some point.

I don't hear anything for a few weeks, but then, out of the blue she emails me.

The photos are shocking; I'm so sad when I see them. This man has battered her. She's been too scared, for too long, to do anything about it.

Her investigation is picked up by a specialist team, and I hear nothing more.

I often think about her, and hope she has a positive new life. Her story still brings tears to my eyes.

***

Two appointments down. I have to get out and about for the second two.

But first, I have to figure out how to use a police car. Apart from last week when I had my driving skills assessed by the sergeant, I haven't driven a police car since starting this job. My tutors always drove.

So not only do I have to decipher what the whiteboard's saying about which keys I'm allowed to select, I then have to get keys out of the cabinet. *It's locked.* Turns out I don't have access.

One of a multitude of things that don't happen automatically when you join or move location. I add it to the long list of things I've had to request from IT – every software platform I need to do my job, and now access to drive a police car.

I then have to find the car matching the keys someone else had to release for me. I walk around the police station car park, clicking keys, looking for flashing indicator lights. *Got it.*

I load all my stuff into the vehicle – some on the front passenger seat, some on the backseat, depending on what I'll need immediate access to. *It's one of the shit cars.* All the good ones are already taken.

I have to check the vehicle over, test blue lights, red lights, indicators, check tyres, make sure there's enough cones in the boot.

After all that, I have to figure out how to turn it on and drive the thing. Every car's different, and I've been driving automatics for years. *This is manual, heavy on the pelvis.*

None of these cars have sat nav – we must use mobiles as navigation. This wouldn't be a big deal, but the cars don't have anywhere to sit a phone. Every shift you must figure out where you're going to put it because you won't be in the same car.

By the time I finally pull out of the police station car park, I need a lie down.

Diary car again

Day five of this set, day three of being FIP. I get the diary car again. I'm starting to suspect that while the team's so low on resources, and with Kim on holiday, I'm going to be stuck with this job a lot this month. My workload's going to rise, fast.

Five appointments, all out and about, spanning the entire stretch of Northcliffe. *How am I going to get through them all between 3pm and midnight?*

I quickly plan my evening based on the most efficient route – starting south, heading north and back to Northcliffe for the last one.

Every incident's different. A concern for welfare where a sociopathic father's using his children to deliberately hurt his ex-wife. *There are way more sociopaths out there than I was aware of.*

Then there's a 14-year-old girl groomed and threatened by a man on Snapchat. She thought she'd been speaking to a teenage girl for months, shared photos of herself. Fortunately not revealing, otherwise she'd have committed a criminal offence herself of Creating and Distributing an Indecent Image.

The scariest thing for me is how naïve people are about how dangerous some apps are. I have to explain to her and her parents what sharing her location with everyone she's connected with on Snapchat means. How easy it is to put yourself at risk.

This man knows where she goes at all times – school, home, friends' homes. She can be tracked constantly. I advise them to lock her phone down, only allowing her location to be known by family and closest friends, people she completely trusts.

Everyone else needs to earn that trust. You must have met the person in real life, really 'know' them before sharing your location. This should be a blanket rule for everyone.

This young girl's also using her mobile very late at night, impacting her sleep and mental health.

Until we start putting our devices down long before bed, poor mental health will continue to rise. If you're using a device when everyone else is asleep and you get yourself in trouble, *it's a very lonely place* – as this young girl found out when she started getting threatened.

At the time, people weren't widely talking about the hugely negative impact smartphones are having on children. I'm delighted and relieved that this has started to change. Just watch Channel 4's Swiped: The School That Banned Smartphones with Emma and Matt Willis.

***

I've called everyone in advance, given them rough timescales of when I'll arrive. But after each visit, I have to call the next person to say I'm going to be later than planned.

As I leave a family – now locking down location services on all their devices and looking into security cameras – I call my next victim with my new ETA and start making my way north of the county.

I then ring one of my best friends. *I've been on the road for three and a half hours without a break.* My head spins with all the information and emotions I've already absorbed this evening. *And I really need a wee.*

"Please can I come and use your toilet? I'm about fifteen minutes away." I plead over the phone.

"Of course, see you soon."

When I arrive, she answers the door, gives me a huge hug, calls her daughter, who's upstairs. "Mia, the police are here to see you."

Mia comes tentatively down the stairs. Takes a moment before she recognises me.

She runs down the rest of the stairs, gives me a huge hug too – slightly trickier for a little person as her hair becomes entangled in the kit attached to my tac vest.

It's wonderful to see them. I don't feel quite so alone as I have over the last few hours.

What a relief. Thank God I know someone in this area – I have no idea where there are public toilets I could use at this time of evening. As a female, walking into pubs on your own, in uniform, to use the toilet is awkward. *I don't need the stares and jeers right now.*

Sadly, I can't stay. No time. So I head off for my next visit.

***

I arrive at a large detached house to take statements from two teenage boys. They've been victims of a robbery while visiting London.

I feel for them, but at the same time, they're slightly too unaffected by what's happened. It's the parents who've called police. So I assume nothing, believe no one, challenge everything – my Copper's nose is making me suspicious about their story.

They say two lads came up to them, threatened them to the point they chose to separate from their other friends and follow these two lads across a road, into an area they thought was out of sight.

They had mobile phones taken which contained their bank cards. The suspects made them unlock their phones before running off.

It turns out, when I check the location on Google Maps the next day, that it took place directly under a CCTV camera.

I already know this investigation will be passed to the Met – the crime happened on their patch, so won't stay on my workload for long.

The parents know they need a police crime reference number to claim insurance. *I doubt they'll want their kids involved further down the line* if suspects are caught and there's enough evidence for court.

I wonder what the Met officer investigating will find on that CCTV. Were these teenage boys trying to buy cannabis? I'll never know.

***

I visit my next victim, not far away. She's been burgled by her ex-partner and father to her four children, all under seven. She doesn't think he's taken anything, but he's broken a piece of furniture on his way in through a window.

People get burglary and robbery confused: burglary is when someone enters a building or part of a building as a trespasser with intent to commit theft, grievous bodily harm, or criminal damage. Robbery is the action of taking property unlawfully from a person or place by force or threat of force.

She doesn't want to support police action, despite me asking numerous times. Like many people, she wants this incident logged to help build a picture of abuse patterns. *I get it.* This investigation's unlikely to go anywhere due to lack of evidence. She knows that. I know that.

There are already multiple investigations underway involving the two of them. She really doesn't need the hassle of speaking to yet another police officer over coming weeks, or dealing with admin involved, including me taking a statement at this late hour. Especially now her three-year-old is awake and looking at me with concern.

As I leave her home, I realise it's so late it doesn't feel right to visit my fifth and final victim. He's accusing someone of threatening to kill him, and a historical sexual offence against his mum which she hasn't reported, but that he feels should be reported.

These allegations are too serious to deal with at this hour. This appointment needs more time than I'll have.

I try to radio in, update where I'm at with appointments, contact colleagues. *I can't get through – no service. Same with my mobile. How interesting: I have no way of contacting anyone right now. I'm completely alone. I'm not sure how I feel about this. Exhaustion has suddenly hit me, blurring my ability to make sense of anything.*

So I head back to Northcliffe, trying to get through to people while driving down the by now very familiar A road. This is a challenge. Driving a police car while trying to look down at and find the right number to push on the radio attached to your chest is hard to do safely.

When you're new it's really hard to get your brain to fully function, well over seven hours into a late shift, having had no dinner, having dealt with ten different people's emotions, on my own, haring all over the county, with eleven weeks policing experience.

Please remember this if you ever try to flag down a police officer that hasn't been sent to you, and you don't get the response you want.

I finally get hold of the sergeant, explain my dilemma: "Hi sarge, I'm not sure what to do. I've got another diary car appointment, but it's so late and I have loads of crimes to build in the crime management system."

"Don't worry, get back to the station, and we'll sort it out when you're here," he says reassuringly.

By the time I get back at 11pm, I'm so tired and hungry I just can't get my brain to work. I don't have the capability to ring my final appointment and give the guy the service needed. Nor do I have the brain power to assess whether a crime's been committed. *Eating now will mess up my sleep – just not worth it.*

I've been out since 3.30pm. Most of the team are there, it's Q (we never say quiet out loud) and they're dealing with their workload.

The report writing room was so overwhelming when I first started, but now it's a place of respite.

Such a relief to get time back at a desk and stop, even if just for a few minutes, and catch your breath.

Right now, my thoughts won't join up. I can't even remember what's happened this shift. So trying to string a sentence together to explain to the team that I still have another diary car appointment, and what it's about, is too hard right now. *I need a few minutes to decompress.*

I think there's a pattern emerging – I often remember the first and last incidents of my shifts but remembering what happened in between is starting to become difficult.

The sergeant has been busy since I got back, so when I finally find a way to string a sentence together, I ask the team for advice: "I've got another appointment to do but it's so late. Do you think I can rebook it for tomorrow?"

Ed kindly offers to call the guy: "I'll call him, what's the log number?"

The log is the computer summary of what the reporting person (RP) has initially reported; along with questions the Force Control Room (FCR) has asked; and the answers.

It's found on WebStorm, but also because this is a diary car appointment, I can find it on Storm. I've also written it down in my pocket notebook. *Come on brain, which one will I use?*

Ed is another kind person, empathy in bucket loads; I really have been lucky to land on this team.

With his experience, and what he very quickly sees from reading the log about 20 times faster than I could, Ed says: "This is going nowhere."

He calls the RP, who is clearly not happy about the time, despite having been given a 10pm until midnight appointment slot.

Even though I can only hear half, Ed's clearly caught up in a conversation I could never have handled as expertly as he does. I listen in, because it's a brilliant way to learn, and I'm not getting any opportunities like this.

It gets heated at times, many of our conversations do because people raise their voices at us, and sometimes don't stop talking, to get their own way. Many people use the police as a weapon against people they don't like.

Ultimately, Ed convinces the guy there's been no threat to kill. He's deduced that the RP has committed an offence against the person he's complaining about; something we come across a lot. It's basically two men having an argument, their egos getting in the way.

The offence of Threat to Kill is only committed when someone threatens to kill another person, or themselves, without a lawful excuse, and intends that the victim will fear the threat will be carried out. It's rare that the suspect has that intention. They are usually just gobbing off. They don't have the means or the inclination to actually kill anyone.

And because both sides are culpable it won't get through the CPS, so there's no point wasting more police time investigating, and building a case file.

Under The Code for Crown Prosecutors, the CPS must be satisfied there is enough evidence to provide a 'realistic prospect of conviction' against each defendant.

After having all this explained to the guy, it's clear the conversation has diverted to his complaint that the suspect has sexually assaulted his mum. Ed's voice and manner turn sympathetic and caring. He explains that the RP's mum needs to report the assault if that's what she wants; and he talks through some of the services available to her for support.

So, there's nothing more we can do tonight on this appointment. What a relief. I've got four crimes to put onto the crime management system following this evening's other appointments, and 45 minutes to do it.

That's going to be impossible, considering my lack of brain function. I'm exhausted. And I feel guilty for Ed having to do that appointment.

I am failing at this job.

Because we're under pressure not to do overtime, I can't get all the paperwork done. I take advice from the team on what bare bones I need to input, and the rest will be done next shift, although I do work for free for half an hour, trying to do as much as I can. At 12.30am I look up, and everyone has gone. This set of shifts is seriously exhausting, even for the experienced officers.

In one week, you go from a set of night shifts (10pm until 7am), less than two days off, then 7am start for training day. The next day starts four lates, with differing times because the weekend is public order: 3pm until midnight, 5pm until 3am, 5pm until 3am, then 3pm until midnight.

Try adapting your circadian rhythm around that.

Or managing life outside work.

I'm doing none of the things I love. I'm really missing time with my wider network of friends and the energy I used to have to do things other than work. I'm just surviving: eating, sleeping, washing.

Is this job worth it?

The madness of police paperwork

After going to bed around 1am, we've had a couple of rest days, during which I've had my third trip to my osteopath in the 17 days since the incident in the car park.

She's working on realigning my pelvis and spine; and unravelling parts of my body that have gone into panic and protection mode.

We're back on earlies, and I feel battered.

Not all the advice I received following my diary car appointments the other night is good.

I'm in trouble for having left without adding everything I should have on the crime management system, to the domestic burglary investigation. Apparently, these should always be completed in full, because of the risk factor. Maybe overtime would have been approved for this? I'll never know.

Another big learning lesson. But why do we have to learn so negatively? *Why do they make it so hard for us to learn?* And if this was such a high-risk domestic situation, why was it allocated in the way that it was.

If someone with experience had looked at the diary car appointments, they'd have seen how my evening was going to pan out, with the size of the area and types of incidents I had to cover; especially as a trainee.

As ever, I'm a bit confused by the conflicting guidance I'm getting, and how much we duplicate information; information that an admin person could process, allowing us to be police officers.

This victim has other crimes under investigation, with all the same details already on the crime management system, but I'm being told that I must input the data that someone has identified is missing.

Just to be clear, someone has been into my investigation, identified missing data that is available elsewhere, and then told me to spend time inputting that data; something they could have done.

So I spend time duplicating, literally copying and pasting information from one investigation into a separate document, so I can then copy and paste it back into my investigation. This is necessary because you can't have two investigations open to do this.

Copying and pasting is something I spend a lot of time doing, because apparently that's a good use of police time. This takes me half an hour, because she has four children, and I must input information about all four of them. This investigation is just going to sit on my workload until someone agrees to close it, because it's going nowhere.

Despite having made it clear in my investigation narrative, I am asked repeatedly in emails from police sergeants and detective sergeants if I'm sure she doesn't want to support police action.

I want to say: "If you're working with the victim on other investigations, why don't you ask her yourself?"

Instead, I'm forced to email her repeatedly, asking if she's changed her mind. She doesn't reply. I made the error when I was with her, not to get her to sign my pocket notebook to confirm her lack of support. Something no one has told me to do, until now.

We must get auditable evidence that a victim is not supportive. Something that makes me feel uncomfortable; as if we don't respect their answer the first couple of times. We can't close an investigation without this evidence or can demonstrate multiple attempts to get that evidence.

Because police officers, who have sat with victims and heard their stories, felt their pain, understood their needs, can't be trusted, it's much better to hound a victim into writing something down. All part of Oakshire Constabulary's 'victim focused' approach, apparently.

Getting approval to close this investigation becomes a total pain in the arse and a total waste of many people's time.

***

The rest of the week continues along the same path.

I get the diary car, again, so more investigations pile onto my workload.

And Tristan and I get an email from a custody sergeant. We are in trouble.

The prisoner we'd dealt with a few weeks ago, the one who'd been strip-searched, had concealed a lighter under his pillow while Tristan was in the doorway of his cell talking to me in the corridor.

It had been found under his pillow; and the CCTV had been reviewed to see how it had got there. The email is highlighting the importance of proper searches. Nothing else comes of our berating.

I'm curious if the sergeant knows I'm only a few weeks into this job, taking all my cues from those with experience, on the rare occasions I get time to work with other people. *If he does know, does he care?*

***

Right now, I feel even less capable of doing much of my workload, than I did back on that training day, when I got in trouble for progressing investigations on my own.

I'm policing on my own so much; and no one seems to be checking what I'm doing, what risks I'm taking to get my now 22 investigations, or the diary car appointments done.

I don't understand how this fits into the ADP; and how this can be described as a year of rigorous training. I feel like I've been dumped out there on my own because there's a resourcing issue. There's no focus on ensuring I'm getting the training I need to progress on the ADP.

I also realise I haven't been told about training I could have been doing while being tutored; to enable me to be more self-sufficient now I'm policing on my own.

And I realise I still don't have access to a load of systems, that I should have automatically been set up on. Everything here feels like it is made way more difficult than it needs to be.

***

It's not all bad; I'm loving being part of this team.

When there's rare moments when we're together, in the report writing room, they ask how I am doing, especially Dom and Max. And Kim and I, now she's back from holidays, manage to do a few walking laps around the car park, as she vapes.

"I'm really anxious about becoming FIP," she says one day.

She's had a few extra weeks with a tutor, and I'm jealous of all that time she's had learning from Dom.

"I'm not going to lie; it's bloody hard," I reply, not one to sugar coat a shitty situation.

We've also got three more trainees on the team; and they are fun.

The other huge positive, now I'm FIP, is that I get a Workplace Assessor as I start the second stage of OneFile. The first stage was assessed by my tutors, and apparently the sergeant.

The moment I meet my assessor, I start to feel like someone has interest in my development; and me, as an individual. I love my meetings with her.

It is rare to hear if you're doing OK or not in this job. But I finally feel like I'm getting constructive feedback; as we talk through the multiple examples of my work that I must submit to her for review and approval.

In advance of our meetings, she reviews my body-cam footage of incidents I attend and reads the laborious reflection documents that we must write, to support each incident I submit for review.

Sadly, our get togethers will only be every few months. And the feedback will come months after the incident has occurred; meaning I'm likely to have learnt so much more in that time. The whole system is flawed.

But I'm not going to complain. I'm just so grateful for the support, and the ability to learn from someone who I really respect.

Despite these being essential parts of our development; my meetings with her are often interrupted by radio calls from the sergeants trying to send me to incidents. She shoots them down eventually, telling them off and explaining how important these meetings are.

Back on St Margaret's public order

My next St Margaret's public order shift is a whole different experience. It's late-September, I'm with a totally different team, no Tristan because I'm FIP, and we're policing a mid-week nightclub event.

We don't expect there to be trouble, tonight is about having a police presence.

As a team, we quickly agree who's going to be partnered with who, who's going to do what, stand where, patrol where.

We're an odd number, so I start the evening with two other officers from the same station, who have naturally teamed up. Two others have got the road closure job – we close off vehicle access to the club, for safety reasons. We agree to check in with each other every hour, to see if anyone wants a change of scene.

A couple of hours into the shift, I volunteer to take over from the road closure team. I'll be on my own, but that's fine. You get to sit in the police car, jumping in and out to speak to the public, and allowing residents trying to get home, licensed taxi drivers, and the DJs and security staff needing to get to the club, through our cones.

It's a busy entrance for people on foot, and some just look completely lost. Others look vulnerable, and many just need to be pointed in the right direction; despite having maps on their phones. To be fair, the walk up to the club is badly lit from the main road.

***

There's a side to this role that really pisses me off, and that's the selfish drivers. Those idiots that think they are more important than everyone else.

As economics take over culture, the UK is becoming a more and more selfish place to live, and I can't tolerate selfishness. I have very little patience for it.

If you want to be selfish, feel free, but don't do it to me or around me, because you'll get to see a side of me you don't expect. And don't think you can drive your car up alongside my police car, and sweet talk me into giving you what you want. Selfishness pisses me off, and has no place when police officers are trying to do their jobs.

This is always a problem during any time we close a road, or a lane. Whether an accident has happened, or if we're guarding a scene, some people think that the inconvenience to them is outrageous.

Try being the police officer whose life is currently at risk because people are still driving 70 miles an hour in a lane next to traffic cones where we've had to park and are dealing with a distressed, ill or injured member of the public. It could be you next time, or your child.

We constantly have to explain to people that no, they can't drive through the police 'road closed' sign, and no, they are not more important than the investigation that is taking place. We are trying to keep the public, and ourselves, safe.

Tonight has been pretty plain sailing so far, despite the longest queue I've seen for an event here. A few people are stopped from going in by door staff. When that happens, we police officers deal with the fall out.

While watching everything that is happening around me, I'm also able to catch up on emails, and even log onto my laptop, and manage some investigations.

Now well into the shift, the event well underway, and the streets empty, I sense a large vehicle pull up alongside me. I look out of the window to see a lorry. There's a supermarket down this road, and lorries arriving during the night are also on the list of vehicles we're allowed to let in.

I wave at him, jump out of the car, and move the cones. With the lorry through, I'm standing in the middle of the road entrance, about to close the gap again with a cone. A car speeds up to the gap and tries to drive through, I get the cone down just in time, and he comes to a screeching-stop, inches from my feet.

The road closure area can become carnage at the end of the night. And it's no different tonight. Uber drivers, and the parents of clubbers, all stop to ask if they can go through the cones.

"No," I explain, trying to contain my irritation. "The road is closed."

They always think their reason is exceptional: "But I've got to pick up...." take your pick: a customer, my daughter, my son, my friend, my boyfriend.

.

I repeat: "The road is closed, you can park over there," and wind the window back up or get back in the car.

Babysitting a kidnapped drug addict

One early shift, straight after briefing, with very little information, I'm sent to the victim room. I take over guarding a drug addict from a night shift officer.

As he steps into the corridor, relief floods his face. "He's OK, he's been sleeping most of the night. But it stinks in there. Good luck."

I step into the small room. The smell slams into me like a physical wall. My throat constricts. There are no windows.

"Hi, I'm Olivia." The words catch slightly as I fight not to gag.

He looks up from his horizontal position on the hard blue modular sofa. "Hello officer, I'm Mark."

The room presses in around us. Most rooms we must share with victims, witnesses and suspects are too small for everyone's comfort. The stale air sits heavy, suffocating.

He's sought solace at Northcliffe police station after escaping from a drug dealer who'd kidnapped him.

Another broken human, underserved by society, sprawled before me. Someone who needs to unravel the pain he's experienced; find a new path.

The source of the stench becomes painfully clear. He hasn't changed his clothes for several days. The fabric clings to his body, saturated with sweat, grime, and God knows what else. My stomach churns.

This is one of those days where no one guides me in what I should be doing.

A couple of hours crawl by. The smell seems to seep into my skin, my hair, my uniform. Slowly it dawns on me that finding somewhere for this guy to go is my responsibility, not that anyone is volunteering to tell me that.

I have no idea what I'm meant to do. I try to get someone in the Council to help. They tell me he'll have to go to a refuge – and it'll be my job to find one.

They email me a list over an hour later, after a couple of chases from me. I know they're busy too, but we're wasting police time looking after someone who should be somewhere else.

My head pounds as I start making my way through the list, ringing each refuge to see if they have availability. I'm already over halfway through my nine-hour shift. The confined space makes my temples throb.

My gut twists with certainty – I'm going to end up driving this guy wherever I can get him a place. I bet it's on the other side of the county. And I bet I end up starting that journey not long before the end of this shift. And I bet I give more free time to the King.

I find a place and we're off. But not before a detour to pick up some clothes from his mum's house. I must get this guy into and out of the property without anyone seeing him.

This is no easy feat. He gets distracted repeatedly, wandering off like a child. My pulse spikes each time. I repeatedly suspect he's going to disappear on me. *That would mean the entire shift would have been a total waste of police time.*

My shoulders knot with tension as I shepherd him through each task.

On the drive, the car windows are cracked open, but his presence fills the space. I breathe through my mouth, counting the miles.

Covering at Harrisville

I often find myself travelling the same route or visiting the same places in batches. One of life's interesting mysteries.

Within six weeks of being FIP, workload spiralling, following five diary car shifts during September, I'm asked to cover at Harrisville police station twice in a row. Night shifts.

It's the first night. I've driven west from home to Northcliffe to join our briefing, pick up a police car, then back east, almost the way I've just come, then north to Harrisville. My spine already aches from the constant seat adjustments, different cars digging into different pressure points; and the incident in the car park.

On arrival I'm quickly partnered with Sarah, another covering officer from another station. Harrisville are that low on numbers tonight. The sergeant tells us we're transporting a child.

Alfie is twelve years old and has been in custody longer than anyone wants a child to be there. Custody sergeants hate having children in custody, especially at night. Nobody does. So we all work hard to get them in and out as quickly as possible.

But this situation is complicated. Alfie can't go home, so arrangements have been made for him to stay with a relative several counties away.

Sarah and I go to meet Alfie in custody, so he knows who we are. He's disinterested. He's met so many police officers and other adults today. He's in no mood to meet more right now. His shoulders slump with exhaustion, eyes glazed over.

Half an hour later, he's ready to be discharged from custody. Sarah grabs a police car, brings it as close as she can to the custody entrance – to avoid the risk of losing Alfie somewhere in the dark police station car park.

She does the drive there. I try to engage with Alfie. He comes across as a sweet child, but he's got a complicated background. We fully understand why he doesn't want to chat to us.

And he's just been given his smartphone back. No one can compete with a smartphone for someone's attention.

He spends the entire journey staring at the screen, catching up on whatever he's missed while in custody. The blue glow illuminates his young face in the darkness. Sarah and I chat about life and policing in Oakshire, as we leave our county and head through four others.

My lower back begins to seize up. The police car seats offer no lumbar support. I shift constantly, trying to find a position that doesn't send shooting pains down my legs.

Hours later, we park up. As we walk Alfie through the automatic doors, tinny music plays in the near-empty, vast service station building. It feels like something out of a horror film. Most shops are closed. Just a handful of tired, random-looking people sit around under harsh fluorescent lights.

It's easy to find Alfie's aunt. We're easy to spot in our uniforms. She walks towards us, saying hello, hugging her nephew. Relief washes over her face.

We have a brief chat, receive lots of thank yous. He's clearly not going to have free access to his smartphone. He's going to be spending time in nature and helping. Sounds like a great place for him to be a child again, without distractions.

I hate driving long distances and motorway driving – it batters my body. I avoid it as much as I can. But it's only fair to share the load and give Sarah a break, so I do the drive back.

My neck muscles knot as I grip the steering wheel. The motorway lights blur past. Every pothole sends vibrations up my already-compressed spine. I clench my jaw against the building tension headache.

When we get back to Harrisville around 4am, we're sent back to our respective police stations.

What a relief. My body needs a rest from being in a car. I've got to do the whole west to east to north drive back to Harrisville tomorrow night.

But then I realise – I still have to get all the way back to Northcliffe now. *My heart sinks.*

By the time I'm back at 5am, it's that weird time of a night shift when the night incidents have calmed down. We've got everything crossed that no one does anything stupid before 7am when the early shift starts.

If you ever hear a police siren around 6.30am, that's some poor police officers about to be off shift late, again – after starting work at 10pm the night before.

Everyone looks battered. Faces drawn, shoulders sagging. It's been a busy night in Northcliffe. The exhaustion hangs in the air like fog.

***

I got a new car a couple of weeks ago. It comes with so many safety features that I often have no idea what it is telling me when it beeps an alert at me. The beeps normally drive me mad, but this morning, as I leave Northcliffe thankfully on time at 7am, heading home for some well-needed sleep, I'm grateful for the beeps. *Keep keeping me awake, please.*

Unfortunately, that isn't the case for the new mum who smashes into the back of me while I'm stationary in traffic on the approach to a roundabout. Double unfortunately, she's driving a Nissan Juke, it has ridiculous bulbous lights which create multiple dents in the perfect rear end of my brand-new car.

I feel for her, she's more tired than me. Her baby had been crying, and she'd been looking in her rear-view mirror to see what was wrong.

She asks if we can sort it out between us, not go through insurance. I don't tell her I'm a police officer, I just explain that it's a brand-new car, I can't take the risk. She's got enough on her plate.

Mental health detainee number two

It's the next night. I've done the home to Northcliffe to Harrisville drive again. My back screams in protest as I climb out of the car.

Arriving around 11pm, I'm sent straight to relieve someone doing a cell watch in custody. There's usually at least one police constable, often two, doing a cell watch at one of the two Oakshire custodies.

The officer I'm relieving has the same collar number as me, just in a slightly different order. We bond over this small but significant thing. A moment of connection in this isolating job.

This will be my second time guarding a mental health patient. Ruby is in her late teens. I've been told she doesn't speak and has been asleep for much of the previous shift.

Now it's night-time. She's awake, sitting in the corner of the hard cell bed, the thin custody blanket wrapped around her like armour, staring at me with hollow eyes.

Another teenager, awake at night, damaging her mental health. But this girl has way bigger issues than that. Whatever happened to her before she started behaving in a way that means police are involved in her life must be truly heartbreaking. Her issues are extremely complex.

She's one of many young people I've met being failed by the flawed system meant to support children with Special Educational Needs and Disabilities (SEND).

I introduce myself, sit down on the hard plastic chair in the doorway of the cell. Cell doors stay open during a cell watch. Depending on the prisoner, we either sit in the doorway or out in the corridor.

Ruby seems unable to speak beyond one-word answers but seems content to sit and stare at me while I watch her and ask questions. I don't fully understand it, but I think she may have non-verbal autism.

While her face is expressionless, her demeanour is expectant. I don't want to stop trying to engage just because she finds it hard to respond. I continue with questions and random ramblings. She continues with one-word answers, yes or no, even a small giggle from time to time.

My chest tightens with hope when I make a breakthrough. I discover she loves Harry Potter books. Despite never having read them or watched a movie all the way through, I've been to the Harry Potter studio tour and loved it. What a fantastic experience that opens your eyes to the complex world of film production, despite being a sensory overload.

So I can muddle my way through Harry Potter-related questions. Ruby smiles. My heart lifts. I get a few more words in answer to my questions. I deduce she doesn't own any of the books herself.

Then, less than 30 minutes later, just as we're getting into the groove of our slightly one-sided conversation, I get the nod. Ruby's going to be sectioned, released from custody, taken into NHS care.

She'd been assessed by an Approved Mental Health Professional (AMHP) before I took over the cell watch.

There's a further breakthrough. Because she has no injuries that would need checking at A&E, she's going straight to the children's mental health hospital at Maplewood.

An ambulance is coming. Two other officers will go with her. I say my goodbyes and wish her well. Sadness floods through me – I can't continue to play a positive role in this young girl's life. I'm a police officer, not a mental health worker.

Knowing she'll be there for at least a few days, I order three Harry Potter books from Amazon and have them sent to her. I'm sure if anyone finds out, I'll be in trouble about that too.

But I hope it goes a tiny way to bringing this girl some joy.

Mental health detainee number three

It's now 11.30pm. The sergeant partners Sarah and me together again, sending us straight to Harrisville General Hospital.

My first time here as a police officer. No surprise we bump into lots of colleagues, including the two we're taking over from. They're on a late shift and desperately want to escape before their shift finishes at midnight. Their exhaustion radiates from them like heat.

After a handover briefing, we take over the job.

Our detainee is Alexis. She's fifteen. She's been arrested, assessed by paramedics, and sectioned under 136 by police.

Because of her aggression, she's been strapped to an ambulance bed in three places. No one wants to do this to a child, but it's essential to get her to Harrisville General Hospital while keeping her safe and protecting everyone around her.

It's devastating to see her. She has one of the angriest faces I've ever seen. I can't tell if she's in mental or physical pain, or both. Her rage fills the space like poison.

Because she's lying on her back, she's handcuffed to the front. Unfortunately, this means she can hit herself in the face with the metal locked around her wrists if we're not quick enough to stop her.

She managed to do this on the way to A&E. A nasty wound gapes on her forehead as a result. It needs checking before she can be medically discharged and also transported to Maplewood.

This means she must be guarded by two police officers. We're playing the NHS and policing dance of who's responsible for the mental health patient.

The two ladies from the ambulance crew also have to stay with us. They can't go anywhere else until their bed is freed up and they can take it back to their ambulance.

We're all in the corridor but then moved into a room allocated for mental health patients. Another airless, windowless room with ridiculously bright lights. If you go in there without mental health issues, you may well leave with them. Bright lights at night again. No good for anyone. The fluorescent glare burns into my retinas.

We get increasingly frustrated by the delays in getting her seen. The ambulance crew could easily check her head wound, clean it up, and we could start the process of getting her a bed in a mental health hospital. But that's not how things are done, apparently. She must be medically discharged by a doctor.

Alexis is seriously angry about something. You can feel and see the tension radiating from her small frame. She waits until she thinks we're not paying attention, then tries to jolt her hands up to her forehead, testing our reflexes to stop her causing more injuries.

My muscles stay coiled, ready to spring. I realise how much stronger I am than when I first started at training school nine months ago.

Eventually, she relaxes a tiny bit. You can see the release of some tension as she starts to talk to us: "I can't live in the community. I need to live in an institution. I wasn't trying to kill myself, I just wanted to get away from those people, be on my own."

As many children in mental health homes do, she'd escaped and run. Then been caught and detained by police near a bridge over a busy road.

Why are we doing this to our young people, ruining their lives before they've even begun? How can a 15-year-old come back from this experience as an adult? The questions tear at my chest.

Without exceptional therapy and a nurturing environment, she may not. And what does that mean for her ability to work and look after herself? How many times will police be involved in her life to come, as a suspect and a victim no doubt?

Aside from the wider team from Harrisville police station that were involved in searching for and detaining her, so far four police officers, two ambulance staff, multiple nurses and doctors attend to Alexis's needs tonight – because our mental health system and approach to SEND is so broken.

If it wasn't, she wouldn't have needed to escape. Her care workers wouldn't have called police. Alexis wouldn't have fought police. She wouldn't have been detained. She wouldn't have felt angry, alone, and out of control. She wouldn't have tried to smash her own head in.

Eventually, she's seen and discharged. I think we're lucky to get the OK to transport her straight to the mental health hospital very quickly after that.

Sarah and I go in the ambulance to ensure everyone's safety.

When we arrive, the mental health team try to have a chat with her, but she's had enough of people. She knows what she needs and just wants to go there. So they put her in the dark green, attractively decorated holding room before they can allocate her own room. It's the middle of the night now.

The room appears familiar to her as I watch her walk in. She sits down on the bed, her shoulders slumping, and then she cries and cries and cries. The anger drains from her face. She's relieved and exhausted.

After hours of torment, she finally feels safe and at home in an institution. She knows while she's here, she'll get the help she needs.

My throat constricts watching her. This broken child finding solace in what should be a last resort.

On the way back to Harrisville, it's just Sarah and me in the back of the ambulance, paramedics up front. We're chatting about how the evening played out, how fast it was from hospital discharge to transportation.

Things have clearly changed since I met Pete two months ago. Is it because the two people I've dealt with tonight were children?

Then it dawns on me. "Do you think the new approach to dealing with mental health patients is being tested?"

Sarah agrees: "Maybe. Something has definitely changed."

"Interesting, we're not due to roll it out for several months."

First developed and launched by Humberside Police, in July 2023 the Government announced that Right Care, Right Person would be rolled out across the UK.

It's an approach to making sure people who have health and / or social care needs get help from the right services. It aims to end the inappropriate and avoidable involvement of police in responding to incidents involving people with mental health needs.

It will stop police attending calls relating to mental health incidents unless there's an immediate threat or risk to life.

Despite Oakshire Constabulary's official roll-out not starting for another few months, by mid-October we're already seeing what a difference testing the new escalation process is making. Some hospital guards are reduced to just a few hours.

Police will be spending a lot less time with mental health patients in Oakshire in future.

I'm interested to know how the NHS is coping with that.

Police emails go missing

One day I'm getting frustrated, not for the first time, that I don't get many replies from victims, witnesses, and suspects. Email is essential in this job because often we are trying to contact people in the middle of the night, when we might get five minutes to deal with our workload.

It's also an efficient, and less intrusive approach. It means you can be clear in your communication and provide people with investigation reference numbers more easily. Also, most people don't answer their phones if they see a withheld number, which ours come up as.

Follow up conversations are generally easier, because they've had time to consume, and process information, and think of questions to ask us. And they can choose to reply in their own time.

However, I'm finding I need make a lot of follow-up calls, because people aren't replying.

Today it's dawned on me, that Oakshire Constabulary emails are getting blocked. They are simply not arriving or going into people's spam folder. I ask around, no one seems to be aware of an issue, and they don't have time to worry about it.

No time to worry about it?

I get that, but this could be a real policing issue. If people aren't getting our emails, they can't demonstrate whether they are supportive of police action, or not. And under our "you've got to have evidence" rule, we are closing investigations under "victim unsupportive" with evidence that they haven't responded to our emails.

Even worse, they might think they've been forgotten or are being ignored, that the police don't care about them and the crime committed against them. What impact will this have on their trust in the police. Will they report other crimes in the future?

In my previous career, this is something I would have jumped on, I'd have contacted IT, given them examples, and pushed until it was investigated, and resolved.

Unfortunately, doing that isn't easy here. Firstly, I don't have much faith that it will be resolved. And, I just don't have time today. Or most days.

***

I've been waiting nearly five months for IT to apply a coloured filter on my laptop. Four months into training school, I was diagnosed as likely to benefit from this, to reduce eye stress.

At the time, I was given a coloured acetate, like the ones we used for projecting presentation material onto screens in the 90s. These days you can place them over white pages when you're reading, taking the glare off.

It was a game changer for reading the Blackstone's books, making my last few weeks of reading those enormous bright white books so much easier, and quicker. I found my brain jumping around way less, and the content going in so much more smoothly.

Engaging with the lovely detective who did our test, and provided the supportive material afterwards, is one of my positive experiences. She talked so engagingly about life as a detective and was one of the few people I met that is supportive of the ADP.

The detectives know how much new detectives are needed, because they are carrying the load.

My interactions with her gave me hope that life after training school was going to be good.

***

Today, I've got some desk time, and after making good progress with them, I take a short break from my investigations. I decide to tackle completing the multistage IT self-service form, to report the potential email disappearance issue.

There's no option to select for this type of report, and I get lost down IT dead ends. It feels like this system has been designed by someone who doesn't use it.

Eventually, I lose patience and close the application down.

I don't have any more time to spend on this challenge right now.

Guarding a rape victim

Policing on my own at night comes with a mixture of emotions. I am brave, comfortable with risk, and pretty sure I can use the conflict (fighting) skills we've been taught. Let's face it, it is fighting, because people fight us to avoid being detained after committing an offence.

But I have an underlying feeling that it's fundamentally wrong to put officers with only a few months experience in this situation.

As a probationer you get all the shit jobs, including scene guards. Although, for me they are a well needed relief from the incessant pace of policing in Northcliffe. While I'm actually really enjoying flying from job to job, reacting in the moment, helping so many peoples' bad days turn good, sometimes it's great to be forced to sit and do nothing, other than observe.

It's time to reflect on what I've learned and assess what I'd do differently next time. And, unless you're unlucky to get a scene guard where you have to stand outside in bad weather, you're often somewhere safe and warm, like a police car.

If you can get internet access, you also get the time to tackle some of your workload. It's not always boring, because like St Margaret's public order stints, you usually get to engage with the public and stretch your legs. You are also a very visible presence which the public want.

***

Not tonight though. Tonight is my most isolating and terrifying scene guard.

I've arrived for a night shift on a mild but windy autumn evening. Walking into the buzzing office, I hear talk of the rape of a woman in her own home. Nausea rolls through my stomach. As well as colleagues involved in the actual investigation from the late shift, two officers from that team are doing the scene guard. They'll need to be relieved.

Lucky for them, with the two-hour crossover between late and night shifts, they'll be relieved in time to return to the station and get home on time. Whoever takes over from them will not.

As most of my team are experienced response drivers, or a tutor and tutee combo, I'm allocated the scene guard. My chest tightens. I grab my bags, pick the only available shit car from the car park, and make my way there.

I drive down the incline of a tree-lined road and into the victim's street. I see multiple side streets and alleyways providing easy access for the perpetrator. *Must keep an eye on these.*

My mind races with questions. *How did they pick this victim? Do they live locally? Were they working in the area? How were they so brazen to commit such a hideous offence in such a residential area?*

But also, *why are we guarding her home when her friends have come to stay with her following the attack?*

I have no choice but to double park the police car. It's late, everyone's at home, every space is taken. My hands shake slightly as I lock the car. I walk along a dimly lit footpath to where my colleagues are parked outside the victim's house.

I think they've been lucky to be partnered together for their shift. They're a tutor and tutee, the obvious choice for the late shift sergeant allocating the job.

We swap car keys, I'm taking theirs; they're getting my shit car. The experienced officer shows me the scene log; explains what to do. I've never used one before. He completes his section before heading off. I complete mine, then survey the area, identifying all routes in and out. *There are places people could hide and homes that have a view of the victim's home.*

Most houses are in darkness. It's 10.30pm and it's eerie. The wind picks up and leaves rustle in the trees nearby.

I shiver, though not cold. My skin crawls. *Someone is watching.*

A few hours into the shift, Tristan and his current tutee Emily come to relieve me, enabling me to have a change of scenery, a walk and a wee. I think to myself that maybe if someone is watching, this change in officers will make them think twice about doing anything.

I count my blessings because I'm relieved twice. So grateful for my team's support again.

I'm there nine hours in total. So long that my laptop battery dies and my phone batteries drain so low I can't do any more of my workload. But I've managed to review and update all my investigations, send a long list of questions to my sergeant about how to progress them.

Because I avoid social media, there's not much you can do in the middle of the night. You can't start messaging friends. If only I'd brought my Kindle. Instead, I make the most of the break from blue-light-emitting screen glow and try to meditate.

As night turns to early morning, I can't shake the feeling that I'm being watched. The sensation crawls up my spine every few minutes.

As always on a night shift, relief doesn't arrive until after my shift has ended. I'm back at the police station an hour late. *Thirty more free minutes for the King.* The rest of my team has gone.

Days later, I hear that another woman, in the same street, has also been raped in her home. Ice floods my veins.

***

The next night, putting my kit back on, I realise my baton is missing. My heart skips a beat. I must have left it in the police car. I'd taken it off my tac vest because it was digging uncomfortably into my thigh while I tried to work on my laptop.

It was a new lightweight baton I'd only just received. Despite being so much stronger, I was doing everything I could to lighten the load, stop the feeling that I'm constantly being pulled forward by the kit on my tac vest.

So I'd asked if I could swap out my medium weight one for the lighter version. Making that swap, and buying myself a lighter weight torch, made a huge difference to the pain in my lower back.

I hadn't written down the vehicle reg of the police car I'd been in during the scene guard. No one else could tell me what it was. So when I get a couple of minutes, I walk round the car park, shining my torch into all the vehicles. Nothing. I ask my colleagues to check the vehicles they're out and about in too. Nothing.

How can a baton go missing from a police car? They're not easy to miss. I'd left it in the cup holder between the two front seats. Someone would have seen it. The next officers in the car would have seen it.

I send an email to the team that took over the scene guard from me, to see if they found it. I never get a reply. No one is owning up to finding it. *Someone must have it.*

I dig around in the wheelie bin in the kit room that's used to return stuff we can't use anymore. Miraculously my old baton is still inside. I'm back to carrying around the heavier weight. It won't be for long. I'll be out of here soon, leaving Response and on my way to CCID.

As well as never finding time to report the missing baton, fear of what communication will follow that admittance also stops me from mentioning it.

The second time I nearly quit

I've been a police constable for four months, and it appears that it's broken me.

It's Saturday morning. I've hardly slept. My alarm screams at 5am.

I've worked so hard to carry on, to motivate myself, to teach myself this job, to push myself well beyond my comfort zone every shift. But this morning I have an overwhelming feeling that I am not fit for work. I feel so low that I can't physically get myself out of bed. *This never happens to me. My limbs feel like lead.*

No one is line managing me. I feel like there's no one to turn to. I don't understand why this organisation is so bad at looking after its people, particularly its probationers.

I don't think this new career is worth being made to feel like this. I've worked damn hard and long hours my whole working life, but it's never impacted my personal life to this extent. The only time I got this low at work was when I had Covid.

Six months earlier, the Police and Crime Commissioner announced that Oakshire Constabulary had recruited more new officers since September 2019 than its target.

Sadly, this isn't helping on the ground yet. Officers are leaving. The average officer service time is at an all-time low. The reality is resources are still seriously low compared to demand – or at least the number of incidents those up the hierarchy are insisting that Response officers attend.

Working in the police is a bitchy environment. People bitch about the job constantly, bitch about other people. I imagine it's worse than it used to be in this ME, ME, ME obsessed world, driven by social media.

Despite all the bitching, I feel like nothing ever changes for the better. No one is doing anything about the concerns or issues. No one is writing these problems down.

I'm spending my rest days beating myself up. *Surely I'm capable of getting through this. I'm resilient. I'm hardworking. I've dealt with tough times in my life. It's only another couple of months before I finish this part of the ADP and move on to what I came here for: to be a detective.*

My brain is in overdrive. I'm totally overwhelmed. Now it's impacting my ability to sleep. I also realise I've stopped contacting my friends because I don't want to drown them with negativity. I'm retreating from the world.

I feel like I only have energy to do the basics of survival. My life has become consumed by work and trying to get enough sleep to survive work.

I realise I'm heading for burnout. I know I need to put the brakes on. But I can't walk away from my out-of-control workload. It won't go away. It'll be there when I get back. It's a no-win situation.

I'm not the first, and I certainly won't be the last to go through this. It's happening right across the organisation.

I just know there's no way I can go in for the set of four earlies I've just got up for.

My hands shake as I send a text to my sergeant to let him know I won't be in. I feel sick. I know I'm not fit for work, but I've always felt terrible about taking time off.

He tells me to get some rest and keep him posted. The relief is palpable. My shoulders drop for the first time in weeks.

I go back to bed and sleep for five more hours.

My long email

There is a saying in the police: if it's not written down, it didn't happen.

As someone who loves the written word, I often find it a more powerful and engaging medium than spoken words. Those can disappear into space, be misheard or misinterpreted, and result in problems not getting solved.

I'm also way more articulate through the written word when having to discuss serious concerns, about something that really matters to me.

When I wake up after those extra hours sleep, I know I must take serious action. I know I won't be able to explain everything I'm feeling in a verbal conversation.

So like I did with the email I intended to send to Inspector Thornton during training school, I write it all down. But this time I send it. To my sergeant and inspector. It goes pretty much like this:

From: olivia.gray@oakshire.police.uk
To: sergeant@oakshire.police.uk, inspector@oakshire.police.uk
Date: October2023
Subject: In need of help

Hi Guv and Sarge
I'm reaching out because I need help, I'm feeling burnt out and not fit for work.

Before I joined, I never got headaches, or had a problem with my sleep. Now I experience both all the time. This job is making me physically and mentally ill and I fight back tears every day.

I fear coming to work because I'm overwhelmed by my workload. I have more investigations than others on the team and can't get time or support to work on them. I can't even get one investigation underway before more come in.

I'm usually such a resilient person but this is too much.

My short time with a tutor didn't even cover some of the basics and I was forced to go FIP before I was ready.

The systems are so difficult to see on the screens we have, and we waste so much time retyping or copying and pasting content. The relentless 'paperwork' is too much on top of the day-to-day job that I actually really enjoy and think I can be good at, with the right support.

A sergeant from CCID put an unnecessary comment on one of my investigations, simply because of my lack of experience. I've put hours into that investigation, including on my rest days.

I seem to be covering other stations or doing St Margaret's public order more than others, each shift not touching my workload or OneFile.

I'm really conscientious but can't serve my victims properly as we don't have time. Surely doing things badly at this stage just causes problems later?

I'm not the only one struggling, many of us talk about leaving because the organisation ruins us, and so early in our careers. It's clear why there's a retention issue. The way we're feeling isn't acceptable, it's dysfunctional.

I'm worried I either won't make it to CCID, or I'll get there broken.

I'm sad at the impact the job has on our personal lives and health. I'm sad at how officers, who put their lives on the line for others, have so much crap to put up with in the poor working environment of the police station:

- *excessive heat making it hard to focus on workload*
- *bad and broken chairs; plugs, sockets and cables that don't work (there's no time to report these)*
- *emails telling us off for not clearing up dirty crockery that we've made drinks for victims, witnesses and suspects in; should we be*

policing or cleaning?

- *emails from the hierarchy that simply lack understanding of the pressures of frontline policing; how did they forget so quickly what it is like?*

The job is so relentless there isn't time to keep hydrated, or take toilet breaks. Most shifts we don't get time to eat properly. This has such a negative impact on our ability to stay fit for the job.

Getting the right uniform has been such a challenge. Unexpectedly this week I was sent a stab vest that fits properly. For four months I've been wearing one that's been causing neck pain and contributing to my headaches. The positive difference wearing the new one has been huge.

I'm finding policing on my own after such a short time in the job horribly isolating. We'd been told we wouldn't police alone at night. This is such a risk when we're new.

There's a serious issue with resourcing and how it is managed. Even though those of us who are trainees aren't counted in the numbers, we're still used as a resource when the organisation needs us to be counted. We're told there's not enough people in for us to take a seriously needed day off, but people on the team are then sent to cover other stations.

I don't think the ADP should be called a 'programme' and I certainly wouldn't recommend it. Someone needs to review what is important and essential for somebody to be accelerated to detective and the fact we're not given the four weeks on NPT to learn the basics.

Sorry for sending such a long email, thanks for reading it. It's the only way I can fully explain how things are. I want to get through this and do my best but need your help to do that.

Sarge, I really appreciate the support you gave me recently, it really helped me get through some of my workload. But we haven't been able to get time together since because of the pressure you are also under.

I just don't feel mentally able to take on any more, before tackling my current workload. I'm not fit to be at work, but I can't face being off sick and coming back to the same workload and the pressure of more coming in.

Can I suggest while I'm off for the rest of this set that I spend a couple of hours each day tackling the urgent bits of my workload, and preparing an email with questions for you?

Please let me know what you think. I'd really appreciate having a chat and deciding on a plan to help get me through the next few days and then the next couple of months.
Kind regards
Olivia

***

After such a strong urge to get it all out, I feel such an amazing sense of relief writing it all down, that I actually consider not sending it.

But nothing will ever change if I don't. So, I hit send.

Things change after that email.

My sergeant sends me a message, and we agree to talk on the phone. He's kind and makes me feel a whole lot better. I realise how much I needed this support. I'm so relieved he's back from CCID, and able to provide it.

He does tell me I need to be off sick, and rest, not work. And we agree to meet face to face at the police station the next day, to talk about it all.

I still work – I don't feel like there's any other option. If I'm going to avoid cancelling a suspect interview in two days' time, I must plan and prepare. It's only my second one, and the first on my own. And I'll lose time tomorrow with the meeting with my sergeant.

***

During training school, we spent about half a day on witness statement writing; and similar on suspect interview training. It was nowhere near enough to make me feel competent at doing a suspect interview on my own.

I learnt so little from watching my cohort muddle through role-plays; and doing them myself. There's no substitute for watching footage of real interviews and analysing them, but this isn't part of our training.

Since then, I've watched Tristan do one short "no comment" suspect interview, before he sat in during my first, with a domestic abuse suspect. He'd actually given me good feedback and clearly felt more confident than I do about my ability to go it alone.

But I'd had weeks to prepare for that interview. It took ages to get time to work on the investigation and then track the suspect down to invite him in.

I'm surprised that providing interview templates isn't a thing at Oakshire Constabulary. I'm baffled as surely that would be one of the most efficient ways of supporting trainees; and ensuring great interviews. When watching suspect interviews on TV, it's clear there's standard questions that need to be asked.

Fortunately, before we left training school, Janos shared with me a set of templates he'd got from a friend. And that's how I'm able to prepare for my first interview on my own. On a crime I've never dealt with before.

***

Back at the police station the next day, the meeting with my sergeant goes well, I feel even better, there's light at the end of the tunnel. I feel supported, and I believe things will improve.

I'm back at work the following day, it's one shift, I can cope. I am resilient.

And, I've got on top of my urgent workload, by being off work. And that feels so good. I feel like I can do this job now; and make the most of my remaining time in Response.

Move to Birchdene

The next set of shifts I'm told I'm moving to Birchdene.

I pack up all my kit, find a shit car and drive over. I lug everything up the precarious metal staircase attached to the outside of the building, and step into my third new work base in 10 months. I'll be based here for eight weeks, or until I get the OK to move to CCID.

I go through the process of getting a new locker for my kit, a new PAVA locker; and then trying to navigate what seems to be unnecessarily complicated office politics.

Not long after my arrival, someone puts the Christmas decorations up. It's the end of November. Somehow, this becomes political too. Notes are left telling people not to change the settings, without a care for anyone who struggles to work with constantly flashing fairy lights in their faces.

Birchdene is a tiny police station, in a small town not far from Northcliffe. It's part of the same policing area so I'm still part of the same team. We share the building with Council staff who rarely work beyond 5pm; unless there's an event going on, when you can hear the clinking of glasses and merriment from other parts of the building.

I'm often on my own here during a night shift and it's rare to see anyone walking the corridors at that time. Going to the toilet gets my heart racing. When you step through the internal door that separates the police station from the Council offices, and into the shared corridors, they are in darkness, until the sensors kick in.

There are way too many closed doors behind which I have no idea what lies.

I think my move is because I've caused trouble, and been critical of life at Northcliffe, by sending my big email to my sergeant and inspector. I'm told it's because it's quieter at Birchdene, a slower pace, and that should help with my workload and learning.

I've only recently been told, because I had no idea what to do with them next, that I must build case files for two of my investigations, then they need to be submitted to the CPS.

I've not remembered any of the very short session we had, explaining what a case file is, at training school. And building a case file is not something we're taught how to do. Unless you count the high speed, tough luck if you get left behind or need time to process your thoughts, crime management system training.

That was over five months ago. And I'm not getting any desk time to teach myself how to do my first one now.

Case files are a critical element of the justice process, and hugely time consuming when you first start out doing them. They must be totally accurate; I mean crossing t's and dotting i's level of accuracy. If not, you can get caught in a game of 'throw the hot potato' with the CPS; and files can bounce back and forward for months on end.

My two first case files sit on my workload for weeks, until I get time to even consider looking at them. Life at Birchdene turns out to be no slower. I don't even get time to enjoy the multiple places you can get a decent coffee, something Northcliffe doesn't have, and something I had really looked forward to. No such luck.

I have to repeatedly beg my sergeant for zero eight (08) time, to work on my case files. 08 time is when you are protected from getting new incidents to deal with so you can work on urgent workload.

But when I'm lucky to get it, just when I'm getting into the flow of teaching myself the case file process, I'm sent out to an incident. I lose my focus and have to start all over again, another shift.

Not being shown how to create my first case file means that I end up wasting time muddling through a chaotic learning approach. A learning experience that means it doesn't cement itself in my brain, and means I have to relearn for each file, which all have different elements to build.

"Just look at the crime management system help guide," I'm repeatedly told.

But we don't all learn well that way, especially for the first case files we build.

Missing girls

I was a missing person more than once. But no one noticed.

While my brother was studying hard, going to bed early and being the model child, I used to sneak out of the back door, through the side gate, walk in the late-night darkness down to the local station, and get a train into the city, on my own.

I'd go clubbing and get the night bus home. No one knew. I never told my mum before she died at 63. I only told my dad when I was in my 40s, and he was in his 70s.

If anyone had noticed I wasn't asleep in my bed, I would have become a missing person.

The College of Policing defines a missing person as: "Anyone whose whereabouts cannot be established will be considered as missing until located, and their well-being or otherwise confirmed."

The level of police activity for missing people is based on risk, from very low to high. Aged 14 to 15 and with my background, I would have been considered medium risk. No one would have had a clue where I was, or anything about my welfare.

Someone is reported missing every 90 seconds in the UK.

Over 170,000 people are reported missing every year (96,000 are adults and nearly 75,000 are children).

There are nearly 350,000 reported missing incidents every year (nearly 130,000 relate to missing adults and over 216,000 to missing children).

Most of the people who are reported missing may be experiencing some kind of vulnerability or risk. One in 10 looked-after children are reported missing compared to one in 200 children. Looked after children who are reported missing will be reported on average six times.

I spend about 10% of my time as a PC, looking for missing people; a skill that I started to hone during my Ride Along in 2022.

***

During a late shift, my sergeant sends me to find my colleague Emily. "Emily can't be reached on her radio or mobile. She might be in a poor service area, but we need to check if she's OK. Can you go and look for her?"

"Yes sarge, no worries."

Emily isn't considered missing. She's at the start of an investigation into a missing 13-year-old girl who hasn't been seen since leaving school at 3pm. It's now 9pm on a Friday in winter. Cold and very dark. They live in a remote area of Northcliffe that's not easy to access on foot.

"Can you head up to the family home, see if she's there?" my sergeant orders.

"Will do, I'll keep you posted."

I plug the address into my mobile, balance it precariously on the dashboard, and make my way over. *My hands grip the steering wheel tighter than necessary.*

I arrive at the large detached house, sitting in the middle of an exclusive estate full of multi-million-pound houses. Each home has its own unique style, most with large gates to keep trespassers out and residents safe inside.

I ascend the steep drive, parking my police car behind the one already there. *Found Emily.* Miraculously, I manage to get some radio service and let my sergeant know.

The mum of the missing girl answers the door. "Good evening, I'm PC Gray and I'm looking for my colleague. We haven't been able to get her on her radio, so we've been worried."

"Please come in, she's here," she says. Welcoming me in with a smile and showing me into a large living room, where I find Emily sitting with the dad of the missing girl.

"Good evening," I say to him, and to my colleague: "Hi Emily, everyone's worried about you. No one could get hold of you."

Unfazed, Emily says, "I'm fine." *Do I see irritation flash across her face?*

I take in the room, noticing many pieces of classic old furniture. The mum takes a seat next to the dad on an expensive-looking large dusky pink patterned sofa, that looks like it's been in the family for years.

Emily sits on one of two matching armchairs. I take the other.

Emily is twenty-one and outwardly confident. I'm impressed at how she's engaging with the parents, but *this is not a job for just one very young, very inexperienced police constable.*

Now I'm here, but not wanting to tread on her toes, I try not to interrupt, waiting to see how the situation pans out and how I can help.

Emily's also on the ADP, a couple of months behind me. She's only been FIP for a couple of weeks.

We're hardly the dream team to be dealing with this situation. Seriously lacking experience, I say, "I'll stay and see how I can help," I can see the parents' relief that there'll be two of us looking for their child.

They have no idea how little experience I have, but my age puts a lot of people at ease. *It's much easier for a middle-aged couple to trust someone their age than someone three decades younger and only a few years older than their missing child.*

The dad's phone rings, he takes the call, then says: "Hold on."

Then, turning back towards us: "It's the mum of my daughter's school friend. Her daughter is missing too. She wants to know what's happening with the investigation."

Emily takes his mobile and shares as much as she can with this other frantic parent, she then asks a few questions and writes a few notes in her pocket notebook.

At the same time, I get a call on my mobile from our sergeant.

"Olivia, how's it going there?"

"Yeah ok, sarge. Just getting as much as we can before planning and starting the search."

Before I've had the chance to tell him who Emily is talking to, he says: "There's another missing girl, they are friends. We suspect they're together."

"Yes sarge, Emily's on the phone with her mum now."

"How on earth?"

"She called the dad here."

"Ah, makes sense. I want you to stay and work with Emily on this. Keep me updated."

"Yes sarge, will do. Thanks."

Emily and I finish our calls at the same time, both with: "I'll keep you posted." And she hands the mobile back to the dad.

Funny, that's two mobiles working here. I'm puzzled how some calls get through in this remote area and others don't.

We gather information from the parents we're with, including a recent photo, and these help us decide our next steps.

The mum's recently lost both her parents and their home is standing empty while being gutted – maybe the girls have gone there. They don't think they've been before, but it seems an ideal place to hide out.

Emily and the parents have already searched the house we're in – it's one of the first things we do. *You'd be amazed how many kids are actually at home, not missing at all.*

So we decide the empty house is the next place for our search. The parents give us the code for the key safe, telling us there should be a key inside, so we don't need to take one with us.

As we drive over in our separate police cars, we keep our eyes peeled. *Getting out on foot is pointless at this stage*, with just the two of us and so much to do first, we plan to do that later.

We're retracing a route I've already done this evening. I think about two young girls I'd seen walking through the town on the way to work, around 4.30pm.

They'd been dressed in fluffy onesies, happily walking in the autumn sunshine. *But my gut had told me at the time that something wasn't right.*

***

We park up in the busy residential street at the edge of a nearby town – a stark contrast to the remote home they're living in now. From the design of the townhouse windows and lack of window dressings, it's clear to see that inside it's in darkness. The parents told us there's no electricity, so if someone was inside, they'd have to use a torch.

I notice a food wrapper on the floor. Inside is a half-eaten wrap – the bread's still fresh and hasn't been taken by foxes yet. *We suspect the girls have been here, but are they inside?*

We knock several times. No reply, no movement, no indication of life inside.

"Shall we try the key safe?" I ask Emily.

"Yeah, look it's just there." She replies, pointing in the darkness to a corner not far from the front door.

I fumble and can't get it open. "This is seriously tricky. I can't get it to work. Do you want to try?"

Emily tries, and after a few attempts the little box pings open. No key.

"I wonder if the girls have been here and taken the key," I say to her. "Or maybe someone else has taken it?"

These are the moments your mind goes into overdrive. Not only are we concerned about the safety of two young teenage girls who may have taken the key, but who else could have taken it? Who else could be inside?

The house has been emptied and all the old-fashioned décor stripped out, so it could be any tradesperson who's been there before. Could they have given the code to someone else? *Is there someone in there that we don't want to encounter in the dark?*

As well as being new and inexperienced officers, there's no potential for immediate backup. We've radioed in our location, but we're too far away from our colleagues for anyone to get there in less than fifteen minutes. *Anything could happen in that time.*

I have no doubt we could put up a good fight, but how long could we control whoever may be inside? *What if there's a few of them? There's only so much our training will protect us.*

We manage to get through the back gate. There's a window open on the middle floor. The parents told us there shouldn't be any open.

Then we kick ourselves – why didn't we ask for a key, just in case? Sometimes it's the little things you don't think about when you're new and struggling to figure out how to do this job.

I call them, and we agree to go back and get one.

***

Back at the house, key in hand, we open the front door, stepping into the eerie quiet. Once a loving family home, now gutted this house lacks character. *It has no soul. I wonder if it's because no one's living here.*

We use our torches to search each floor, room by room, finding nothing. *The silence presses in around us.*

We reach the top floor and check built-in wardrobes in a bedroom, off which we discover a small ensuite tucked in the corner.

Right in the hidden most corner, behind the door and easy to miss, is a shower cubicle.

Inside it are bags. We pull them out. They are school bags, containing school jackets and empty chocolate wrappers.

The girls have been here. And they're smart – what a brilliant hiding place, easy to miss. It must have been them that took the key from the key safe.

Now what? They could be anywhere.

Emily and I decide to split up and agree to meet back here in an hour.

She heads over to the house of the other missing girl, to speak to the parents, get a photo, and search the area over that way. I search from the area they were last seen, around the town, and back towards the first missing girl's home.

They could be constantly on the move at this point – we'll need to retrace likely routes a few times. We've got to search several square miles, just the two of us, separately, on our own.

But that's policing. These aren't the only missing children tonight. We're under pressure to get this job wrapped up and join a huge search with our entire team for a high-risk missing 16-year-old lad who's got himself in trouble with a drugs gang.

It's getting to the stage of the evening where late-night revellers are starting to spill out of pubs. *Not a time for vulnerable young girls to be out on their own.*

I wander in and out of as many pubs as I can, checking with bar staff if they've been seen. Nothing.

My phone rings – it's one of the mums. An elderly neighbour and old friend of her parents has seen the girls going into the empty house in the last few minutes. I call Emily and we head straight there, travelling from opposite sides of the area. She brings the other mum with her, who waits in the car.

We still have the key, so we open the front door and as we step inside, we shout: "Police, is there anyone in here?" We continue to shout this, so the girls know we're there and who we are.

They appear on the landing above us, their young faces sheepishly looking down at us.

Finally.

"Come downstairs please," I ask up to them.

Emily says, "I'll go and get mum from the car."

We all meet in the hallway, which has some streetlight illuminating it, making it easier for us all to see each other. They both appear small for 13, but Emily and I are both tall.

They're wearing fluffy onesies. The same ones I saw earlier.

There's a lounge area down a further flight of stairs which seems a better place for us to go through the usual question set that we must do when a missing person is found.

Later, Emily and I will each log the answers given by each girl on the missing person system, when we finally get back to the police station.

I doubt they'd tell us if they had, but they answer no to each question:

"Have you met or been with anyone else? Have you had any alcohol or taken any drugs? Were you scared?"

They do admit to being cold. *I expect by this point they're extremely tired,* and their bodies no longer staying warm with adrenaline from the fun they were having earlier.

I ask them, "Do you have anything you want to tell us, any concerns?"

"No," is the simple answer.

"You know you can call 101 anytime?"

They nod in reply.

There's way more to this story than we're getting, and I can tell it won't be the last of their contact with the police.

To provide some reassurance I say, "I'm happy to come and see you if you'd like me to."

They smile in response. *I hope they'll feel comfortable contacting the police if they need us. Hopefully I'll be involved next time as well and provide some consistency for them.*

I feel it's a good place to end this conversation and get them home as it's really late now.

"Shall we go?" I ask Emily what I think is a rhetorical question and make a move to leave the room and head back upstairs.

But before everyone has the chance to follow me, Emily unexpectedly and sternly says: "Now the bad news. Your parents have been worried sick. I don't understand why you've done this. You both live in lovely homes. I don't want to hear of you doing this again. Do you understand?"

For God's sake. I know all our hard work has just been undone. *I don't blame Emily – she's young. She doesn't realise this isn't just children having fun. She doesn't understand there must be a complicated backstory to all of this.*

There are parts of this story I won't share, because they're too personal to everyone involved, but what I will say is that returning the girls to their homes isn't easy. I don't get back to the police station for another hour and a half, around 1am.

I have little time to decompress, go for a wee, and add details to the missing persons system, before heading out to join the other search.

We're searching outside until after 4am and do a twelve-hour shift in the end.

Missing again

It's two weeks later, and the second 13-year-old girl goes missing again.

My sergeant tasks me with the search on my own, we don't have enough resources for more officers to join me: "Go work your Misper magic. I'm sure you'll have her home in a couple of hours."

I'm chuffed with his confidence in my capabilities.

First stop is the family home, where Emily was less than two weeks ago. I meet the parents and do the obligatory search of the house. It's a labyrinth, easy to get lost, easy to hide. I have to be really thorough.

It's always awkward, looking through people's cupboards, under their beds. They are always embarrassed, apologising for the mess, even when there isn't any.

During our chat, I find out that the girl was meant to walk to her dad's place of work after school but never arrived. I get some ideas of locations she may be, including the local pub, just round the corner.

"Thank you, I'll start at the pub, and then I'll head over to her friend's house, to see if she knows anything. I'll keep you posted. Here's my number in case you hear anything in the meantime."

At the pub I chat to the staff and show them a photo of the girl.

One tells me: "She's been in here at other times on her own but isn't here now."

I ask: "Please can you call 101 if she comes in? Also, if there's ever any children that come in on their own, please can you call 101? It could save significant police time searching for missing children, and parents a lot of anguish."

Next step, searching enroute on the way to the other girls' home.

I realise on the drive there, that there is no way this missing girl could walk to her own house on pavements; only cross country, or on narrow 60mph country roads. It's pitch black. I ask myself how on earth she could get home by herself. *She certainly couldn't do it without risking her life.*

I pull into the familiar steep drive, knocking on the familiar front door, and get a familiar hello from the other mum I'd spent so much time speaking to, just two weeks ago. She welcomes me back into the familiar living room, and I take a seat in the familiar chair.

We chat about the missing girl; the tables have turned. It's no longer her child that's missing, but she knows what the anguish is like.

She tells me the girl hasn't been here: "She's not been here since they both went missing. My daughter has been here since school. We collect her now. She's in her room. Apart from coming down to grab some snacks, she's been up there the whole time."

"Can you get your daughter to come down so we can have a chat please?"

"Of course," and she heads upstairs.

I hear them chatting as they come down. The girl takes a seat in the chair Emily had sat in.

She has a new hair cut which makes her look so grown up, I say: "I love your new hair style."

She smiles shyly, not expecting this from me: "Thanks."

We do the whole awkward small talk about life and then I say: "We are really worried about your friend. Do you know where she is?"

A shake of the head in reply.

"I'm more concerned than when you went missing together before, because this time she is on her own. When you're together you are safer. Everyone's very worried about her. Can you tell me anything?"

For 10 minutes we go through everything I can think of, she is cagey, but responds to all my questions, with what seem like honest answers. She keeps checking her phone, sending a couple of messages, typical teenager.

As I'm coming to the end of the usual questions, I ask mum if she's searched their house. She hasn't.

I ask her: "Do you mind if I have a chat with your daughter on her own, while you start searching?"

"Of course," and she leaves the room, heading straight upstairs.

I ask the girl: "Are there any issues you want to talk to me about, while mum isn't here?"

She looks at me closely, wondering whether to trust me, and then tells me: "We're being bullied at school."

She waits for me to say something; but I know from life experience, rather than any police training I've had, that it's important to let her talk without interruption.

"There's a girl at school. We were all friends. She was here in the summer, and she took my brother's mobile phone."

She goes quiet and then continues: "Our parents don't believe us. We've been scared to walk in certain places after school."

That's all she's going to be saying without probing so, trying to join the dots of this disjointed story, I ask: "Why is she bullying you?"

She replies, quietly: "Coz last time she was here, my brother took the phone back off her. It had the girl's sim in."

This is all starting to make sense.

I ask about the bully: "What does she look like?"

As she starts to describe the bully, I think I might have met her before: "Do you have a photo of her?"

"Yes," and she gets her phone out to show me.

***

A few months back, when I was with Tristan, we dealt with a disturbance on the top of a four-storey block of flats. A bunch of school aged kids were mucking about in a dangerous spot from which they could have fallen. A concerned member of the public had reported them, and we'd broken up their little party on the roof.

We'd been particularly concerned about one girl, she was really tall for her age, and was halfway up a wall, in a short skirt. There was no way she was going to be able to get down with her dignity intact.

I'd been glad I was with Tristan that day. Despite his flaws, he is very respectful in that kind of situation and dealt with it brilliantly.

It made me think back to my rebellious school days and how, if I'd ever been unlucky enough to get involved with the police, that he would have been the kind of officer I would have respected. It's funny how differently I feel about him now he's not my tutor.

That day, I'd also thought about some of the guys at training school, and I dreaded thinking about their reaction, and abilities in the same situation.

From the short conversation we had with her, it was clear that the girl was from a troubled home, and I really felt for her. She refused a lift home from us. I could understand why.

It was a beautiful summer's day, why would she want to go home, when she could be out with her friends in the sunshine; and why would she want to bring police officers to her home. Or more interestingly, why wouldn't she.

***

I look at the photo and it's her. The same girl. This story is all falling into place. I understand what's playing out here. And my Copper's nose is clearly at work again.

As my brain starts to work out what my next steps are going to be, I hear the mum coming down the stairs. She walks into the room, and looking at her daughter says: "Is there anything you'd like to tell the officer?" She asks the question twice. Her voice is stern, yet soft, this is clearly a difficult relationship that she is trying to navigate.

The girl looks at her blankly. An expression I now realise she has clearly mastered. She doesn't answer.

Mum looks at me: "She's hiding in the cupboard in the bedroom at the end of the corridor."

I raise my eyebrows in response, take a quick glance at the girl and head straight upstairs. As I try to push the door open there's resistance.

With no sound of a person pushing it from the other side, I stick my head round the door to discover there's a piece of furniture up against it. I squeeze my way in, just enough room to fit myself, and my bulging kit through the gap, without scraping the woodwork.

The wardrobe door is ajar, I open it fully to find the missing girl, crouching amongst her friend's clothes. I think I see a glimpse of relief in her face.

"Are you OK?" I ask. She nods and I radio in the news immediately.

My sergeant calls me and says: "Well done, good work, do you need anything?"

"I'm all good thanks sarge, I'll let her mum know now."

"Get yourself back to the station as soon as you can, I've got another job I need you to deal with."

Her mum receives the news with mixed emotions. She's relieved her daughter is safe, but angry. "I can't believe it, has she been there the whole time? Why didn't anyone check?"

I can't answer that question so I divert to action: "I can drive her home now.

"No, dad will come and pick her up."

"OK, thanks," I reply and then to the girl: "Dad's on his way, come on then, let's go downstairs while we wait for him."

She follows me downstairs, and the two girls scurry into another room together, sit on a step and start whispering conspiratorially.

I update mum: "Her dad's on his way to pick her up. I'm just going to have a quick chat with the girls on their own, while we wait for him to arrive."

I wander into the other room and crouch down in front of them, there's nowhere to sit except for the floor. And then I get the full story.

The missing girl was too scared to walk to her dad's place of work after school. It would have meant she was entering the territory of the bully. Without her best friend by her side, because she'd had a lift home, that walk was too risky for her on her own.

That was today, but this story had started months ago, at the beginning of the summer holidays. I can't imagine how difficult it must have been for them to go back to school in September.

During the summer they'd all been friends and had been hanging out at each other's houses. The story is slightly different to earlier and now I'm told one of the girls had leant the bully her brother's mobile phone. She'd broken it.

During the bully's visit to their house one day, the brother had taken the mobile back off her and refused to give the sim back, until she paid for the damage to the phone. The bully didn't have any money. This resulted in a stalemate that has been going on for months.

And because of this, the two girls became a target for bullying. Neither girl's parents believed them. That's why they started going missing.

To move or not to move – who decides?

I've had a meeting with my Workplace Assessor. As ever, she makes me feel good about my progress and sympathises about the unnecessary challenges we experience.

However, the narrative I'm starting to hear is that I won't be moving to my first detective placement on time. There's too much outstanding on my OneFile.

I'm furious, because no one is doing anything to enable me to achieve the things I need to get ticked off. The rigorous training is non-existent, and the ADP is ignored, out here in Response. No one has time.

"There's no way I'm going to get stuck in Response because this organisation isn't supporting me," I tell my assessor. "Does no one care? We really are just numbers, aren't we? I'm done with this; I'll leave if I'm going to be messed around like this."

She calls the PDU (Professional Development Unit) sergeant to join our Teams meeting and I tell him the same thing, adding: "Surely, we can do some of this OneFile stuff later? Spend a day or two back in Response during our second year?"

They agree to think about it; and come back to me.

And then I message Rosie and James:

"Good morning, how's your worlds? Have either of you had your meeting with the PDU sergeant yet? I had mine and one with my assessor. As predicted, the impression was they weren't going to let me move to CCID on January 2 due to lack of OneFile. So, I said that the move is what's keeping me here and if they don't let me go to CCID I won't come back to work after Xmas. I said it was totally unfair to treat people the way they do, and the organisation doesn't support people on the ADP at all. So now I have a 2.5-hour meeting with my assessor tomorrow to look at OneFile to make sure I'm done. Stay strong people."

James replies: "I've only had one meeting with my assessor, haven't had one with the PDU sergeant. At 5.15 this morning I got a compliant arrest, with a section 32 vehicle search, a seizure of Class B and a section 165, all from one bloke. I learnt today, if you want potentially easy arrests, go onto the crime management system and search for court warrants."

I think to myself: *wouldn't it be nice if we all got a consistent experience and were all told things like that from the beginning?* We're nearly at the end of our Response journey.

I reply: "Well done." James is clearly more on track than I am.

There's a man on a bridge

November is proving to be a very interesting month. With more of the trainees becoming FIP, I don't get the diary car anymore. It's such a relief, because I don't want my workload to continue to spiral, with only a few more weeks before I'm hoping to move to CCID. I'm yet to get an answer from my Teams call about this.

The British weather still doesn't know what it's doing. Sometimes warm, sometimes cold, it feels like the trees are taking longer than usual to shed their leaves. It's difficult to work out how many layers to wear each day.

I'm still policing on my own most of the time, but I'm getting used to it; and with help from my sergeant, I'm finding my workload more manageable. It's still too much, but I feel more competent which goes a long way towards feeling more motivated to stay.

I'm on a night shift. I've been out to a couple of small incidents and am back at Birchdene police station when the radio sparks into life. I hear one of the sergeants from Marsham ask for assistance.

With resources low, single crewed, he's attended a location where a member of the public reported seeing a man on a bridge.

This sergeant is one of the good ones, I've covered in his team before. It's also the same team, bar quite a few people changes, that I joined for the Ride Along last year. I always feel welcome and at home working with them.

In the middle of nowhere, surrounded by fields, on a deserted country road, the sergeant has managed to convince a man in his 30s from achieving his latest suicide attempt, and secured him in a police car.

As ever, the Ambulance service can't get there for another five hours, and it's too risky for the sergeant to drive him on his own, this is a two-person job. I think to myself: this isn't even a police job, it's another mental health situation.

My sergeant tasks myself and Max to pick up the transportation job, and Max calls me with the news.

Max likes to drive, and with the really crap cars at Birchdene I'm happy when he says: "I'll come and pick you up, I'll be there in 15 minutes."

***

It has crossed my mind that police vehicles come to die at Birchdene. The one I've been driving has done over 170k miles, a manual with a clutch that feels like it's going to collapse at any minute.

If that's not available, then I have to drive a van. This was something I'd never done before, and had to learn one late shift on the way to an incident by a canal. In the darkness I'd missed the gates, behind which was a terrified woman who we believed had escaped from her abusive partner who was apparently wielding a hammer. The road wasn't wide enough to turn the van around.

Fortunately, my colleagues weren't far behind me. They came in a car, easier to turn round, after they too missed the gates.

I eventually caught up, having travelled half a mile down the road to a space big enough to turn around.

***

As we head towards the location, Max says me: "You know they're going to make us take this guy to St Margaret's City Hospital."

Rolling our eyes at each other, we both know what that means on a night shift. *Here we go again.*

Once again, we'll be on a hospital guard well beyond our 7am shift finish time. Our relief colleagues won't start until 7am and could be coming from anywhere in Oakshire. We'll then have to get back to Birchdene, and Max then back to Northcliffe, in rush hour traffic. *My heart sinks at the thought.*

Max is already formulating a plan to avoid all of that. *I can see the wheels turning.*

We radio the Marsham sergeant to say we're on our way. He gives us the What3Words combination that helps us find the isolated location.

This app is an absolute godsend for emergency services trying to find people, pinpointing them to a three-metre square location. If you're ever anywhere remote, please make sure you have it downloaded. You'll be found so much quicker if you get into trouble.

We arrive at the muddy layby, tyres squelching as we try to avoid the giant potholes. *We don't want to get stuck out here tonight.* We introduce ourselves to the guy, and once again my heart goes out to another person who just can't figure out how to fit into this world.

We get him settled into the back of our police car, I jump in the back next to him, and Max sets off. He misses the turn towards St Margaret's. *Wait, what?*

"Where are you heading?" I ask.

"Maplewood Mental Health Hospital," he replies.

Bold move. I question his decision while being totally in agreement: "But we haven't had the OK to take him there yet?"

"This guy doesn't need to go to A&E. There's nothing physically wrong with him."

"Absolutely, let's try and work our magic," I agree. *Please let this work.*

The guy also agrees. He's been in this situation before. He knows as well as we do that A&E isn't the place for him right now. We all want to avoid him being passed between multiple medical professionals. He recognises and appreciates what we're trying to do: "Thank you," he says with gratitude and sadness in his eyes.

That look breaks my heart.

Enroute to Maplewood, Max starts making the relevant requests over the radio. The FCR make some calls. Maplewood says there's no beds. We're told he needs to go to St Margaret's.

Of course they say no. But we continue on. We want to try. Arriving at the gates we're refused entry. One last try fails.

Damn it.

So we're off to St Margaret's City Hospital, and we say goodbye to finishing at 7am. Yet another mental health patient is going to have an unnecessary wait in A&E with police officers, until there's space at Maplewood.

The system is broken, and we all know it. At least we've wasted some time driving around. It's nicer for all of us in the police car.

Because he has no physical injuries and doesn't appear to be a risk to himself – because we've stopped that from happening – he doesn't get allocated a room to wait in.

So the three of us hang out in a small waiting area, watching the hustle and bustle of the busy hospital around us. Getting the usual stares from the public who are uncomfortable not knowing why the person we're with needs a police guard.

How many consider that the person is detained for their safety, not because they've committed a crime.

The fluorescent lights buzz overhead. My eyes feel gritty from the long night. The plastic chairs dig into my back as I shift position for the hundredth time. *Soul-destroying.*

Our handover colleagues arrive at 7.30am. Max has to drive me back to Birchdene before heading back to Northcliffe. It's rush hour traffic, so by the time I get back it's gone 8am, and Max another twenty minutes after that.

My body aches from sitting in hospital chairs for hours. The morning sun streams through the car windows, mocking our exhaustion.

After wrapping up our night's urgent paperwork, neither of us leave for home until 8.30am.

I don't have to tell you that we'll only get paid for 60 of those 90 minutes overtime. Once again, the King gets his free 30 minutes.

The rage bubbles up in my chest. We'll also have to find an inspector to sign off this overtime, write the correct words, along with the relevant incident log number on our resource management system. If not, it won't get paid.

More hoops to jump through. More unpaid admin time. The system squeezes every last drop from us.

There's a body in the countryside

Homicides are more frequent than people think in Oakshire, there's many that don't make the headlines.

Continuing to manage to avoid the diary car, one early shift I'm sent to another scene guard. This time I won't be alone; I'm joining a few other colleagues who have also been drafted in from other stations across the county.

I'm told there's a body, a potential murder victim, and our Forensics colleagues are yet to complete their tasks, so we must keep the public away.

Birchdene has been my base for a couple of weeks now. I've gotten into the groove of the quieter office environment. And got over the fact that it's no quieter from a workload point of view.

The move had seemed like an ideal scenario, but it is starting to mean way more time in the car, adding a lot of time to my journeys, particularly in rush hour.

I've started my shift in Birchdene, having driven west across the county. Now I'm driving all the way back east again, to join the A road – this time travelling as far south as you can go in the county.

All this driving, in the shit Birchdene police car, is starting to take its toll on my body. *Must book another appointment with my osteopath.*

Battling the rush hour traffic, I arrive at the scene around 8.30am. The poor night shift officer I'm relieving is already an hour and a half late off shift. He must now battle the A road.

I get my police car in position, trying to block the unusually wide country lane entrance. A few cones assist in trying to ensure the public don't gain access. The crime scene is 50 metres up the road from me. Another police car is parked in front of it, and another 20 metres up from that.

A mile up the road is another officer in another police car. Turns out it's Tristan. So our team is down two officers today.

This is one of the reasons we so often have an issue with resources, and vehicles. For the next eight hours, four of us, and four vehicles will be here.

The sun is shining, taking the edge off the cold winter's day. The countryside is beautiful, and peaceful; vast fields and hedgerows surround us.

I wander up to say hello to the guys and then radio Tristan to explain the setup down here. He's too far away to see us, the country road is long, winding, and the other side of a small hill; where a few houses sit, isolated within the cordoned-off road.

I realise the body isn't here anymore, but we can see the spot where the female victim was found. The ground is burned where her body has been set on fire. Barbaric.

Who is she? Who is her killer? Or killers?

The gossip around the force is rampant that day, there's a lot of speculation. Is it an OCG (organised crime group) killing? Was she a drug addict with a debt?

We're guarding a bit of concrete, and I wonder if all of us are necessary to do that. At this stage of the investigation, surely no more than two cars and two officers would suffice.

Back in the police car, I try to get service and internet connection on both my work and personal phones, so I can hotspot to my laptop. I want to use the time effectively and crack through some workload. But it's too remote, there's little service and no internet, so I can't do anything useful.

Several people pull up to the road block in their cars and ask if they can come through; some ask where they can turn around. The first question is easy, it's a no – the second I have no idea. I've never been here before.

I'm surprised how many people I have to deal with in this remote area. Some are polite and understanding, others moody, with no idea why we are there, because we can't tell them. Most would be shocked. I'm sure they will be when the media get the full story.

Three hours in, and four and a half since I left Birchdene, having kept the thought from my mind until now, I'm starting to consider where I'll go for a wee. I can't see any hiding places.

Sitting down I can feel the pressure on my bladder. I'm going to have to bite the bullet soon and have a bush wee.

A white van and a car pull up at the road entrance. I get out and walk over to see what they are up to.

The lady explains: "We're Police Federation reps."

I've not seen any since training school when they came to chat to us about joining them. I had, of course. You'd be mad not to in this job.

I move the cones, to give them access to drive through, put them back in place and walk up to join them. They park up alongside the police car that is blocking entrance to the scene we're guarding.

We all introduce ourselves and chat about the job; they look at the scene, and have a moment of quiet as they take it in.

"Why are you here?" I ask.

The guy slides open the side door to the van.

Inside is a hot water tank, and boxes of tea, coffee, savoury snacks, and biscuits. We stare, wide-eyed and wide-mouthed, blown away. The guys are so happy they dive straight in, rummaging through the boxes. I hear them muttering in excitement about what they are finding.

Then I realise, there's no way I'm drinking tea. It's a diuretic, and just the thought of it reminds me how much I need a wee.

And then the guy says: "There's something else," leading us to the back of the van.

He opens the back doors. There's a toilet.

"Oh my God," I say. "I'm going in." Inside it's like a Portaloo, but more spacious.

Having a cup of tea is back on the agenda. I'm so happy right now. With very little mobile service, chatting, drinking tea, and eating biscuits is what is going to keep us going today.

I radio Tristan: "I've got some great news, we've got tea, snacks and a toilet down here."

We all agree to rotate our positions so he can get access to conversation with colleagues, and the van.

It's yet another off-late shift. We must wait for relief because this scene guard is going to run well into the next shift, maybe even into another night shift.

The guys kindly let me go first because I've got the furthest to travel back. Here we go again, this long journey in reverse, in rush hour, across the entire county.

An hour and a half late, another free half hour to the King. I'm just used to this now.

Choosing our detective placements

In September, Rosie, James and I had been sent another one of those 'pick-your-location' emails; for the three placements we do as trainee detectives. We'd already provided our choices back in training school.

We'd been asked to choose which of the three custody locations we wanted for our Central Crime Investigation Department (CCID) placement, which of the Oakshire police stations we wanted to be based at for our Local Crime Investigation Department (LCID) placement, and which Public Protection and Safeguarding Department (PPSD) we'd like to experience working in.

Each is due to be four months long. Just long enough to get a taster, but not too long that you pick up too much workload, before moving on to the next. Although, the way things are going with my workload in Response, I'm not sure how true that is going to be.

I choose Southpine for CCID, because I'd like to build relationships with people that I may end up working with when I move to LCID.

I don't want to be driving to Harrisville, past Southpine and Westrock to get there. It's more than double the journey which I could do without. I have caring responsibilities for my 83-year-old dad, whose health is deteriorating. It's highly likely he's going to die in the next six months.

***

Five years ago, dad passed responsibility to me for his entire life. He was living alone, very ill and couldn't cope. He called me one evening, just as I was organising a huge conference for 300 people.

"It's over to you," he told me, and I'd had to unravel and fix a giant mess over the coming months.

I moved him into a care home for some respite, and he decided he wanted to stay living in that type of environment. I'd had to renovate and sell his house to pay for the fees. The whole lot, including his savings, and pensions, have nearly run out: over £400,000. *I don't have time to think about what happens when the money runs out.*

It's been two years since dad was given the diagnosis that his 15-year-old prostate cancer had metastasized and was now in his lumbar spine. Dad doesn't remember that diagnosis, he doesn't remember that he has cancer; because he also has vascular dementia.

***

In November, we get an email telling us where we will be for CCID. I'm given Harrisville. So is James. Despite both of us living way closer to Southpine. He has children. None of this makes sense.

I write immediately to the team who manage the ADP, asking if I can be at Southpine, explaining my caring responsibilities and likely imminent death of my dad. I hear nothing.

In the meantime, I focus on the fact that everyone is still telling me how I will have so much more time to work on investigations, and that the workload isn't anywhere near as bad as in Response.

"You'll find it so much better," my sergeant reminded me this week. "You'll have more time to learn and get through your workload, it's a slower pace."

He also tells me: "You're lucky, your CCID sergeant is brilliant."

I'm relieved. I need a great sergeant; it makes all the difference to the learning journey and feeling of psychological safety; desperately needed when working in an organisation that is proving to be so dysfunctional.

So, I'm on a mission to get there, into the detective world of CCID, where the promised land lies.

Move or leave

December passes in a blur, there's more of the same, but I feel marginally less out of control.

Every day I long for the move to CCID, being out of the uniform, out of uncomfortable police cars and vans, away from the terrible chairs at Birchdene and Northcliffe, back in a professional office environment, hopefully more back in control; and doing the job I came here for.

Another St Margaret's public order shift, and another one covering Marsham. Nothing has changed to help me complete the necessary elements of OneFile to enable my move.

As someone on the ADP, and only in Response for six months, I seem to have been allocated St Margaret's public order a disproportionate amount: four times in total.

There are certain things they insist you do for OneFile before leaving Response, but I've spent too much time over the last few months being allocated jobs that don't provide those opportunities.

A month after the initial threat that I might not be allowed to go to CCID and two weeks before I'm due to move, I haven't made any progress with my OneFile, and my Workplace Assessor tells me that my move will likely be delayed, she can't see how they will let me go.

It's what I'd suspected, and dreaded, but wasn't prepared to hear. I feel like this organisation is sticking its fingers up at me and saying: "We can treat you as badly as we like. And you're just going to have to take it."

It's also been weeks since I requested to have my CCID placement moved to Southpine, and I still haven't had a reply, so I chase. The reply comes back quickly: "Sorry it won't be possible. Speak to your CCID sergeant, I'm sure they will ensure some flexibility when you need it."

Really? My dad is at the end of his life and you're sending me to the other side of the county. Other people have swapped. In fact, many people, me included at the moment, aren't even moving to CCID when they are meant to, because the organisation hasn't supported our ability to move.

Decision making and allocation of resources are seriously flawed. I once again face the fact that I'm a number, not a human here.

Realising that I can't fight the move to Harrisville, I've decided I'm going to put my foot down about my move date.

I have another chat with my Workplace Assessor. "I've made the decision that I'm either moving or leaving. I'm not prepared to be used as a resource in Response indefinitely. I'm meant to be on a fast-track programme to be a detective. I'm not going to be another Paul, never knowing when I'm moving to CCID."

She replies: "I feel your pain, Olivia. I'm so frustrated for you. I don't want you to leave, but I know this organisation doesn't treat people very well. There needs to be more flexibility. I just know that you'll be a great detective, you've got the right skills."

Once again, I'm chuffed at the rare and positive feedback on my capabilities – and the recognition that life at Oakshire Constabulary is difficult for many.

I also chat to the PDU sergeant, explaining how I'm feeling about my Oakshire Constabulary experience.

He says: "See how you get on in the next couple of weeks. Ask for some 08 time to get your OneFile stuff written up and ask to be given jobs so you can get the rest ticked off."

I know getting protected from new incidents with 08 time, so I can deal with my OneFile isn't going to happen. I've already asked for this, and time to build case files.

Despite the team having grown, the never-ending demands of life policing Northcliffe means 08 time is never guaranteed; and rarely allowed.

And then I'm back covering Marsham for another two shifts. My team can't do without me, so I can't have 08 time, but I can be transferred to cover another team.

Once again, I'm left wondering how resources, and the ADP are managed here; and whether I want to work for this organisation.

***

Luckily, the team at Marsham are super supportive of my OneFile needs, enabling me to get two more incidents ticked off.

I'm forever grateful to that team, and the PDU sergeant who relents, allowing my move with one more incident for OneFile outstanding.

"I'm going to let you move to CCID as planned in January. Make sure you get that final bit of OneFile done asap," he tells me.

"I will, I promise." I'll need to organise time back in Response during my second year to get it done; hopefully back in Marsham.

He warns: "Other people have let me down when I've allowed them to move on before completing everything."

"Why would they do that? Don't we have to complete everything before we finish our probation period? And where's the integrity in that?"

He rolls his eyes and says: "Not everyone has integrity."

"Honestly, I'm true to my word, I won't let you down. Integrity is one of my values. I really appreciate your support, thank you."

And I really do. Considering my experience so far, it's such a relief to have a few people, who I really believe have my back in this organisation.

Divas

I have a wonderful friend called Daisy, who I used to meet up with two to three times a year. I haven't seen her since January.

We usually travel to London and do something cultural. Our time together normally involves cocktails. We love exploring London together. It's the best city in the world and has so many hidden gems.

During December, Daisy and I visit the DIVA exhibition at the Victoria and Albert Museum in South Kensington. It's a Saturday and London is really busy.

It's so different to the weeks when the UK came out of lockdown, when you could explore cities by yourself, empty streets, never needing to book ahead, being more impulsive about your choices on the day.

I'm always early, for everything. I just can't help it. Friends are always apologising for being late, even if they are not. Because I'm always there waiting.

"So sorry," Daisy mouths as she bursts into view across the crowded museum. Dressed in an emerald green flared jumpsuit and huge furry white coat, I admire how stylish this woman is. I am always impressed by her. Everyone watches as she walks past them; she doesn't notice.

"It's fine, honestly, you know how much I love to just be. I love an excuse to stop and absorb what's going on around me," I reply as she comes in for a hug.

I love this girl. I'm eternally grateful for the remarkable women I have been able to surround myself with. And I always thank my truly inspiring mum for this. I'm convinced her spirit lives on in my friends, and other people I have met along the way.

As Daisy and I walk into the exhibition, through the narrow and dark entrance, showing our tickets to the friendly staff, I say: "God it's good to see you. I've missed days like this." And I really have. It's time to get my social life back on track.

The exhibition is celebrating the power and creativity of iconic performers, exploring, and redefining the role of 'diva', and how this has been subverted or embraced over time across opera, stage, popular music, and film.

The place is full of information about many inspiring women: Cher, Tina Turner, Rihanna, Theda Bara, Marilyn Monroe, Amy Winehouse. And some men such as Prince and Elton John, who are also well known as divas.

Amongst the many incredible women I learn about today is Joséphine Baker. An American-born French dancer, singer, and actress who lived from June 1906 until April 1975.

Her career was centred primarily in Europe, mostly in France, and she was the first black woman to star in a major motion picture, the 1927 silent film Siren of the Tropics.

The plaque above one of the stunning photographs of her says: "Josephine Baker: always takes the difficult route."

I instantly feel a connection, and an increased understanding of who I am, and why I'm doing this job.

I need to continue this journey. It's not time to leave.

***

In my final week in Response; there are no longer enough chairs in the briefing room for all of us. People stand or balance on windowsills, due to the amount the team has grown.

This might sound like a good thing, but when I started, the team was mainly made up of very experienced officers.

Three of them have moved on to other areas of the organisation, one to another police force.

Nearly half the team now has less than six months service; and a third are under 23.

Several are still with tutors; slowing down the remaining experienced officers, causing them frustration, and more stress.

Part Four: Central Crime Investigation Department

I've made it

JANUARY 2024, I'M ABOUT to start the first of my three detective placements, in the Central Crime Investigation Department (CCID). In Harrisville.

As I embark on what should be the best part of the ADP, I suddenly realise that I have no idea what a day pans out like, here in the detective world.

We've had no input from the people who run the ADP; there's not even a checklist of what we need to achieve during this second year of the programme.

I must use the word trainee before the word detective until I am made substantive. This means I've got to complete the OneFile I brought with me from Response and which measures PIP1; I'm currently at 55% after six months there. Most of the outstanding stuff I need to do, I can complete while being a detective, all bar the one I'll need to do on a day back in Response.

I also need to complete several PIP2 training courses and do a further PIP2 OneFile.

PIP is the Professionalising Investigations Programme; all police officers do PIP1. PIP2 is the training programme for detectives, focusing on investigating serious and complex crime.

It feels like a lot to do in the next 12 months, as well as the on-the-job training I'm expecting to get. But this is what I signed up for and I'm ready.

For now, Rosie and James don't have a move date and are stuck in Response.

James is waiting for sign off on his final OneFile elements. He's had the OK to move from his assessor, but it needs to go up the chain, a painful wait for him.

Unfortunately for Rosie, her assessor has gone AWOL, and no one is doing anything about it. As a result, she has so little of her OneFile signed off, there's no end in sight for her.

She's also not getting the 08 days that have been promised to her, so she can write her reflection documents.

I feel so bad for her, while counting my blessings.

In CCID, shifts are slightly different, so I'm starting another change to my circadian rhythm.

Earlies and lates match those in Response, but we don't have to work nights, although at weekends the shifts are still 10 hours long, with lates running until 2am instead of midnight – we pick up the other end of the public order chaos, those who've been arrested.

Day one in CCID

It's very early morning and I'm on my way to Harrisville. Cold but dry and clear. Very dark. I'm back in a suit and smart shoes, something I haven't worn for many years. *The soft fabric feels strange against my skin after months in police uniform.*

I've emailed my new sergeant twice in the past few weeks. I'd suggested visiting the team before joining. I'd also wanted to find out where to go, and if there's anything else I need to know before arriving on day one in this new job.

No reply. *The silence gnaws at me.*

I tried one more time yesterday, hoping I'd at least be told where the office is in the labyrinth that is Harrisville police station.

No reply. I'm really surprised, and a bit disappointed, considering the impression I've been given by others of her style, and how much I've looked forward to working with her.

We all have different needs and the "you've got to figure it all out yourself" attitude at Oakshire Constabulary makes some of us feel like shit. *If you want people to feel anxious, and therefore less productive in their new jobs, then this is an ideal way to treat them.*

So I don't know where I'm going after I arrive in the car park. One final check of my emails while sitting in my car. Nothing. *My chest tightens.* At 6.30am I make my way to the building.

Because I've covered Harrisville three times in the last three months, I find my way into the building, retracing my steps into the Response report writing room that's become familiar, and ask someone for help.

One of the officers kindly gets up: "I'll show you. Go up here to the first floor," he says, directing me down the corridor and pointing to one of the multitude of staircases.

I'm grateful for the energy he's mustered to help me – I know he's been on shift since 10pm last night.

As I enter the first-floor corridor, I bump into another kind man: "Good morning, can you tell me where CCID is please?"

He gives me the final directions, pointing me to the CCID office: "Through those doors, turn right. Good luck."

These moments of kindness make so much difference in an organisation where many people's attitude to trainees is to let us sink or swim.

***

As I turn left, I can see the office is huge – a vast open space with banks of white desks, all with two screens. *This is posh,* so different to Northcliffe and Birchdene. There's a block of lockers at the far end, behind which sits a couple of tables which I assume is a breakout area, if you ever find time to do that.

All the grey blinds are down. Still pitch-black outside. Despite being smart and well equipped, I notice how clinical the space is. *Absolutely no soul.*

There's one person in the room – my new sergeant, Sophie. Apart from the tapping of her keyboard, there's not another sound in here right now. *The silence feels deafening.*

She hears me approaching and turns around with a genuine smile. "Hi, you must be Olivia."

"Yes, I am. Good morning." *Relief floods through me at her warmth.*

"I'm so sorry I didn't reply to your emails. It's been hectic here."

I've learnt that I need to sit as close as I can to those I can learn from, so I take a seat next to her.

"Custody has been relentless over Christmas and New Year. I've never seen it so busy."

Over the next half hour, the office fills with the rest of the team. Loads of them, lots of chatting and introductions. They seem like a great bunch of people. *I breathe a sigh of relief. My initial concerns subsiding.*

***

Before long, I'm head down in my workload – all the investigations and cases I've had to bring with me from Response. *I'm trying to figure out what I can get done before going on holiday in a few days.*

It's been four days since I last removed my police boots after my last shift in Response. I still have the indentations from where they used to hug my ankles and calves.

As I find myself sitting at a desk for longer than I have in ages, the stiffness and pain in my Achilles catches me off guard. *I find myself unable to walk properly when I get up.* Sharp pain shoots up my leg.

During Response this wasn't a problem – except for scene guards, we rarely sat down long in the same place, so no time to seize up. We kept our boots on all the time. But once I'm back at a desk for hours on end, and my ankles are no longer constricted, it starts to become an issue.

The irony is, during my time as a police constable, I only ran a couple of times. Quite frankly, in all that kit and ill-fitting boots, you can't run that fast anyway. *So damaging my Achilles, learning to run to pass the damn bleep test, just wasn't worth it.*

My holiday can't come soon enough. I still need to shake off my Response experience and hopefully start to heal my Achilles.

I'd tried to book a holiday to sit neatly between Response and CCID, but because of the last-minute details of when and where I was being posted, that wasn't possible.

I have no idea if Sophie, who insists we don't call her sarge, knows about my holiday.

I intend to talk to her about it, but the shift sparks into action immediately at 7am, with allocations of prisoners and discussions around workload for the day. *There just isn't time.*

First custody prisoner interview

In CCID, we get the low-level crimes, the ones the specialist teams don't deal with, the supposedly non-complex crimes. *Which is why they send us here for our first trainee detective placement.*

Because of the large number of prisoners held overnight at Harrisville custody when there's no detectives on duty to deal with them, Sophie decides to take one.

Sergeants don't normally do this unless things get really desperate from a resource point of view.

She explains: "Normally we call people in from one of the teams at Southpine or Westrock, but they've got too many prisoners to deal with themselves."

"Can I join you, so I can see the process please?" I ask her.

"Yes of course, good idea."

So she runs through the plan at breakneck speed. *My head starts to spin immediately.*

"We review the evidence, like CCTV, photos of injuries, statements, body-worn footage. If necessary, we chat to the Response officers involved from the night shift, but they've probably gone home now because it's 8am. We review the custody record, look for any issues and if they want a solicitor which I hope custody will have booked. Sometimes they may need an appropriate adult which we will need to book. They can take a few hours to get here. If they don't speak English we need to book an interpreter, that can take a while too. We also do a PNC check on the suspect. That helps us decide what outcome we can agree on, based on their offending history. We will plan the interview, making sure we cover all the points to prove, and do disclosure for the solicitor. At some point before the interview, we'll pop down and meet the suspect, say hello. This should be a quick one. It's likely to be an out-of-court disposal."

Unfortunately, that information is not delivered in one go. It's constantly interrupted by Sophie having to speak to other people in the room, the phone ringing, or her getting distracted by a constant stream of Teams messages and emails.

My brain feels like it's fragmenting, trying to hold onto pieces of information while new interruptions keep coming.

As she's talking to me, she's also showing me where all this information comes from – multiple places, different software platforms. *My head is spinning.*

My focus is lost so many times that I know I'm going to have to be told all this again another day. *I like Sophie's positivity, but I'm thinking, wow, that's a lot. Surely that could take all shift.*

In Response we had weeks to set these interviews up because they were invited to come in voluntarily. I've never had to do all of what she's just mentioned and certainly not all in a few hours.

I'm finally starting to understand how everything joins up – something that has never been explained. Unless I missed it at training school, in amongst the chaos.

You never get to follow an investigation from beginning to end. From arrest, to custody, to interview, to building a case file, to engaging with the CPS.

No one explains the connections, or brings to life what happens with prisoner handovers – a briefing document that we complete to explain the investigation so far, and the details of all the officers involved.

If I'd fully understood what happens at the CCID end, I'd have appreciated what really mattered when completing a prisoner handover.

"OK, what can I do?" I ask her, *hoping she'll repeat some of what she's already told me.*

"Why don't you look at the body-worn footage."

Now that I know how to do. I open the relevant system, and I type in the arresting officer's camera number which I've found on the prisoner handover.

As I'm watching the footage of the suspect's out-of-control behaviour, I'm beginning to think that maybe I should have asked for a workload day today. *I have a crucial suspect interview to do during the next shift, and two case files to complete before I go on holiday.*

I feel overwhelm starting to creep in again. The familiar tightness spreads across my chest.

***

While watching the body-worn footage, I spot one of my colleagues from training school and reflect on how little training school prepared us for the reality of life on the streets.

I'm also reminded of how much more useful it would have been to spend more time watching body-worn footage and analysing what went well and badly. The more I see in this job, the more I believe it's far more beneficial than much of the practical stuff we did.

This student was great at training school. She'd also been a police cadet and seemed to know what she was doing. But even though we've been in the job for over six months, what I'm seeing in this footage is a young officer really struggling to deal with someone with mental health problems.

I get to see a lot of body-worn footage of training school colleagues during my time in CCID. It's fascinating to see them out of that environment, where some were so judgemental and cocky; and see them dealing with the reality of policing.

***

At some point in the day, I manage to speak to Sophie.

"I've brought some case files with me that I really need help with. And I've got a really big interview on Friday." I give her the highest-level detail of the investigation.

She's experienced enough to know that I need someone else in that interview and says: "You can't do that interview on your own. I think Gavin should join you."

I'm relieved at this latest opportunity to work with a colleague.

Before we leave for the day, I brief him on the very long story that is my Kimberly investigation.

Is it still day one?

Kimberly – the one that will always live with me

A month after becoming FIP back in Northcliffe, I picked up a complex harassment investigation.

At the time, I didn't know it was complex, because no one was reviewing my workload or supporting my learning journey.

It was very clear by then that you must crack on regardless of whether you have any idea about what you are doing. I put on a brave face, did my best and hoped that the members of the public I interacted with believed in me.

During one of the multiple diary car shifts I was allocated during those weeks, I had visited a mum of one called Jessica who was being harassed by her neighbour. She felt silly reporting it, but it was clear from what she initially told me during that first visit, and from the impact it was having on her, that this was serious.

Jessica was physically shaking, as I sat in her living room, while she told me how this other woman, Kimberly, was hounding her from outside her home.

It was causing so much distress and anxiety, and Jessica was struggling to keep her small child from hearing the abuse. Kimberly regularly ranted and swore at Jessica, with no regard for Jessica's child.

In her ranting, she accused Jessica of all sorts of outrageous things that were untrue. It was really disturbing, and causing Jessica to hide in her home, avoiding other neighbours who were hearing it all.

They lived horribly close to each other, so Kimberly could conduct her harassment with ease.

During my first visit, Jessica showed me recordings of this behaviour. I was shocked at the malice and during our discussion, about how to safeguard her and her children, we agreed she should install cameras.

It was clear Kimberly seriously had it in for Jessica, and this problem was not going to go away. Kimberly's behaviour was often delirious, and her face often contorted. She was usually inebriated with drink and / or drugs, and it was often late at night, but also sometimes during the day.

Jessica installed multiple cameras, and over the course of the investigation I processed over 30 recordings. There were more, but we didn't need them, the ones she shared told a compelling story of the harassment she was on the receiving end of.

Watching the disturbing recordings, I could totally empathise with Jessica's growing fear that Kimberly could become violent. This woman was out of control and really nasty.

It had already been going on for seven months before Jessica reported it.

***

Most people who report harassment to the police are not being harassed. As a result, we waste a lot of time investigating spats between adults who are behaving like children.

There are a lot of people in the UK who cannot manage relationships. They are often selfish and / or entitled individuals, who think the world should revolve around them.

As you know, I don't have time for selfishness. And I don't have time for people who blame everyone else for their problems.

But in Jessica's case, she was very definitely the victim of a disturbed offender. I was compelled to do everything I could to help her.

This is the type of investigation I joined the job for.

***

During my tutoring phase with Tristan, we'd started work on a domestic harassment investigation which ended up on my workload. Once FIP, I continued to work on it on my own. I'd put my heart and soul into that investigation.

My team had arrested the offender one night, when we felt there was enough evidence. Detectives in the Public Protection and Safeguarding Department (PPSD) interviewed him and took it over from there; because it was complex, due to the amount of evidence and offences.

That arrest, one I'd supported rather than done myself, as another probationer needed an arrest for her OneFile, was the most satisfying of the handful of arrests I was involved in.

The offender was a cocky shit who thought he could get away with throwing his phone inside the house, and trying to shut it, as my colleagues grappled to get him in handcuffs before transporting him to custody.

He failed, we seized it. It had great evidence of the harassment he was putting his ex through, including stalking her and damaging her property.

I hadn't really known what I was doing, but I knew that I was supporting the victim as best as I could; and doing the best I could on the investigation. It meant that the detectives had as much as I could provide with my inexperience, to create a case to go to the CPS.

As well as Harassment, I hoped they had enough to add Controlling and Coercive Behaviour to the case. The victim had been on the receiving end of domestic abuse for many years.

***

I knew that Jessica's story would mean a similarly time-consuming investigation.

I also knew that I would be working on it alone, with my experience so far in Response, there'd be no one to help me.

They always say there are investigations that live with you forever, and this is one of mine.

What is harassment?

The offence of Harassment is governed by the Protection from Harassment Act 1997.

Section 1 prohibits harassment:

1 (1) A person must not pursue a course of conduct:

> a. which amounts to harassment of another, and
> b. which he knows or ought to know amounts to harassment of the other.

1 (1A) A person must not pursue a course of conduct:

> a. which involves harassment of two or more persons, and
> b. which he knows or ought to know involves harassment of those persons, and
> c. by which he intends to persuade any person (whether or not one of those mentioned above):
>
> (i) not to do something that he is entitled or required to do, or

(ii) to do something that he is not under any obligation to do.

1 (2) For the purposes of this section or section 2A(2)(c), the person whose course of conduct is in question ought to know that it amounts to or involves harassment of another if a reasonable person in possession of the same information would think the course of conduct amounted to harassment of the other.

Then there's the actual offence of Harassment which I add to the investigation details and ultimately the case file which goes to the CPS, this is outlined in Section 2:

2 (1) A person who pursues a course of conduct in breach of section 1 (1) or (1A) is guilty of an offence.

The offence can result in up to six months imprisonment and / or a fine.

Kimberly the sociopath

It's clear to everyone involved that Kimberly is unhinged. She's either ranting a monologue, or quiet and calculating. In moments of lucidity, she is intelligent and articulate.

I recognise this controlling behaviour and know it well; it's in my family. Once I got to know Kimberly, I knew I was never going to be able to reason with her, like I never could with them. People like this are sociopaths.

Antisocial personality disorder, sometimes called sociopathy, is a mental health condition in which a person consistently shows no regard for right and wrong; and ignores the rights and feelings of others.

Like autism, there is a spectrum of this behaviour, but unlike autism much of it is choice. People can choose not to commit offences, or deliberately hurt people. They can also choose to get help for their behaviour, learn how to tame the urges to do bad things, to deliberately make life difficult.

Understanding antisocial personality disorder is something we should be taught more about in the police. It would help officers to deal with, and understand criminal minds, and sadly some people who say they are victims, when they are not.

Apart from the hell she's putting lots of people through, I have little tolerance for Kimberly's insistence that everyone else is to blame while always claiming to be the victim herself.

I know she is in pain. She needs help. But I know she will never get it. For her, it's easier to blame others than look inward at herself. Again, something I'm very familiar with, seeing in people close to me.

My first interview with Kimberly

I've done one day in Harrisville, followed by two rest days, and now I'm heading to Southpine, for Kimberly's interview, with my colleague Gavin, who I've only met for one day.

Since starting this investigation a few months ago, Kimberly has been arrested twice, before I've had the chance to bring her in, for what was meant to be her first interview.

Instead, while in custody, she was interviewed by people who didn't know my investigation; and only questioned about the specific incident she had been arrested for at the time.

I've spent a significant amount of time preparing, including on my rest days; and my interview plan covers the full harassment investigation. I intend to question her and put all the evidence I've gathered to date.

It's taken me three weeks to get Kimberly to agree to this date. I'd started trying, when, in mid-December, I'd received an email from a detective sergeant from the CCID team who'd first interviewed her.

She'd copied in my Response sergeant, saying she'd noticed I was on holiday in January, when I was meant to be dealing with Kimberly's bail return appearance.

I had no idea what any of this meant, or that I'd be responsible for that. This investigation had seemed quite complicated to me, and I didn't understand why it would remain with a trainee like me, once it had been dealt with by detectives. My sergeant was equally surprised.

It's usual for a bail return date to be fixed for three months after an arrest; to give officers time to conduct outstanding enquiries and build the evidence.

Unfortunately, the date set by those who had interviewed her clashed with my holiday, so I needed to bring it forward. Funnily enough, no one else wants to step in to do this interview.

Kimberly had been so difficult to deal with on the phone, making excuses, making little sense and then hanging up on me, when I caught her out in a web of lies as to why she's been avoiding me.

Because of this, I hadn't been able to get any direction from her, about who she wanted to be represented by, or if she wanted a Duty Solicitor.

All this was before her second arrest around Christmas which I found out about when I turned up for three night shifts.

I emailed the solicitor that represented her during this latest interview. Explaining the situation, I asked them to sort out her attendance; warning that we'd have to arrest Kimberly if she refused to attend the interview.

If you're a suspect, and don't turn up voluntarily when asked to attend an interview, you can be arrested. And when someone is wanted by the courts or police, they find out that their family and friends will be repeatedly disturbed, while we try to track them down.

Usually, their arrests will happen in the middle of the night, or very early morning – it's the best time to catch people unawares.

***

Unfortunately, for Kimberly's latest arrest, no one connected the dots between that offence, my investigation, and her earlier arrest. So, she's now got two different custody records, two different bail clocks, and two different investigations.

I only find this out from the custody sergeant when I get to Southpine today.

We agree to use the original bail clock, which has nine hours left. That time includes every minute, from the moment she is booked into custody, the interview, with any breaks for her to talk to her solicitor, until she is booked back out again.

During the interview, she answers every one of my questions, each in endless detail. Lies and more lies, blame and more blame, tying herself in knots, going round and round in circles, repeating the same denials, despite the evidence being undeniable.

I show her multiple pieces of CCTV footage which she doesn't flinch at. She seems to think her behaviour is acceptable.

After well over an hour of denying the offences, we take a break for Kimberly to speak to her solicitor, one of the most patient women I've ever met.

After what feels like a lifetime, we restart the interview, she admits the harassment and apologises for her behaviour.

Eventually, we've got the result I needed.

I've learnt a lot today, about how long an interview can last, when a suspect answers all the questions. The process has taken us from 10.45am until 3.30pm. It's been a painful but brilliant experience, and Gavin has been a joy to work with. We tag team well.

I wish I could work with people like him more, or come to think of it, just work with any colleagues with more experience than me. It would make my learning experience so much better.

Gavin and I are both exhausted as we leave Southpine to head back to Harrisville. A journey I'll be doing in reverse a bit later. We spend a lot of time debriefing the day.

"What do you think I could have done differently? Do you think I asked too many questions?" I ask as I drive. We've travelled in my car; using a job one was too complicated today.

They've changed the system for booking cars out, and it's not going very smoothly.

"I think fewer questions would have been better. But if she'd gone no comment, we'd still have had to ask them," he answers. I appreciate his honesty. It's what you need when you're learning.

Kimberly had to have the opportunity to give her side of the story, and I had to put all the evidence to her. Any gaps left, if we didn't, could be pulled apart by a good Barrister later.

I'm delighted that I can update Jessica, and the witnesses, with the positive result, and do so as soon as I'm back at Harrisville.

I'm less delighted that I can now start working on the case file, so the CPS can make a charging decision. I still have two other case files to finish before my holiday, two days to do it; and little idea how.

I leave for home an hour late, making today an 11-hour shift.

"CCID will be so much better," they'd said.

"You'll have so much more time to do your workload," they'd said.

There's no turning back now.

***

Lots of officers try to change direction, deciding they are not right for the entry route they've chosen into policing; or simply wanting to move to other parts of the organisation. Gavin is one. He's come to CCID from Response for a few weeks and wants to stay. It's a much better fit for him and his skillset.

Even though there are really obvious gaps in some teams. Most people, like Gavin, are refused a move, meaning the only option is to leave, or wait for positions to be advertised. Even then, there's no guarantee of a move; and it can take months to transfer, even when you've been successful at getting an advertised job.

Why would an organisation that is spending millions of taxpayers' money, recruiting and training people, make it so hard for them to be in a role that's best suited to them; or simply let them go?

I've started to hear about a few of my cohort who have left, three so far, in just a year. Others have been moved into the Force Control Room, not their choice. It was that or leave.

Thinking about this, made me remember that at the end of training school, it was announced that five of us were not going straight to become police officers. Despite spending five months training, five had to go to the FCR for a few months, due to critically low staff levels. I think being on the ADP saved me that fate.

First week in CCID

It's day three in CCID, a Saturday. This set of three shifts are known as mids. They usually sit between earlies and lates. You can work from the office or home, doing your paperwork, or get out and about conducting your investigations. Gavin and I have already used one of this set to do the Kimberly interview.

Our whole team are in the office because we're mostly inexperienced in CCID and learning. I'm relieved that I have two days with lots of people around me to ask questions, including Sophie, as I build my case files.

I hear her planning the following set of late shifts. It sounds like there's going to be lots of changes coming. Most of the team are moving roles, or going back to Response after a short placement, so won't be with us anymore.

In fact, the team will be shrinking significantly while I'm on holiday.

Shit, I haven't mentioned my holiday.

"Sophie, I'm really sorry, I'm on holiday for the next two weeks."

"Oh, OK, thanks for letting me know," she replies.

I ramble on, feeling guilty: "I wanted to take a break between Response and CCID. Unfortunately, I had to book the holiday before getting my start date which I only got three weeks ago."

As well as not being able to book a holiday as early as I would have liked, once again I've not been able to make any plans for 2024 yet, because I didn't know what shifts I'd be working.

All the CCID sergeants' workload is crazy, and Sophie's is no exception. As I listen to her discussing workload with the team, I don't know how she juggles being on top of it all.

And managing the constantly changing members of her team must be a nightmare. This seems to be the norm here. I'm discovering that people come to CCID on placements from Response all the time, and at any time, there's no consistency to when they start.

Then there's those of us on the ADP, and those who have been in force longer and training to be detectives – we're all on four-month placements. And until now, we all come and go at different times.

However, this month has seen the start of a new approach to the trainee detective placement rotations. We've had an email announcing, that from now on, we will all rotate every four months, to enable some consistency. That fits with my move to CCID anyway, but for those behind me on the ADP, like Emily, it means staying in Response for several more months.

***

My first four shifts in CCID are done, they've flown by in a whirlwind of activity, and I've met a load of new people I won't be working with again.

Thanks to the set of mids, I've managed to get some work-load time, and even completed two case files, with a lot of help from various people on the team. Time to count my blessings again.

Despite the detectives in CCID dealing with similar crimes repeatedly, there don't seem to be templates to follow for interviews or case files. So everyone contributed something different, usually with differing opinions.

My body and brain are very ready for our first two-week holiday in four years; we're off to Thailand.

***

I have one day to prepare before we fly, and I need to visit my dad.

I'm still smarting from the organisation's lack of care that he is dying; and how it has been made so much more difficult to see him. My journey to Harrisville has already taken away time I could be spending with him, and our holiday is going to take more.

Dad's health is really declining now, and I'm constantly waiting for the call from his care home to say he's died.

I'm really concerned he might die while we're away.

Miraculously, he's still clinging on when we're back, two weeks later.

Kimberly's been arrested – again

Believing one of my first priorities, when I'm back at work, will be building a GAP (Guilty Anticipated Plea) case file, unfortunately the first thing I hear, is that Kimberly has been arrested again.

She clearly had no intention of stopping harassing Jessica.

While I was away, she's convinced my new colleagues to change one of her bail conditions, one I had in place to stop her from going to her home without a police escort. This condition was keeping Jessica safe and providing some desperately needed respite for the whole community.

The day after this was removed, she was arrested.

In my follow up conversation with Jessica, taking yet another statement from the poor woman, she explains: "It was the third time that week she'd come at me."

Confirming the exact dates with her for the statement, I realised it had started while Kimberly was negotiating the amendment to her bail condition.

By now, Jessica is utterly exhausted by Kimberly's behaviour, the constant interactions with different police constables and detective constables and the frustration over how long it's taking to get Kimberly dealt with.

So much so, that she hadn't even bothered to report these new incidents. It was only when police arrived, to deal with a separate matter involving Kimberly, that Jessica flagged officers down.

***

So, now I have the challenge of getting Kimberly back for another interview and fighting to get the bail condition reinstated. Unfortunately, I'm told this can't be done until she's physically in custody. And it takes another three weeks to get her back for another interview at Southpine.

Things are now really complicated because on her third arrest, the Response arresting officer created a new crime. And for some reason, the decision was made not to arrest her for Breach of Police Bail, which she had clearly done. A third custody record and bail clock have been created.

I'm beyond confused about what I'm meant to do now.

The day before, Sophie suggests: "I think we should remand Kimberly when she comes in for her interview tomorrow."

So, as well as preparing the interview plan, to ask more detailed questions than the latest interviewing officer has done, I must also prepare to arrest her for Breach of Police Bail and a remand case file. I don't know how to do this.

Fortunately, Sophie has joined me at Southpine and is partially, amongst her own out of control workload, able to support me through the process. It's detailed and time consuming, and causing me anxiety, because I'm getting closer and closer to Kimberly's arrival time.

I'm also distracted by the fact that, for the first time in ages, I'm back in a room with Rosie and James. I'm so excited to see them and so jealous they've ended up on the same team. James had managed to move to CCID a few todays after me and Rosie just over two weeks later, with multiple outstanding incidents for her OneFile.

I hear my name called over the Tannoy, Kimberly's here with her solicitor. This time, I'm interviewing alone and I head downstairs.

Interviewing on my own doesn't daunt me now. In the four weeks I've worked in CCID I've already done multiple interviews alone. It's the process around it that I still don't have a clue about.

As I walk into reception I see Kimberly, and a duty solicitor I've worked with before. We'd met a few months back while I was in Response. He'd represented a vulnerable teenage suspect whose interview I'd planned and coordinated while off sick.

Here we go again.

"Hi, good to see you, shall we head in?" I say as I lead them through multiple sets of doors to custody.

"Hello, have you moved?" he asks, noticing I'm not in uniform.

"Yes, I'm on the fast-track detective programme. I'm in CCID for four months, before I go to LCID." *Pride swells in my chest despite everything.*

While booking her in at the custody desk, I arrest Kimberly for Breach of Police Bail, so I can ask her questions about the offence during the interview. *My hands are steady as I go through the now familiar process.*

The custody sergeant is reading the case details on the crime management system while I do this. When I'm finished he says, "I'll review the request for remand while you're in interview."

The solicitor overhears and asks: "Are you going to remand her?"

"We might," I reply. *Finally, some consequences.*

He's surprised and clearly not been briefed on the extent of Kimberly's offending to date: "Oh wow."

Kimberly starts to have a meltdown. She's got plans and responsibilities that could completely unravel if we keep her here overnight and straight to court tomorrow. She's crying with no tears. *The performance begins. I fight my natural instinct to feel bad for someone in distress. I'm torn between believing this is genuine or her usual manipulation.*

"Has she been searched?" asks the custody sergeant.

"Not yet."

"I'll get someone to do it."

"It's fine, I can do it," I reply to him. And then to Kimberly: "Are you OK with that?"

"Yes," she splutters, still half crying with no tears. *She might not like me, but she knows me, and knows it will be quicker.*

Once calm, we go into an interview room for a much shorter interview. Kimberly is in complete denial about her behaviour again, despite the latest evidence. *Her lies flow as easily as breathing.*

I watch her weave her web of excuses. My jaw clenches with frustration.

I take her back to the custody desk and prepare for the fallout of remanding her, assuming it's a done deal, considering the evidence. *This has to stick this time.*

The custody sergeant asks me to go to the next cubicle – not that it will stop us from being overheard – and asks: "Why hasn't she been arrested for breach of police bail before now?"

My stomach drops.

"I don't know sarge." *The truth sounds pathetic even to my own ears.*

I wasn't the arresting officer, the interviewing officer, or a sergeant involved in reviewing the case at the time. I've been on holiday.

"Well, we can't remand her because the CPS will ask why it's so urgent to do so now. I'll have to bail her for another three months."

The system fails Jessica again. My shoulders sag with defeat. *All this work, all this evidence, and she walks free again.*

The only good news is that I can finally get the bail condition reinstated, stopping her from going home. *Small victories in a broken system.*

I break the news to Sophie when I get back upstairs. She seems surprised about the remand situation. *It seems we're all learning, all the time, in this job.*

I dread to think how many more months Jessica is going to have to wait until we can get a charging decision from the CPS. The weight of that failure presses down on my chest like a stone.

Prize fighter

Along with many of my wider circle of friends, I haven't seen my ex-colleague and friend Esha for eighteen months. Now I'm not working nights, it's a bit easier to see friends. *My social life is slowly getting back on track.*

We usually find somewhere new to try, and tonight we're meeting up at a fabulous Thai restaurant, giving me a wonderful reminder of my recent holiday.

The inviting and salivating smell of Thai food hits me as soon as I walk through the double glass doors off the pretty courtyard, into the colourful and stylish restaurant. We sit in a corner by the huge, floor-to-ceiling windows that look out onto the street and green outside.

So much to catch up on, we talk nonstop, entertaining each other with our tales of joy and woe.

Halfway through our meal, I hear the guy at the table next to me say: "Apparently the manager is on the phone to the police."

My police radar instantly activates. Then a waitress appears at their table, apologising for the wait.

My concern peaks. I ask: "Are you OK? I'm a police officer. Let me know if you need any help?"

At training school, we'd been told that we should step in if help is needed – especially if we're using the benefit of free train travel. We can travel for free on the local trains using our warrant cards, the only benefit of being a police officer, but not if you're planning to get drunk.

The waitress explains: "There's a guy causing trouble, saying he's having an allergic reaction to the food."

I know they always ask if customers have allergies. Apparently this guy had said no.

"Just let me know if you need me. Are the police coming?"

"I'm not sure, I'll check with my manager."

Poor Esha is trying to talk to me, but I'm completely distracted by this point. Minutes later the waitress returns to the table: "My manager would really appreciate some help."

"Sorry," I apologise to Esha, leaving her at the table and making my way over to the manager.

She points out the problem customer: "He's over there. He's been intimidating staff and other customers. His behaviour has cleared that entire area. Everyone's moved to other tables."

I can see he's sat on his own, at a table for four, surrounded by empty tables.

The manager continues: "He's been ordering food nonstop, and vodka. We've had to stop serving him alcohol, and now he's saying he has reacted badly to some seafood and refusing to pay the bill."

He's been telling staff that he's a prize fighter, and was in a big fight last night, that he won. *I can believe he's been fighting* – he's got multiple facial injuries. From what he's been saying, the staff don't think he's local.

The manager tells me: "I've spoken to the police and they said to call back if things escalate."

Things have clearly escalated so she says: "I'm going to call them again." I assume my colleagues will arrive soon.

She and other members of staff are clearly upset by this situation, and unsure what to do with this guy next.

"I'll go have a chat with him," I say. *My pulse quickens as I walk across the restaurant.*

I take a seat opposite him – sitting being less confrontational.

I calmly and kindly ask him if he's ok. *You never know, he could really be having a reaction to food.* Not that anyone believes this. It's always obvious when people have pre-planned to get out of paying their bills. *The stories they come up with are ridiculous.*

I've seen this trick before, and I'm sure it won't be the last time.

I'm surprised at his initial reaction. He's open to talking to me and begins chatting, slurring his words in a strong accent, retelling me his story of woe: "Um awright, bu'um avin lergic raction ta seafood."

The table is covered in food that's been picked at and dropped. Multiple plates are strewn across the table, most with food left on them. *What a waste of delicious food,* especially if he had no intention of paying for any of it.

Somehow, even the menu is covered in food, as is the floor. Food dribbles from his mouth as he talks. There's also food and an unidentifiable liquid running down his front. *The man is a mess.*

"What happened to your face, it looks pretty painful?" I ask.

"I was in a fight last night, you know. I won so."

"Oh, congratulations, well done. Do you have money to pay the bill then?"

"Who are you?"

The atmosphere suddenly changes. My heart starts to race. *Maybe I'm out of my depth here?*

"I'm an off-duty police officer, I'm having dinner here. I heard..." my voice trails off.

His hands go to his pockets, fumbling around for God knows what. *The risk level has significantly increased.* I start to move out of the seat, trying hard not to trip over it while stepping backwards.

He starts shouting at me as I move away: "Whaz ya number? Whaz ya number? Fake police officer. Fake police officer."

Still on the phone to the police, the manager and the waitress have seen the change in mood and headed out of the glass entrance doors.

As I make my way over to them, I can hear the guy getting up from the table behind me, stumbling and crashing into tables and chairs as he moves. *The sound of destruction follows in his wake.*

As I get onto the other side of the door, I turn to see how close he is to me. *He's right there, on the other side of the glass.* And he's got his mobile phone out, trying to film me.

Panic floods through me. I hide my face, while pushing my body weight against the door to stop him from pushing it open. *It's impossible.* This man is a giant. He's got to be at least 6 foot 5 inches tall.

The manager is relaying everything that's happening over the phone to the Force Control Room.

I'm trying to shield my face while holding the door against the giant, but he bursts through it. *I simply don't have the strength to hold it.* The door slams open, nearly knocking me backwards.

Now we're all in the courtyard. I'm still trying to shield my face to stop him from filming me. *My heart hammers against my ribs.*

He's chasing me with his phone, and I'm heading for another door. As I try it, I realise it's locked. *I'm cornered.*

For a second everything becomes a blur as I try to get my bearings. *I hope my colleagues get here soon.*

I turn around, expecting the worst, but he's gone. *He's vanished without anyone seeing.* How can a giant just disappear like that?

It's the best-case scenario for everyone. He was never going to pay his bill, and he wasn't going to hang around knowing police had been called.

My colleagues never turn up.

On the way home, I drive past a police car – two officers speaking to a driver they've stopped. *What made this incident more important than the one I'd been involved in.*

***

Over the next two weeks, this crime keeps coming back to me. *No one takes responsibility for it.* It should be picked up by the team who cover the area to investigate, but somehow people think that because I was there, it should be my crime to investigate. *Even though I'm not a police constable in Response anymore, it's not my patch, and I was off duty.*

I do spend time on my rest days trying to get the CCTV footage from the restaurant. *They never supply it,* so in the end it goes nowhere. After much wrangling and multiple emails from the FCR, the log is closed.

I will never step in again.

Learning to love custody

I hated trips to custody when I was working in Response, but that changed the moment I joined CCID. Harrisville custody becomes one of my happy places.

The custody sergeants and detention officers sit at a long, elevated bank of desks. This position gives a deliberate air of authority, ensuring compliance and respect from prisoners and officers.

In front of them are Perspex screens behind which are five charge counters, where prisoners are booked in and out, each separated from the other by tall walls that provide a little privacy.

Each counter has an old-fashioned red phone handset with a long, coiled red cable which inevitably gets tangled. Many prisoners ask to speak to their mum, especially the men. There's also a height chart. And there are boxes of gloves in small, medium, and large. It's a good place to stock up – we go through a lot of these gloves.

At each end is a curve, additional protection that stops people from easily accessing behind the desks. Here you'll find detective and police constables hanging out while the custody process runs its course. It's a great place to catch up with people you haven't seen for a while.

Somehow, I only ever bump into colleagues from training school that I'm happy to see. It's great to hear how they are surviving their policing journey, each experience completely different.

There's a hip-level blue strip around all the walls that you can hit in case of emergencies. An alarm sounds across the entire police station, and the words: "Affray in custody. Affray in custody. Affray in custody," repeatedly blast from the Tannoy system, bringing officers into custody at breakneck speed.

For those of us without PPE on, we stop still until the alarm goes off, hoping for the best for our colleagues dealing with a troublesome prisoner.

Because of its height, the strip is regularly activated by accident, so that gut wrenching feeling, fearing for our colleague's safety, is ever present.

There are emergency strips in all the interview rooms, giving us some level of protection when we interview completely on our own. Sometimes a prisoner won't want a solicitor, so it's just them and me during an interview, and those blue strips are a lifeline to back up. A sense of safety.

WIFI is sporadic in custody, and daylight is hard to find. But somehow it feels like a good place.

I love working with the custody sergeants and detention officers, especially those on shifts aligned with mine. They make the painful moments less painful.

Custody is full of people whose freedom has been taken away, for a period of up to 24 hours. But here prisoners are treated kindly and respectfully – it's this team's responsibility to ensure prisoners' welfare is maintained. They have an amazing ability to ensure calm in an environment which could be anything but.

Custody is a place where we can stand for many hours, waiting for somebody to be ready to deal with us.

That could be the custody sergeants, who have a queue of other prisoners to deal with. Or a solicitor who is already representing another prisoner. Maybe a suspect who is deciding whether to give their correct name or not before interview.

Or an AMHP (Approved Mental Health Practitioner) who needs to decide whether we can Section 136 someone. Sometimes there's even a doctor, to decide whether a prisoner is fit for interview as their drugs or alcohol wears off.

Over time, I get to know a lot of the duty solicitors – they are a fascinating and eclectic mix of people. Most of them are decent humans who want to work with us for the most appropriate outcomes for those they represent.

While standing around can be infuriating, as the end of a shift is nearing and you know you've got so much more work to do before you can go home, my time in that strange place will forever remain a fond memory.

Settling into life in CCID

Two months in, I've realised that life in CCID is formulaic and monotonous. Each shift we get a prisoner and go through the motions for nine to 10 hours.

While I love preparing interview plans and liaising with the team in custody, building case files and all the other paperwork is boring, inefficient, and unnecessarily complicated. It's not what I expected.

I never get out of the office to investigate, so I'm starting to feel like a caged animal in this soulless office space.

The team has shrunk significantly, and Sophie is increasingly out of the office. With various covering sergeants, there's no consistency and absolutely no focus on my learning.

Having arrived into what was a thriving, energetic, motivated, and happy team, things are very different now. What once felt like a vibrant office environment, despite the dull decor, is now starting to suck the life out of me. It doesn't take long for me to lose motivation.

I realise that fatigue is starting to become a real issue for me, and the impact starts to take hold.

It's so bad, I have to take a day off sick in the middle of a run of four early shifts. As I know from my time in Response, that set of shifts is the worst to get motivated to come in for, especially when you're feeling low. I take the time to rest and message friends who are becoming worried about me again.

I just know that I can't get through four in a row, each day getting a new prisoner, a new investigation, and a new case file. I've been a trainee detective constable for two months, my CCID workload mounting up, and I still have no idea what I'm doing.

I'm saddened at how much time off I've had to take in the short time I've been working for Oakshire Constabulary, just to cope with the dysfunctional work and learning environment. I can't understand how this is allowed to happen to trainees.

The good news is that I've got rid of all the workload I brought with me from Response, except for the Kimberly case. My two completed case files are finally making their way through the court system. *I can do this.*

Thinking about quitting again

In March, out of the blue, we get an email saying they are changing the amount of time we will be spending on our placements as trainee detective constables, extending each from four to six months.

Apparently, there's been a consultation involving lots of people. But when we discuss it on our WhatsApp group, Rosie, James, and I haven't found anyone who was involved in it.

Having started in CCID in January, we were all due to move to LCID at the end of April. There's only meant to be another two months in CCID, and my travels to Harrisville, before hopefully getting a police station closer to my dying dad.

But now there's four months until that move. My gut is screaming at me again.

I'd worked hard to start my detective rotations, but no one tells you what it's really like. No one tells you that CCID is known as the sausage factory until you arrive in it.

And LCID is the placement I'd most looked forward to, now I've got to wait what feels like so much longer.

Rosie and James's CCID team at Southpine has two great sergeants who are consistently there, and their team is much bigger than mine. I realise how unlucky I've been in my team.

The people around me seem miserable. We don't have time to bond as a team because of our workload; and our health is being impacted.

Out of the three of us that joined the team in January, two have a few years' service but are new to the detective role. So while they've got much more policing experience than me, in CCID they are ultimately trainees like me.

One of them has been consistently off sick, and now the other joins her – their time off amounts to a significant number of shifts.

This means the rest of us – me, an investigator, and our only non-trainee detective who just recently became substantive – get prisoners every shift and rarely get to touch our workload.

By now, neither of them has time to help me, although they really do try.

On top of that, sergeant Sophie has been removed from the team, 'voluntold' that she's off for five months to teach on a residential training course. One that sounds significantly better than my training experience. One that sounds more like the old days I've been told about.

As a result, I'm really struggling to learn the job of a detective, and I'm starting to get that familiar feeling of overwhelm.

My workload is back to out of control again, and I have no one to turn to – we have no line manager.

I try so hard to teach myself the job, but I'm starting to get back and neck tension, and banging headaches.

As if all that isn't enough, I hear that our one substantive detective constable has been successful at securing a job in another team – she will be moving in a few weeks.

I'm gutted, I really like her, and she's been key in maintaining some level of sanity.

New sergeant

We've had a few weeks with no sergeant and therefore no line manager. Other sergeants have been taking it in turn to cover our team, sometimes remotely.

I've seen a short red haired lady loitering in the office recently, chatting to a few people. I find out one shift, when I come in to find her sitting at one of the CCID desks, that she's our new sergeant, Harriet. She'll be my third line manager in three months.

I find getting to know people interesting, hearing their stories, but over time, as most conversations with her go off on multiple tangents, I get lost in a whirlwind of information that I don't need to hear when I'm horribly under pressure.

I don't want to be rude and ask her to stop talking, but it's all too much when I'm trying to learn. And because I'm feeling so low and overwhelmed, I get irritated because the time she spends talking could be used to teach me stuff.

She can clearly sense I'm not in a great place, but for some reason, she asks other members of the team if I'm OK instead of asking me. I'm clearly not OK, I'm clearly out of control. Maybe that's why she's not asking me.

Or maybe it's because the rest of the team are in more of a mess than me, so I'm last on the list to get the support I need. She has inherited a shit show of a team.

At the end of one shift I get left in the office on my own, wondering what I've done wrong to get this kind of treatment. It's after midnight, and the whole team has gone home, I'm alone and broken.

I put my arms on the desk, my head on my arms, and cry. Even as I do it, I'm thinking that I don't have time for this moment of despair, I need to crack on. But I feel like I have nothing left to give.

I've been so clear that I need help, and because I haven't been taught how to do something that I need to do this shift, I've done it wrong. And now, at this late hour, on my own, I must unravel it and do it all again, teaching myself as I go.

I have no idea how I get my brain to function, but I do, eventually getting out of the empty and dark office around 1am. Another 30 free minutes to the King.

On the way home, I think about how bad all this unnecessary stress is for me. And how, once again, I feel like I have no one to turn to. I just can't believe I'm in this situation again.

I seriously consider going home and never coming back.

Life is too short to be in an environment that makes you feel so awful.

***

I do go back, because I'm diligent, conscientious, and have investigations I can't give up on. But I know that I'm never going to get the support I need before my time in CCID is over. I start to retreat from the others, feeling that I can't ask anyone for help.

Rosie and I chat regularly, keeping each other going, focusing on the light at the end of the tunnel and our move to LCID in a few months' time. But after this experience, I tell her: "I don't want to do this anymore."

I know I can do anything I put my mind to if I decide to leave, a thought that is becoming stronger and stronger.

If only they hadn't extended our placements – I'd have been out of CCID in a few weeks.

***

I try hard to remain positive and consider that maybe Harriet isn't aware of my lack of experience. So when we finally have a one-to-one, I explain how I'm feeling.

"It's a really difficult learning environment – I'm not getting any support because everyone is so under pressure. We've all got out of control workloads. Will I ever get someone to support me, a tutor, coach, or mentor?"

She tries to understand, but she's new on the team. She tells me: "I'll be your tutor and mentor."

But this doesn't happen, no on the job support ever materialises. Because, despite having a significant number of years of policing experience, she's not worked in CCID before. It's a very different environment, and she's having to learn herself.

She's also learning how to be a sergeant, acting in the role as she develops her management skills. And she seems to be out of the office a lot for holidays and training.

Aside from monthly workload check-in meetings, where I get some useful pointers to progress my investigations, often I'm told to look at the crime management system help guide. I try to explain that I don't learn well like that and that I've heard and said this before.

As if the pressure wasn't enough, we get a constant stream of probationers joining the team for very short periods of time, all needing to get things ticked off their OneFile list.

Somehow, they get priority for support from everyone on the team, including Harriet. Ironically, I even have to teach them stuff.

On the rare occasions I get out of the office, it's to support other people's investigations, and no one ever does the same for mine. In fact, each time I try to leave to do the follow up enquiries for my investigations, I'm told I can't, there's another prisoner to deal with.

My investigations start to slip, and I have a nagging feeling I will never look at some of them.

PST refresher – 'Day Two'

It's been just over a year since we completed Personal Safety Training (PST), and I've not heard when my yearly refresher is. Rosie and James have got dates for theirs, and I wait patiently for mine.

The invite doesn't come through, so I chase and quickly get dates: my next two training days, those precious days I would have used to progress my workload.

The first month I'll do 'Day Two', then 'Day One'. This makes sense to someone, but not me.

A few more things happen over the coming months that make me question how I was set up as a new starter. Aside from the endless software platforms that I wasn't signed up to, I'm also not on certain lists, and the pension provider was given the wrong address.

I also discover that I'm not invited to the Chief Constable's staff event, when everyone else is.

Ahead of PST, the fear of the bleep test has set in once again, and I decide to request to do the treadmill version. It will have way less impact on my damaged Achilles than running up and down a hall.

I get no reply to this request. So I email again. Still no reply.

By this point, 14 months into this job, I'm seriously fed up with the unnecessary anxiety that is caused by the lack of response to emails. What is it about this organisation?

***

Today I'm back at Oakwood Grange sports centre for PST Refresher 'Day Two', and I am relieved to hear that I'm down to do the treadmill version of the bleep test. I'm the only one doing it, so I can do it straight away, I just need to go for a wee. No middle-aged woman, or woman who has had children, wants to run without taking this precaution.

There's a couple of my training school colleagues here too. I'm curious as to how they are still allowed to do their jobs in Response with such a delay in their refresher.

One decides at the last minute to do the treadmill test, and when I get back from the toilet, I find she's jumped the queue. She's standing on the treadmill ready to go, and now I have to wait over ten minutes before I can start.

She fails seven minutes in. She's a vaper.

While it's so much kinder on my Achilles, it's still bloody hard work. You don't have to run, but you do have to walk very fast up an ever-increasing incline. The incline becomes so high that I feel like I'm going to fall backwards, and this feeling means I lose concentration and my breathing goes haywire.

After three months being back at a desk and struggling to find motivation to exercise, I'm definitely not as fit as I was, but I pass.

The trainer is brilliant at motivating me to keep going. I enjoy the one-to-one interaction, and not having to take the test with lots of other people. Although trying to have a conversation while not falling backwards off a treadmill adds to the challenge.

When I'm done, she says: "Well done. I'd recommend you come here once a month and practice on the treadmill to build and maintain your fitness."

And then she says something that triggers a load of questions for me: "If you really want it, you'll do it."

Do I really want it? Is this for me? Will I be able to do this test in a year's time? Or each year as I journey through my 50s? Will I be forced onto an action plan at some point?

The rest of the day is spent doing health and safety training. It's vastly improved since training school the year before, and I feel much better equipped to save lives than I have until now.

Aggression from a colleague

Two days later I'm travelling to work on a Friday mid-afternoon for a late shift.

The traffic is really bad because there's been roadworks for what feels like forever. I end up stationary in extremely slow-moving traffic for about twenty minutes, slowly navigating my way round multiple roundabouts.

There are hundreds of vehicles, but I'm pleasantly surprised that everyone is good natured while navigating the congestion. People give way to each other, using the one for one rule as traffic merges onto roundabouts and from two to one lane in parts.

No one is aggressive, no one sounds their horns. Although hugely frustrating for everyone, the traffic flows very slowly without issue.

I'm approaching the final roundabout before a straight stretch. *Amazingly the traffic in front of me is moving freely onto the large roundabout, so I follow. It's great to be moving faster than five miles an hour at last.*

As I round the large roundabout in the left lane, the straight road comes into view. As it does, the cars in front of me come to a sudden stop, as we join another long queue of traffic.

With no choice, I come to a standstill, still on the roundabout. Another car does the same behind me.

Unfortunately, we're blocking the two lanes to our left and other cars from joining the roundabout. There's nothing we could have done, and those drivers have seen how we've ended up in this predicament.

While awkward, because I wouldn't have chosen this situation, everyone continues to be patient, seemingly understanding the situation.

What feels like a minute passes. Then I hear a car horn sound. *It's the car I'm blocking to my left.*

My stomach tightens. I turn to see who and why someone would have done this. I see a young guy and shrug my shoulders, mouthing to him: "I can't do anything."

As I turn back to face the queue of traffic, *I think how aggressive that was.* Why is he the only person, out of all the drivers inconvenienced today, that has chosen to behave this way?

Finally, the traffic is moving slightly. I'm able to join the straight road ahead but come to an immediate stop again. I look in my rear-view mirror. Interestingly, the car behind me has not moved and is still blocking one lane, but there's enough room for this guy to squeeze through between our cars.

As he does, I see that he's wound his window down. Instead of facing forwards or looking towards the traffic coming from the right as he navigates the roundabout, *he is looking directly at me*. His left arm raises in a gesture towards me.

I have no doubt what is coming next. I will not have him berating me without challenging his behaviour, so I wind my window down and shout: "You are so aggressive."

I'm not prepared to put up with aggression, particularly on the roads, especially by men towards women. The knock-on impact can be huge, causing stress for so many people.

I'm still not able to move my car forward any further. I sit and watch him drive away. *But he doesn't.* He pulls over on the left of the roundabout, stopping his vehicle, and ironically blocks the left-hand lane.

Now he's getting out of his vehicle and walking towards me amongst the other cars that are trying to drive through the gap behind me.

Then I see POLICE, clearly visible on the edges of his short sleeved black shirt. *A colleague? No way!* Not one I know. But he is a police officer, and he should know better than to behave like this.

Because there's no lights flashing on his vehicle, indicating he's a police officer, I assume he's in his own car because it has no markings.

As he approaches my car, he's also not addressing me as a police officer. He does not show his warrant card and asks: "What do you think you're doing? You shouldn't block round-abouts like that."

I can't believe what I'm seeing and hearing. This is so unprofessional. I repeat: "Your behaviour is so aggressive."

I also say: "By the way, I'm a police officer too. We're probably heading in the same direction."

There's a slight change in his demeanour, but he doesn't stop berating me: "You shouldn't be blocking the exit of the roundabout."

I try to explain: "I had no choice. I didn't intend to do it." *But he's not listening, or hearing.*

To someone else this would be intimidating. But I'm annoyed at him. How dare he?

Then he decides he's finished with his lecture. He looks at me with disdain, *a look I've seen from a few officers in this organisation already,* before walking back to his car and driving away.

As I make my way through the rest of the painfully slow traffic, I wonder what police powers he thought he had to deal with this situation in this way. It reminds me of the Response sergeant ten months ago asking me after the search I did: "What powers did you use?"

My sixth sense tells me that this officer is likely to be based at Harrisville, and that we will bump into each other sooner or later.

And that fills me with dread. I just don't need that awkwardness – this job is difficult enough as it is.

I will never drive this way to work again.

No respect

I've been sitting at my desk for an hour when I realise my water bottle is empty. I head to the kitchen and find someone else in there, his back to me as I walk in.

He turns round. *It's him. I feel tension in the air. Very uncomfortable seeing him so soon.* I haven't fully processed what happened earlier.

However awkward, I know it's important to tackle and hopefully resolve the situation now. "Are you the person involved in the incident at the roundabout earlier?"

"Yes."

"Do you want to talk about it?"

"Sure."

My muscles tense. "Do you know how aggressive it is to use a car horn at someone, especially considering the situation we were in?"

He disagrees: "It wasn't aggressive, and you shouldn't have blocked me. It's an offence to block an exit of a roundabout. You shouldn't have done it."

I explain what I thought was obvious about the traffic situation: "It was unavoidable and not my intention to block you. Can you understand that?"

I get that same look of disdain. He clearly can't. He just wants to continue telling me that what I did was wrong. And he does, repeatedly.

One of my team walks into the kitchen, *picks up on the tension*. None of us say a word until they leave again.

I'm not ready to back down on this. "Do you understand how your behaviour could have come across to a woman in my situation?"

He doesn't acknowledge this. Something about this guy is making me uncomfortable. It's clear we're never going to meet in the middle on this. *He has no intention of learning anything from this situation.*

He thinks he's right. He thinks I'm wrong. And he has a point to prove. He is also not backing down.

I'm frustrated because if he had any respect for me as a colleague, instead of denying being aggressive, he could try to recognise the impact his behaviour has had. He could choose different language, saying something like: "I didn't mean to come across aggressive."

But he can't recognise or explore the possibility that there's an alternative view. *He's just shutting me down.*

So I change tactics: "What was your intention when you used the car horn against me?"

I cannot believe what comes out of his mouth, or the attitude and tone of voice he uses: "I was teaching you that you were in the wrong."

"I don't need you to teach me," I say. I'm barely able to contain my irritation.

His response: "I didn't know you were a police officer."

"That is irrelevant. You shouldn't behave like that towards anyone."

I simply don't understand how he thought his lesson was going to be received or understood in the way he delivered it.

It is not his place to use his horn to teach people how to drive and then confront them in the way he did, by getting out of what turns out to have been an unmarked police vehicle to challenge them.

Sounding a horn should only be done when your vehicle is moving and to warn other road users of danger or a potentially dangerous situation, like if they are about to crash into something or someone. It should never be used in aggression, and certainly not to teach someone a lesson.

I challenge him about stopping his car to speak to me: "Do you think it's acceptable to get out of your car and confront me in that way? Not identifying yourself as a police officer?"

And once again I'm flawed by his response. He says: "It's because some woman was screaming at me."

I explain: "I was shouting, not screaming." *Just because female voices are higher pitched than male voices does not mean that we are screaming when we shout.*

It's clear we're getting nowhere. He's completely incapable of assessing the situation or having empathy or understanding for the position I was in. *He's not prepared to accept that I didn't deliberately block him.* He's simply not prepared to hear me.

He moves to leave the room, and with a smug look on his face says: "We'll have to agree to disagree."

I try to remain professional: "I'm glad we've had the opportunity to have the conversation."

I get no such respect in return.

As he walks away, *I realise I'm going to have to see this officer on a regular basis.* Life in CCID has just got a whole lot harder. *I just don't need this extra stress in this job.*

As soon as I get back to my desk, one of my colleagues asks what's going on.

"I heard some of what he was saying. I can't believe how he was speaking to you. How arrogant he was." *I can tell he's disgusted at the lack of respect.* I fill him in on the whole story.

Harriet, now listening in with concern, walks over and asks: "Are you OK? I overheard some of what you were saying. Do you want to go into an office to talk about it?"

"Yes please, I definitely do."

When I've finished relaying what happened she says: "Send me an email with the whole story. I'll think about whether to speak to the Professional Standards Department."

PSD investigates complaints and allegations of misconduct against police officers, staff, and special constables.

I'm not sure at first if speaking to them is necessary. "Do you think we can resolve it by speaking to his line manager?"

"Let me think about it. I know his line manager, so I'll talk to him."

I feel so much better when I come out. I really needed her support. It's only the beginning of the second shift of four lates, and we're here until 2am tonight and tomorrow. *I need someone to make me feel like it's worth being here.*

***

With personal safety training, this incident, and four public order late shifts in less than a week, *I seriously need a break from the relentless sausage factory that is CCID and the tension in the office.*

Fortunately, the next couple of weeks pan out that way, and I can finally unwind a bit. *Otherwise I would have had to have more time off sick.* It pains me to think this way about how to survive this environment.

During the first week, I only have to work two shifts because of how my rest days fall, combined with bank holidays. At training school, we'd been told that as trainees we wouldn't have to work bank holidays, but I did in Response, including Christmas Day and Boxing Day.

Here in CCID, I discover that I don't have to, and the long Easter weekend is a welcome relief – *a break that keeps me going.*

I've also managed to work some magic with my shift pattern because the following week I get four days of PIP2 detective training. That's two whole weeks where I only get two new prisoners to deal with and all the paperwork that goes with them.

The PIP2 training is brilliant. It's really inspiring and motivating – the trainers do such a great job.

Although there's some awkwardness at the beginning of day one.

As we go round the room introducing ourselves, I discover that out of the twelve officers here, two are from the same team as the officer I'd had the confrontation with.

This quickly subsides when I realise they are really decent guys, and they don't know who I am and what has happened.

Nearly four months in, I finally feel like I'm learning the skills required to be a detective – which would have been helpful to learn before starting the role.

***

The confrontation situation goes unresolved for weeks. *The increasing tension and uncertainty is eating away at me.* I now think that this officer needs professional support to change his attitude. PSD are best placed to instigate this because this could be the start of future problems.

I know Harriet has spoken to his line manager and she tells me I'll be getting an apology. Nothing is ever mentioned again about PSD. *I don't really want an apology.* I know it won't be genuine – that much is very clear from how this entire situation has and is playing out.

What I do want is this officer to understand that his behaviour is not acceptable, for someone with authority to help him change his behaviour before it becomes entrenched, if it's not already.

Before others are on the receiving end of it, especially other women.

Eventually, I get an email from Harriet about the incident. She is forwarding me an email from the officer's sergeant. Below that is the apology from the officer.

In his email, he addresses his sergeant, not me. He apologises to his sergeant for sounding his horn, not me. *This issue has not been resolved – it's going to be swept under the carpet.*

I continue to encounter this guy on multiple occasions. We walk the same corridors and use the same kitchen. *I can't stand to see him.* I must contain my irritation at his arrogance and his presence in my life.

Feedback – it's been a while

In my time so far in CCID, I've had no feedback on how I'm doing. With my two one-to-ones so far with Harriet being all about workload, I'm just adding to my to do list.

And then I get an email that lifts my spirits, and gives me hope.

From: harriet@oakshire.police.uk
To: olivia.gray@oakshire.police.uk
Date: April2024
Subject: Feedback

Hi Olivia
Sophie has shared some feedback for your OneFile which I attach below.
I also want to say I'm impressed by your resilience.
The Harassment file you're working on is testing, and you come in every day ready to go again, with a fresh perspective.
Thank you for your hard work.

Kind regards
Harriet

Sophie's feedback

During Olivia's time in Response, she demonstrated core investigative skills on a complex harassment. She's taken full ownership of the investigation, managing numerous statements, obtaining key evidence, and conducting multiple interviews. An eye for detail and organisation are clearly key strengths.

Olivia's tenacity stood fast as she navigated breaches of bail, overlapping bail conditions and a challenging suspect. She has seen this investigation through from day one to a full file submission to the CPS which I have no doubt will secure charges.

Olivia comes in each day with a positive mindset and willingness to learn. She is a great addition to the team and an asset to the organisation, working well on an individual and team basis; she openly shares learning with others.

It would be a pleasure to work with Olivia again.

***

So, along with the knowledge that I'll be getting regular breaks from CCID over the coming weeks, to do more PIP2 detective training, things really do brighten up for a few days.

I message Sophie to let her know what a huge difference hearing this feedback has had, and what a great leader I think she is. And that I'm sad we're not working together. Her management style is more nurturing that Harriet's, and I felt heard and supported.

I cling on to the positive impact that the short time I got to work with Sophie had on my policing journey, and I hold out hope that I'll get this experience again.

Placement lottery

With my experience in CCID panning out very differently to how it was sold, I'm also clinging on to the hope that I get a Local Crime Investigation Department (LCID) in an area that I am keen to police in, for the six months from July 2024.

It feels like forever waiting for the posting sheets to come out which will seal our fate or positive future.

And then I get the email. I have got my second choice, Marsham, I'm so pleased. I'm familiar with the police station, some of the people, and the area, having spent time there on my Ride Along and during my time in Response. So it won't feel like starting all over again.

I'm happy, excited, and relieved. Once again, I have hope for my future policing career.

I'll wait for the dust to settle before reaching out to my LCID sergeant.

I know sergeant's inboxes are insanely full, and he will have received a few emails about people moves on his team ahead of the next rotations.

I'm filled with hope that I will be moving to a team that truly feels like a team, as I send an email saying hello a couple of weeks later. I suggest a few dates that align with both our shift patterns for me to come in to meet him and the rest of the team before I start.

I hear nothing. I email again. I still hear nothing.

PST refresher – 'Day One'

A month after PST 'Day Two', towards the end of April, I'm back at Oakwood Grange for 'Day One'.

I'm losing my training day, or workload catchup day, again. And again, this will be immediately followed by four relentless public order late shifts. I'm already dreading it. It was a seriously tough week last month.

Sadly, it's also been a really tough couple of weeks back in the office after my PIP2 training, and my friends have been telling me I look pale.

So the fact that today is more physical isn't ideal. Unfortunately, we're doing our conflict training and getting up close and personal with colleagues again.

We're in the stinky padded room, the Dojo, where we throw each other around to learn and test our skills. In pairs, we're being taught a new technique to incapacitate someone by hitting them on the back of the shoulders.

Before we even start practising this move, I don't think it's a great idea and can't see how we will apply this technique in the real world. I'm also slightly concerned that my partner, an inspector, hasn't been listening to the instructions.

Your partner is meant to catch you as you fall backwards after they've wacked you on your shoulders. Neither experience is pleasant, and my partner definitely hasn't been listening to the instructions.

He stumbles to catch me as I fall backwards, and my head hits his knee on my way down. In exactly the same place that the police car door frame hit my head eight months ago.

I'm dazed and confused, and I hear people asking me if I'm OK. I have no idea. Once again, I don't think it's possible for someone who has just had a head injury to make that call.

Unfortunately, this environment doesn't lend itself to people being comfortable saying how they really feel when they are injured. We just suck up the pain and carry on. Which is exactly what I do.

Fatigue sets in

With two members of my CCID team still regularly off sick, a third has also been struck down and off for most of April.

My team are dropping like flies. *At what point someone will figure out that stress is causing all this sickness?*

And as the month ends, our most experienced detective moves to her new role.

So, adding into the mix the fact that Harriet is acting as a sergeant, our team, who are never all in at the same time by this point, are now entirely made up of trainees, plus our one investigator who is being forced to do the job of a detective but not being recognised for it.

I have so many questions right now.

If we're all supposed to be training, who are we supposed to be learning from?

How are we supposed to develop in our roles?

Who is responsible for making sure that our training journey is consistent and of a good standard?

Why is no one noticing what's going on here?

Does anyone care?

***

I've just about dragged myself through the four public order shifts since PST and my second head injury, and I'm not in a good place.

Trying to fit in all the detective training means I'm getting no time to work on my investigations and cases which have piled up since joining CCID four months ago.

It's the end of April and my second rest day. If they hadn't changed our rotation placements to be six months each, I'd have left CCID and would be moving on to LCID. *Time is really dragging now.*

The feeling of being trapped in CCID hangs over me like a black cloud.

I don't think I can carry on without a break. I don't have enough holiday, and I shouldn't be using holiday to deal with this. Why is it so hard to do a good job and not burn yourself out here?

I'm feeling exhausted, and my brain is not functioning. The last few shifts I've been pale and dizzy. And despite now being on day two of two rest days, I've continued to feel totally wiped out and still quite dizzy.

Luckily, I've got an appointment with a GP to review my HRT and take my blood pressure. I've been on HRT for years, and it's been a game changer for me. If I wasn't on HRT, this journey would be a whole lot more difficult.

I honestly have no idea how women get through a job like this while going through the menopause unaided. I suspect they don't. In the UK, only around 14% of menopausal women are currently prescribed HRT.

This is shocking to me because HRT makes all my symptoms go away. There's also scientific evidence that it has a hugely positive impact on women's future health, reducing the risk of dementia, osteoporosis, brittle bones, and therefore breaks and fractures as we age.

Unfortunately, there's still stigma around it, and a lot of doctors still prescribe menopause age women antidepressants instead of HRT.

My GP tells me my blood pressure is very low, and I'm likely to be experiencing fatigue. She wants me to have some blood tests. I manage to get a blood clinic appointment for the following day when I'm due back on shift. I need to put my health first and get this investigated, now.

I know Harriet isn't going to be in again, so I send her an email after my GP appointment, explaining how dreadful I'm feeling, what the GP said, and the plan for the blood test.

I also explain that I've got two appointments with SOCO (Scenes of Crimes Officers) to progress an investigation that I've not been able to touch for a month. If I don't go to the office to do them before my blood test, it will be another month before I can get evidence processed.

I also really want to meet with SOCO because it's an important part of my learning journey and will hopefully give me some sense of satisfaction that I'm doing some actual investigating.

She replies saying she hopes the blood test goes well, and she'll let the stand-in sergeant know about my commitments. I'm relieved. I feel like I'm being supported in this, and the stress of having to take time out is released.

***

Back in Harrisville the next day, and the stand-in sergeant is surprised when I explain that I've got meetings and need to leave five hours into this nine-hour shift for my blood tests.

No one has told me that you're not allowed to take time out for health-related appointments at Oakshire Constabulary. Even if the job is breaking you and making you ill.

So I innocently drive to St Margaret's City Hospital, the only place I could get an appointment this quickly. This wasn't something I wanted to wait weeks for.

During the rest of the day and into the evening, my body and brain get progressively more drained. There's no way I can run the risk of going to Harrisville the next two days and getting prisoners to deal with.

So I speak to Harriet about it on the phone to see how we can manage the situation.

I explain: "I really don't want to go off sick, I've got so much workload to do, and I'm due to spend a whole week doing more PIP2 training in two weeks. I need to get on top of things. I don't feel mentally strong enough to deal with the pressure of handling prisoners each shift, but if you're supportive of the idea, I could work through my investigations and case building at home. This way I can ease the pressure and make sure my existing workload doesn't lag behind. Do you mind if I work at home for the next two shifts."

She's supportive of this, seeming to understand, but asks: "Are you sure you shouldn't be going off sick?"

"I just can't, I just need to get on top of my workload."

We discuss the fact that next week we're on mids, where we shouldn't get prisoners. And when we're usually able to work at home, unless we're called in to support another team.

So I feel like I'll have a bit of respite and have time to teach myself how to progress my investigations.

Those missing police emails

More than six months since I first identified there could be an issue where people don't receive police emails, I also decide to try completing the dreaded IT self-service form again.

I call a couple of witnesses who I've not heard back from, and they confirm that they have not received my emails. They are not even in their spam folders.

Now I have evidence that this problem is real.

And this issue is holding up progress on a serious investigation involving multiple crimes that has a chance of going somewhere.

I'd covered at Southpine one day in April, interviewing a prisoner for multiple drug and driving offences. High on nitrous oxide at 2am he'd smashed into two parked cars. The personal impact on the victims was huge, for reasons I can't go into.

I'd been told that the investigation wouldn't stay with me. It did. And dealing with it is way beyond my skillset. I expect I'll be taking it with me to LCID, as there was no way I'm going to get all the work done during the initial three-month bail period.

This morning, I find a way to bypass the IT Service Desk question set that, months on, still doesn't fit my needs.

Incredibly, I get a call not long after from a helpful guy who asks me to send examples. He's not heard of this email issue before, and asking around the room, apparently his colleagues haven't either.

So I send over the examples I've got.

To be sick or not to be sick?

The next day, I get an email from Harriet. It opens with an update on a review she's done of one of my cases, one that I've been trying to get feedback on for a few weeks, and then this:

"Tomorrow, please could you email me the actions you have been able to complete so I can update my list of your workload. I want to keep as up to date as possible while you work remotely.

When you are on earlies next week, you might be called in to deal with prisoners. Your role requires you to come in if needed, so if you are not well enough to do that you need to report in sick.

Working from home is not guaranteed.

For each day you are working from home, please send me a list of what you have completed that day.

Let's have a one to one about your workload when we are both back in next week to see what is outstanding before you go on your PIP training."

I'm too broken to figure out if this is just her management style, or if I'm being asked to provide evidence of the work I'm doing. *Am I being paranoid? Or maybe this means I'll get the help I need at last.*

I'm so relieved I'm at home right now, so I can have a good cry.

I'm trying my best, teaching myself how to do this job; and trying to make sure my investigations move along.

But we're not set up to be able to do this. We're constantly firefighting, due to the number of people ending up in custody. I don't want to fire-fight. I want to investigate and solve crime and support victims. That's what I came here to do.

It's starting to dawn on me that maybe there's an issue with the number of people who are being arrested. Maybe there's too many because everyone has to make arrests to evidence them for OneFile.

Maybe the huge number of new officers, needing to make arrests, is creating a knock-on impact on those who have to do the interviewing?

I'm trying to stay at work, but I'm getting the impression that I may have no choice but to go off sick, let the workload pile up, and come back after some time off to the same problem.

At least for these couple of days, I have permission to be at home. *And thank goodness, I've then got three days off. It's another bank holiday weekend.*

Once again, I find the positives, and count my blessings that there's so many bank holidays during my time in CCID.

***

The Early May Bank Holiday weekend makes a huge difference, time relaxing, and lots of time with friends reminds me what matters in life, and how much I'm sacrificing my happiness for this job.

Back on shift, working mids at home, I pour my heart out to my Workplace Assessor during a meeting to review my progress.

She and Rosie have continued to be brilliant at motivating me; helping me to feel that I'm not the only one feeling like this.

I'm honest about just how much this job is sucking the life out of me. How much the additional time in CCID has impacted me, considering the poor experience due to the team dynamics, and lack of support to learn effectively.

She gets it, she's seen it all before; and tells me: "I have faith in you Olivia."

***

The next day Harriet wants to see me face to face for a meeting. It's a relief to have felt strong enough to drive back to Harrisville and see people.

The meeting feels constructive, I feel supported, comfortable, and that Harriet really cares.

Apparently, things are changing, someone new is joining the team, they are a substantive detective constable, and he'll be supporting my learning, starting next week.

And, apparently, I can also have a mentor, if I sign up for one. I just need to go to the intranet and find the form.

Somehow, it all feels a little too late. I've only got five weeks before I leave the team and move to LCID.

And then Harriet picks up a huge pile of paperwork, and starts handing it to me, in sections:

1. **The Discretionary Leave Policy**: 24 pages, that if I read them, may help me to understand what my rights are, in relation to my dad dying.

2. **The Workplace Adjustment Policy**: 16 pages, that may help answer my question about what measures could be put in place, to enable me to deal with the workload, at the same time as teaching myself the job, and manage my deteriorating health, without going off sick.

3. **The Attendance Management Policy and Procedure**: I skim read the 14 pages, and discover that you cannot go to the GP, go for blood tests, or any other health related appointments, to understand why your body and brain are not functioning, during a shift. These must be done on your rest days. Anyone who's ever tried to get an NHS appointment knows that's near impossible.

I leave the meeting with 55 pages of HR policies.

I feel like I'm being used as a case study for Harriet's One-File, for her promotion to sergeant.

Is this organisation where I want to spend the next decade of my life?

Fortunately, next week I have five more days of PIP2 training. I'm going to be learning, in depth, how to interview witnesses and victims. There will be role-play practice; in a supportive environment, with people I can trust and respect.

Ironically, I've already been interviewing witnesses and victims, for nearly 11 months.

Once that, and a couple of other shorter bits of training are complete, I can sign up for the suspect interview training. That will take place just over a year after I started interviewing suspects, and six months after I started in CCID; where all you do, shift after shift, is interview suspects.

My one court appearance

It's May 2024, and about 14 months since I first started familiarising myself with courts, during my visit to Marsham Magistrates Court.

I'd often thought about how long it would be before I had to take the stand, as part of one of my investigations. Today is that day.

Conveniently it's at Harrisville Magistrates Court, on an early shift day; so, I get out of dealing with yet another prisoner.

I never thought I'd thank a drunk driver, for enabling me to spend the morning getting through some of my workload; and the afternoon sitting around waiting for the court process.

Back in November on a night shift in Response, several members of my team and I had attended an incident together. A driver had been found by members of the public, parked in a very peculiar position.

Just off-road, on a grassy area, his car was wedged on a bollard and partially blocking an alleyway. It was clear that he'd tried to drive it, before getting stuck, and deciding to have a sleep.

I carried out the breath test, and he was nearly three times over the drink drive limit. Emily arrested him for the offence. Max further arrested him for Possession of Cannabis, and he and I took him to custody. I was sat next to the guy in the back of the car, Max kindly giving me enough leg room to move.

On the way there, the guy's behaviour was erratic, so Max called for a van, and we swapped vehicles with colleagues from the late shift, who were still on duty.

It was one of my favourite shifts, because I got to interact with so many colleagues, and really feel like part of a team. I even enjoyed being in custody, because I got to see how Max handled things.

The nearer Southpine custody was too busy to take our prisoner, so we had to transport him 30 miles to Harrisville. This happens surprisingly often. It's a long way home for some prisoners, worse if you get released from custody at the end of a late shift, around midnight, and there's no public transport.

It's also a long way there, if you're sitting in the back of the van, facing the prisoner. I'd had to listen to this guy ranting on and on and telling me: "I need a piss."

In a loud drunken voice, he kept saying: "I'm going to piss all over the floor." *Nice.*

I was so tempted to reply: "Listen you twat, we've been dealing with you for 90 minutes already. I need a wee too, but I'm not complaining about it. Us women don't have the luxury of whipping it out, and peeing anywhere like you do, so we have to learn to hang on. Man up, cross your legs, and get over yourself."

Ever the professional, I kept my mouth shut. But really, this job does test my patience!

As a result of that long, and painful journey to Harrisville that night, our drunk prisoner is now appearing at Harrisville Magistrates Court. He pleaded not guilty at his first hearing within weeks of the offence; and has waited nearly six months to have his day in court.

I won't explain the court process, and how much time is wasted; books written by The Secret Barrister talk about it, and how broken it is, far better than I could. If you've made it this far in my book; you'll probably find those a great read.

Mr Drunk Driver represents himself. He's found guilty, must pay a significant fine, and court costs. If he'd pleaded guilty at his first hearing, he wouldn't have had to pay the costs. He also loses his licence for a year.

The man was drunk, we had strong evidence that he was drunk, why he bothered putting himself through all this, I will never know. Many people do, adding to the pressures on the justice system.

Having now experienced court as a police witness; I wonder when the Kimberly case will be heard, when the CPS will ever make a charging decision; and when we will all be called to court.

A day back in uniform

Towards the end of May, something unexpected happens. I find myself digging my police uniform back out of the cupboard, where I thought it had gone to stay. Initially apprehensive, I realise it's an opportunity to try and get the outstanding OneFile action completed and I feel proud when I get it all out again.

We are told there is an unprecedented demand on Oakshire Constabulary, and our Response teams are not able to deal with all the 999 and 101 calls.

All detectives not dealing with a prisoner, not dealing with a witness or a victim interview, or taking a statement, need to get back into uniform, and help to clear the backlog.

We have a lovely Response sergeant, doing a placement in our team at the moment. Dean's been an absolute godsend, because I've finally been able to get some support, from someone with experience.

Learning from him is a dream, he's so patient and brilliant at teaching. His calming nature, and true passion for engaging colleagues, helping us on our learning journey, shines through. He's another of the handful of truly great leaders I meet on my policing journey; and he's usually based at Marsham.

It's starting to feel like that might be a place I'd be happy ending up working long term, if I stay that long; with my people experiences so far, I feel at home there.

All Response sergeants are sent to CCID for a 10-week placement; to learn how to review case files and provide case direction.

I think the idea is to encourage them to become detectives at some point. But more importantly, it eases the pressure on detectives, reducing the need for them to review all case files, and take on the risk filled task of providing case direction. This is a crucial part of the process of deciding what to do with a prisoner, or suspect, and their crime, and what goes to the CPS for prosecution.

Never did I think I'd be happy to be back out there in uniform, but it's a blessed relief. And even better, Dean and I both end up working out of Marsham, we're crewed together, all day. Plus, we're working a shift with the team I have covered with so many times. *Happy days.*

I just know Dean and I are going to get a lot done today. I'm not sure how much use I'll be, but I'll give it a good go and take all the guidance I can get from him.

During my six months in Response, I only worked with a sergeant twice. Once dealing with a bad driver with no insurance.

The other time was delivering an agony message to a mother of young twins, whose husband had been found dead after a night out with friends. I will never forget her scream when my sergeant told her the news. I had the awful job of trying to keep her gorgeous girls out of the room, with her mum, who I then had to break the news to.

Nothing prepares you for the complexity of these situations.

Dean and I smash through logs, because he knows the area like the back of his hand, and of course, he's a sergeant, so can make decisions without needing permission.

We deal with multiple issues, including clearing an abandoned motorbike from a golf course, and removing drugs paraphernalia from a bush. We uncover that a potential child safety referral, and domestic abuse issue is actually a neighbourhood dispute.

And we investigate a potential criminal damage by children in a play area. This is a great example of why there's an issue with police resources and why we're not getting time to do our investigations.

Dean drops me off at the edge of the play area, and I walk around the whole thing, trying to identify the damaged landscaping that has been reported. Eventually, I come across some tree trunks which I think have been positioned in an ideal way for children on bikes, to ride over them like ramps.

As would happen in nature, the outer layer of the bark has come away. Whether this has happened naturally, or because bikes have been riding over them, we will never have the evidence to prove.

Either way, this is not a crime, and certainly not something we should be spending time investigating. Someone has complained that children were playing.

They have no idea what other young people in the area get up to. Because there is a lot of money in Marsham, combined with some very deprived areas, and a lot of students.

If you keep your eyes open, you will see drug dealers daily.

You'll find them loitering in all the parks, and not far from schools and colleges. Their small, often across the body, drug bags are easy to spot. Many are using electric scooters, given to them by those higher up the drugs chain. Most are trying to hide themselves under headwear.

I learn more new things today than I have learnt in the last few months. It reminds me what, and how much, I loved about being a police constable in Response.

We get out and about, showing a police presence in various communities, we get to speak to victims, witnesses, and the public.

It's the policing people want to see us doing. It feels productive, it feels proactive, it feels efficient, and most of all it feels rewarding.

Today, I feel like I'm delivering value in the community; one of the reasons I joined.

Meeting my LCID team

In between all the incidents we investigate, when we're back at the station I notice the LCID team at the end of the office.

I've checked and know it's my new team on duty today, and there's going to be no better opportunity to meet them than now, considering I never received a reply to my emails.

I walk over to the bank of desks and introduce myself to the middle-aged man who is clearly the sergeant. He looks up as I approach and say: "Hi, I'm Olivia Gray, I'm joining your team in a few weeks time."

"Hello," he replies, and then introduces me to the other people at the bank of desks.

The team all appear friendly, saying hello with welcoming smiles, and one asks what I'm doing at Marsham today.

"I'm here to help to clear the logs. We've all been told we have to, if we don't have prisoners, interviews, or statements to do today."

Strange, why are they not doing the same?

My gut instinct is that I'm comfortable with these people, although I am always filled with positivity at the beginning of each new journey. And right now, I won't let anything spoil what I hope is going to be my favourite six months in my policing journey.

One of them is also on a trainee detective placement and will be leaving as I arrive. I will be getting his workload as well as bringing my own workload from CCID – I've already been told I won't be leaving mine behind. Why is he leaving his?

This is playing on my mind because it means inefficiency, with unnecessary travel back to Harrisville regularly. *How can you ever get stuck in and learn the ropes on each placement if you're dragging your old investigations along with you? There must be a better way.*

My future team all need to crack on with their day, and I must crack on with mine, so I say: "Goodbye, see you in five weeks."

There's light at the end of the tunnel. And I know from my countdown clock that's been keeping me going since the end of April, that I've only got 13 more shifts in CCID and another holiday to look forward to.

Later in the day, I bump into one of the team again.

"Hiya, how's your day going?" I ask.

"Yeah, good thanks. How's yours?"

"Good thanks. I'm really excited about joining you and have the opportunity to work with and learn from such an experienced sergeant. I'm just looking forward to feeling part of a team, that's really missing for me in CCID at the moment."

Their reply casts a doubt in my mind: "This team is great, including the sergeant. But he does like to take credit for other people's work."

Alarm bells ring, I know the damage this does to team morale.

This information, along with the fact that he never bothered to reply to my emails or attempt to welcome me to the team proactively, starts to cast doubt in my mind about my upcoming experience.

It's all the small things that build up, never one big thing, during my time at Oakshire Constabulary that make it a place I stop wanting to work in.

More than ever, I need to decide whether I really want to continue this journey.

Do I really want to start all over again, in a new location, albeit one I am familiar with, but with a whole new team and with a new workload, with new working practices and new learning styles?

Do I really need to do that for the fourth time in 18 months?

And it's also only for six months before I have to move on and start all over again.

***

There's something I haven't mentioned about the posting sheet that delivered the great news about my LCID posting a couple of months ago. It also came with bad news.

My last placement as part of the ADP, is in the domestic abuse team, part of the Public Protection and Safeguarding Department (PPSD).

Having grown up living with an alcoholic, it's not somewhere I relish spending any time, let alone six months. Four I could have coped with, but the powers that be changed the goalposts on the ADP and as a result, my entire experience here.

For most of the time, for trainees like me, the work in domestic abuse is just like CCID – the main difference being that it involves family members or intimate partners.

My experience and interests lend themselves to the team that looks after vulnerable adults, the PPSD team I'd applied for. I truly believed it was a place I would be able to deliver value, shine, and enjoy my job.

But no one knows what I can deliver because no one takes the time to understand us as individuals at Oakshire Constabulary.

Sadly, with a dire resource situation in the domestic abuse team, that's where I'm going, along with most of the other trainee detectives.

The even worse news is the posting sheet told me that is the team I'm being posted to, at the end of the ADP.

What this means for me is after six months in LCID, hopefully enjoying an environment I will excel in, I'll be posted to the domestic abuse team for the foreseeable future. And I've seen how hard it is to get out of teams you don't enjoy. I can see where my career is heading, and I don't like it.

Don't get me wrong, it's a vital and valuable team that is doing amazing work. I admire everyone who survives and thrives in it. It just has a terrible reputation, and no one has convinced me otherwise.

And I've recently heard that two of the sergeants there have walked out of their jobs, leaving more gaps to be filled.

Parents at peace

I arrive home from my day back in uniform, and my husband kindly opens the front door for me. I'm laden down with all my kit that needs to go back in the cupboard.

He looks anxious, unusual for him.

"My sister called me. Looks like my mum's dying. I'm leaving in a minute." And then he's gone.

I feel so bad. I can't go with him. I only have one day off tomorrow before starting a run of five shifts, including two PIP2 training days that I cannot afford to miss. *I have so much to do.*

She dies while he's travelling. Finally at peace after well over a decade living with Alzheimer's.

***

Three months into my CCID role, and my dad's vascular dementia had really kicked in. He'd started to make less and less sense when I visited him. His cancer was also taking its toll, making walking more and more difficult. We're blessed that his care home staff have been amazing.

In the past few weeks, he's been struggling to string sentences together and doing random things like tying his bed sheets round his head. *It's been hard to watch* as he gets more and more aggravated. *There's nothing I can do, except be there.*

***

Today is day one of my PIP2 Public Protection training. My mother-in-law died two days ago.

The group I'm training with are lovely. I'm pleased to see my Response sergeant, who is also on the training. We're partnered for a short exercise at the beginning, where you get to know and then introduce your partner to the rest of the group.

Totally unexpectedly when introducing me, he says to the group: "Olivia was one of the more trusted members of the team, so she was sent to Birchdene, as she could be trusted to work in a more isolated role."

He also praises my ability to find missing people, calling me the Misper Spoc (single point of contact). *I can't believe it, I'm so proud!!*

So it turns out that my move to Birchdene was more positive than I thought.

***

During the first break of the day, I'm taking a short walk on my own when I get a call from dad's care home.

"The GP has seen your dad this morning and put him in end-of-life care, he's deteriorated fast," one of the nurses tells me, in a kind and sympathetic voice. *They have to make these calls all the time.* "I'm sorry Olivia."

I fight the urge to cry. I was ready for this call, but nonetheless, it's still incredibly sad to hear someone say it. *Whatever pain this man has caused over the years, he's dying, and before long he will no longer be in my life.*

***

I visit him that evening. He's very weak and clearly on his way out. But not knowing how many days it will take, I make the decision that I will go back for my second day of PIP2 training.

I don't want to stall my detective training. I've come this far. I'll have to wait at least another month for another date. Then longer for all the subsequent training that will open for booking when I've completed this one.

Somehow, I'm able to compartmentalise, something I've never been great at but am learning in this job. I get through the second day of Public Protection training, learning more about the horrors people put others through.

I visit dad again that evening. His decline has progressed, and I'm reminded of how my mum declined at the same fast rate in the days before she died.

Now I have a big decision to make. I'm due back on shift for three lates from tomorrow. Even if I go to see him in the mornings, can I risk driving to Harrisville and being so far away?

No one is saying don't come in, they are asking me if I think I should. I have no idea.

I fight with my conscience all morning, trying to figure out what to do. And I go to the funeral directors to make plans for the inevitable.

Going through the motions of preparing for dad's death finally kicks in my sense of self-care, at last. I'm not going to work. I'm going to be with him, or at least stay local, until he dies.

***

I spend the next day and a half camped out in my dad's room at his care home. He's unable to speak or move. The once tall, broad, strong and intimidating man is now skinny and helpless, struggling to breathe, making a sound like the death rattle that I'd heard my mum make hours before she died.

I should just sit and read to him, or just to myself, while he's dying.

But I'm working. I've set up my work laptop on the tiny table, designed to hover over dad's bed when he used to eat. *It has become my desk.*

My drive to do a good job and misguided determination not to let people down is outweighing my ability to make a rational decision, even at a time like this. I've never been good at figuring out when to stop, when to put myself first, what are reasonable expectations to put upon myself or accept from others – until I break.

So here I am, embracing the time I've now got to teach myself how to complete a new document for a case. Something I should have had time to do in the office but never could.

Dad passes away peacefully, full of morphine the next day.

Finally at rest after a lifetime filled with little peace – an unwanted war-time baby who experienced too much abandonment in his life. *No wonder he engaged in self-sabotaging behaviours that undermined his relationships and pushed people away.*

***

I take the day after as bereavement leave, and then it's rest days. I work every day, to some extent.

Five days after dad's death, I go back to work. This whole time, Harriet has been away again, so I've been liaising with covering sergeants.

Back at Harrisville, today's covering sergeant is so kind to me. *I try hard not to cry.*

He says: "Sorry to hear about your dad. I won't give you a prisoner to deal with today. Just do what you can."

That lasts about an hour. The team is still decimated and there are too many prisoners to deal with. I spend the rest of the shift dealing with two men who have been fighting. *Here we go again.*

I spend an entire shift and more processing a prisoner and start an investigation that is going nowhere. *If I'd had that day with some peace, I might have been able to continue, but the pettiness of the situation and waste of police time tips me over the edge.*

I've come back to work too soon.

With Harriet back the next shift, she advises me to take the next two days off on bereavement leave. She understands parental bereavement. We finally find something to connect over.

Saying goodbye

It's June 2024, the day after my mother-in-law's funeral and two days before my dad's.

I'm having lunch with one of my best friends, the one whose toilet I relied on during my time in Response.

"What's the plan for your dad's funeral?" she asks, as we sip our large glasses of rosé wine, a sure sign of the warmer months.

"I'm doing a direct cremation. We'll just watch the body leave from the funeral directors, in a hearse."

"Do you follow it?" she asks, sadness mixed with surprise.

"No, no one goes. They take the body to the crematorium. A half-hour slot is booked for them to take the body into the chapel. It's basically the same process, but no guests or service." I reply. "Since my mum's I can't stand funerals – don't feel it's the best way for me to recognise someone's death. Plus, there's not enough people to invite to make it worth the energy organising a bigger event."

She looks at me with a smile filled with love and kindness. *She knows me better than anyone.* We've been through over four decades of life's challenges together.

It makes me think, for a second, whether I should have booked this kind of service. But I know it's right.

My husband, uncle and I celebrated dad's life the weekend after his death; with lunch and a pint in a sunny pub garden. *It was the perfect way to send him off.*

"What are you doing after you've watched him go?" she asks.

"I'm going back to work."

Her expression changes. *Now she's looking at me despairingly:* "Olivia, seriously. Do you think that's a good idea?"

"I'm fine honestly, thank you. My workload is out of control, despite doing some work every day of my bereavement leave. And I've only got a few shifts before we go on holiday. When I'm back I only have a few more shifts before I leave. I want to leave everything in a good state, so my cases don't collapse once I'm gone. I don't want my hard work and sacrifices to be wasted."

***

It's the day of dad's cremation. We're up with the birds and head to the funeral directors in the sunshine. *I think how lucky I am that the sun shines on the days I really need it to.*

We take a seat on their bench outside as planned, and the sun finds its way through the tall trees in the distance. *It's shining right on us,* taking the edge off the early morning chill. Another half an hour, and it would be too high in the sky to reach the spot we're in.

The hearse pulls off the main road into the small gravel car park, tyres crunching as they make their way through the open ornate metal gates. We exchange respectful smiles with the funeral service operatives, who drive through a further gate and disappear to collect dad's body.

We hear gravel again as the hearse slowly reappears, pulling to a stop between the two gates to give us a few minutes to pay our respects. The coffin is draped in a bluebell printed cloth. On the top is a single coral coloured rose that I cut from a rosebush at home this morning.

It was as if it had suddenly appeared for the occasion – I hadn't noticed it before today.

As we sit still, my husband squeezes my hand, and I remember the moment the hearse pulled into my mum's road – *the gut wrenching feeling this symbolic moment brings.* Just days before, the same memory had come rushing back to me as my mother-in-law's hearse approached us.

I can't hold back the tears.

They pull out of the gates and onto the long straight road. We watch until they disappear into the distance.

And at that moment, I decide I'm not going to work later today. I think I'm finally coming to terms with just how much I still put work first, even at a time like this.

And that, amongst other things I've been considering, needs to change.

It's time for a new chapter, with a totally new approach to work.

Part Five: Walking away

Final weeks

DID I MENTION I'M leaving?

In between dad dying and his funeral, I decided to resign. People thought it was because I was grieving. It wasn't. I don't make decisions like this lightly. I finally decided it was time.

Around the time of deaths and funerals, the substantive detective constable – who was promised to be my mentor and provide the support I'd really needed during the previous five months – arrived into the team.

Ryan and I haven't spent much time together yet, but now I'm leaving, he's tasked with helping me get my investigations ready to hand them over.

Once again, it's a joy to be working alongside someone, and I have a moment thinking, maybe, if it was like this, I could stay.

As we talk through the Kimberly investigation, he says: "You shouldn't have been working on this on your own, it's a complex case with over 40 exhibits. These usually go to the team that deals with serious or complex crimes."

Nothing surprises me anymore about this organisation, but my hands involuntarily raise into a shrug: "I didn't know they existed? No one told me at any stage of this investigation, and I've been working on it for nine months."

Ryan has no words in response. He knows what this place is like.

I explain more about the investigation, including the issue with the multiple crimes, custody records, and bail clocks.

"It became a nightmare because Kimberly was arrested three times, and I was never on duty. She ended up with four different solicitors representing her. They were from three different law firms. I won't bore you with how much confusion, bureaucracy, and administration time this has caused over the months, trying to unravel and merge these into one case."

I get the impression Ryan would rather be doing the talking, rather than listening to me. He wants to share his knowledge, but now I don't care. It's too late for me – I don't need it now. It's such a shame.

As he takes a break from the deluge of information to get a drink, I reflect on how much of myself I put into this investigation.

I spent so much time engaging with the victim and neighbours who became key witnesses in the case. They weren't always available during my shifts, and my diligence and determination never to let anyone down meant that I worked on many of my rest days. I couldn't let this investigation fail or be delayed in any way.

There were so many people involved that I have over 500 emails in my 'Kimberly' email folder.

I can't let that effort go to waste, so I download them all into a file, just in case someone needs something that's contained within them. Then there will be no excuse to say: "I didn't know," or "I can't find that information."

Responsibility is one of my values and I want there to be no reason for this case to fail – or certainly no reason for anyone to blame me for its failure. The blame game is rife at Oakshire Constabulary.

Five and a half months after starting the investigation, the case file was submitted to the CPS. The very same day, it was rejected because four of the CCTV file links had corrupted. They had been fine for months, then the moment they went to the CPS they weren't.

I have no idea how or why this happened, and nor does anyone else. But this issue had a big impact on the delays in the CPS making a charging decision, partly because I didn't know it was rejected, because I wasn't alerted. I'd found out weeks later.

In the end, the case file came back three times for changes to be made, additional information to be provided. Why they couldn't ask for all of it the first time I don't know.

Each time I went through the pain of trying to get someone to help me get it right. So much time is wasted through this lack of experience and support, I've been so frustrated by the wasted energy.

This has such a negative impact on the victim and us because it's all extra unnecessary time, engaging through emails, calls, and the convoluted way we communicate with the CPS via the crime management system.

Final few days

Early July, originally planned as a break between CCID and LCID, my husband and I spent a week in Italy.

It was a 'fly and flop' holiday, a term I hadn't heard until this summer. We didn't move from our hotel, and we've come back slightly less able to move our bodies because we've been so lazy.

I should be moving to LCID, but because I'm not, I'll be spending my final couple of shifts wrapping up my investigations as best as I can.

I don't have a line manager and no one is really interested in me, or my exit from the organisation. I've had one email from HR, just after I resigned a month ago, and nothing since.

When I resigned, I'd suggested to Harriet a plan for how I could work my final shifts to ensure everyone gets what they need from me. And to make sure I can hand my paperwork over to someone.

But Harriet was moved to the domestic abuse team a few weeks ago, so she has no interest in CCID anymore or what I do with my paperwork.

I was hoping to see Sophie, who's finished her five-month residential training, but she never came back to CCID. She was also sent to the domestic abuse team.

Someone needed to fill the gaps left by the sergeants who exited in a rush.

Final visit to Harrisville

It's my penultimate day and my final trip to Harrisville police station.

My police uniform and PPE are all neatly and tightly packed into the kit bag I'd been given at training school.

I'm relishing this final journey to the place I'd spent six months being a trainee detective constable and what should have set the foundation for the rest of my career.

A career I'd longed for and worked so hard for.

With reservations that it may get ransacked by Response officers if they find it, I take my kit straight to the post room, leaving it on a desk all labelled up, ready to be sent back to where it came from.

I visit custody for the final time and find my favourite custody sergeants on duty. I'm truly sad to say goodbye to these guys: "Thank you for making such a positive difference to my experience."

One starts to say some lovely words about how he'll miss me, and I look up to the ceiling to stop the tears. While he speaks, he starts to choke, and his reddening face makes me giggle.

"Blimey, please don't choke about me leaving," I say.

With a cheeky grin, always looking like he's going to do or say something naughty, he replies: "No one has ever asked me to stop choking before."

"Thank you, what a brilliant final memory of my time in custody." I say while laughing.

I track down one of my favourite detention officers in the fingerprint and mugshot room and hug him goodbye. We wish each other well.

As I leave this unique area of the police station, I reflect on how scary it had been when I first started. The anxiety of approaching the high desks, the pressure to say all the right words.

I really will miss these guys.

Back up to CCID, and I say my final goodbyes to the handful of people I'd worked with and admire so much. As it's the week where everyone has moved onto their next placement, there are new faces on the team. And the team seems bigger.

One is embarking on the same journey I had started six months earlier. He's just left Response and has the same deer in the headlights expression as I did, professing to know nothing.

I genuinely wish him luck. I hope he doesn't become one less detective too.

Two of the new team members have just finished their final placements and are now substantive detective constables. They've been posted back to CCID, much against their wishes, but it seems they are determined to make the best of it.

"Who wants all of this?" I ask the team, as I offer up my pile of paperwork that I've removed from my locker. "I have no line manager to hand it to."

"I'll take it," one kindly agrees, and I hand her all my investigation folders.

I feel bad because I know they all already have their own overwhelming and out of control workloads. I know that this paperwork, and the investigations on the crime management system that they support, will end up with them.

I've done my best with my investigations, but I know some of the work is certainly nowhere near good enough, and someone will have to pick up the pieces. Like I did when I picked up other people's investigations when I started on the team six months ago, including one investigation that had been doing the rounds in CCID for two years and is part of this pile.

Having no idea what is to become of my work plays on my mind, especially the Kimberly case.

I'm curious to know if my paperwork will just end up in a cupboard, to be forgotten. I expect someone will berate my work at some point, say I hadn't done a good enough job, say I didn't keep paperwork that I should have.

But I did all that I knew I had to do. It's all there. Diligent to the last. If there's anything missing, it's because I wasn't told or didn't have time to teach myself that I had to do it.

Now I must let go.

***

I walk slowly out of the building, where I've only just learnt to navigate all its corridors, stairways, and labyrinth of offices, treasuring every memory this walk sparks.

I hear a prisoner banging on a cell wall and shouting profanities as I walk into the car park. I'm reminded of Rob's language at training school.

I pass the marked and unmarked police cars, the forensics vans, and the unmarked detective vehicles.

One final exit through the large secure gates, turning right and out onto the streets of Harrisville, it's time to head home.

Last day

It's mid-July 2024, my last day at Oakshire Constabulary and I'm heading to HQ to return my IT equipment.

Driving there brings a mix of emotions and memories of training school. The building that my 32-strong cohort had trained in is no longer.

I remember wondering if I would feel sentimental about it being pulled down. I'm not. I hope the set up for training future police officers will be so much better. Maybe they'll even provide lockers?

And maybe they will make the signage more user friendly? For now, the signage and ability to navigate the site is still a challenge.

***

Handing over my IT equipment in what feels like an ever-growing faceless organisation is also made difficult. I arrive at an empty counter in an empty corridor. A telephone sits on a desk with a note next to it telling readers to pick up the phone and choose an option.

Following the instructions, I listen carefully to the options. Doubting whether I'm going mad, I listen three times. There is no option to return your equipment when leaving. Frustrated, I mutter out loud: "What if your option is: I'm trying to leave? What do you select then?"

Someone's walking down the corridor, she's overheard me and says: "Just press two."

Shortly after pressing two, a typical looking IT guy appears and reaches out to take my equipment without words. I'm so grateful for any human interaction as I leave this organisation. I have no manager to support and guide my exit, and I've still only had one email from HR.

Determined to use my experience to help others and hopeful that I can help make a change for all the incredible officers I've worked with, and future ones joining Oakshire Constabulary, I'm meeting with someone to do an exit interview.

I don't usually take up this opportunity, always suspecting nothing will ever come of it, but I feel compelled to do it here. I spend over an hour and a half sharing my 18-month experience and making suggestions for improvements.

The guy makes loads of notes. I even explain: "I have a lot of experience supporting leaders with their business strategies."

At the end, he says: "Thanks for your time. You've raised some serious concerns. Someone will need to follow up with you."

I'm delighted and reply: "I really want to help make a difference. I'd love to come back and speak to someone. See how I can help."

And then I leave HQ for the final time. Now I do feel a bit sentimental. I drive as slowly as possible through the security gates and up to the main road.

I have such a strong feeling of sadness at how this journey has panned out and how final this decision is.

***

Two weeks after leaving Oakshire Constabulary, I email the Police and Crime Commissioner. I offer to share my policing and strategy experience to support the Police and Crime Plan.

I never get a reply.

A month after leaving, I've also heard nothing from Oakshire Constabulary.

I send an email chasing, saying I'm interested to understand if there's going to be a follow up conversation and asking what has happened to the feedback I provided.

I'm told that the guy I'd spoken to during my exit interview has left Oakshire Constabulary. My feedback has gone up the hierarchy, they will decide where to send it next. If they need anything they will get in touch. She asks if I'm happy to be contacted.

Of course I am! I reply, saying I want to help Oakshire Constabulary avoid losing more officers. I let her know that I've been writing about my experience while deciding what to do next; and that I've already written 16,000 words.

I never hear anything back.

With no one with the power to make change interested in hearing me, I sit down and turn those 16,000 words into a book. Within four months, I've written over 90,000 words.

Epilogue

Why did I join the police?

I WANTED A NEW challenge that utilised my skills and expertise, my middle-aged wisdom, and I wanted to stretch my brain.

I wanted to solve problems, in areas that mattered, and I wanted to learn, every day.

I embrace and enjoy change, and I love variety.

Policing would deliver all that.

I wanted to do good in, and improve the quality of life, for the community, by being someone that cares, being an ear and listening to people's challenges. Sometimes that's all people need to take them down from the edge, to give them the boost they need to get themselves on a more positive track; or simply to see that there is another way, a more positive way to do things.

I wanted to work collaboratively to do that, be part of a team, with a strong and shared purpose, shared values and principles. I wanted to be part of an organisation and team of people who support each other, not fight against each other, to protect their own world.

I'm also fascinated by the human mind and behaviour. In the police, you get to study that, in real life situations that play out daily.

During my six-month application journey, it really felt like Oakshire Constabulary was authentic; they sold a good story, that I believed.

And my Ride Along experience showed me how a good team could operate.

Why did I stick it out?

I had hope, tenacity, and determination; and I was prepared to work damn hard.

I really wanted to stick it out for those 18 months. I couldn't have left earlier. I wanted to complete at least one of my detective placements, as a trainee detective constable. And I wanted to do my PIP2 training.

I could even have done another six months. LCID was where I really wanted to be, and I'd been allocated a location I was happy with; I believed it would be my best six months.

There are so many elements of policing that I really enjoyed, and people I respected told me I was good at, that I'd make a great detective. I also believed in myself; I knew I could be, with the right learning, support, and environment.

I was so privileged, to have been working with some of the most remarkable people I've ever met, and I didn't want to let them, or my victims down.

I didn't want to leave in the dead of winter. Summer is a much better time to take time out; we're all happier during the lighter days. And summer is a time to start new things, create new habits, be outside more, and be able to think clearly.

A good time to start again.

Why did I leave?

Many people have asked what made me leave, what was the final straw. But there wasn't one thing. There were many, many things.

Life is for living, and I want to feel alive. Sadly, the organisation sucked the life, and motivation out of me. I couldn't be the best version of myself. I became someone I didn't want to be.

I never thought the organisation would cause more stress than the job of dealing with all the people involved in the incidents and crimes.

Like most organisations, the reality on the inside is not the shiny exterior, painted during the recruitment process that is used to hook you into joining.

It is sad to look back, and see how naïve I was, about the reality of how police officers are treated in the UK.

All credit to those who survive this job; but what long-term affect does it have on their physical and mental health? I witnessed the impact this job already had on many people in the short time I was there.

In the end, the environment just wasn't right for me.

I wasn't living in alignment with my values. What was the point of pushing on and making myself ill? Because that's what happens when your life is out of alignment with who you are.

All employers need to remember: it's not all about you, employees have a choice about whether to come and work for you, whether to stay working for you. There's lots of other jobs and options.

And I have no problem reinventing myself, learning new things, and moving on.

1. I missed the warning signs

My gut was screaming at me, right from the start that the organisation wasn't right for me.

I'd missed so many warning signs, telling me this new career wasn't going to pan out as I hoped.

One friend had mentioned how her sister loved her job as a detective, but how she was being refused promotion. This, despite being asked to act in the more senior role that she was applying for, but only when it worked for the organisation.

A colleague I was working with when I started the application process said: "Don't do it."

That's all he said. It was a clear and simple message. I didn't question his advice; I didn't think he knew me well enough. It turns out he knew the organisation well enough to give this advice; he'd worked for Oakshire Constabulary a few years back.

My friend Suzanne talked about how her police friends were all relieved, when they completed their 30-year service, and left with their police pensions; how much they'd seen the job change over those years.

2. I was misled

They tell you all about the exciting detective roles, never giving the reality of what you'll spend many of your first years doing. They talk about teams that investigate major crime, gangs and organised crime, cybercrime, people trafficking and sexual exploitation, and the anti-terrorism, covert surveillance and specialist operations teams.

No one mentions the sausage factory that is CCID, or the desperate domestic abuse team. How your first years as a detective are spent investigating thefts, low level assaults, men fighting with other men, or their families.

That's how it should be, to learn the job. That was fine with me. But they need to be honest about it and do something to make CCID and the domestic abuse team more attractive areas of the organisation to work.

I found out too late about other routes into policing. In some forces, you do your police training, and then get time to study, and consolidate your training in real life situations. With the Police Now National Detective Programme, there's a really structured, and supported approach.

At Oakshire Constabulary, sadly the ADP offered none of this.

Aside to that, police training school did not set me, or my cohort, up for success. Five of us left in the first two years. Rosie and James are still hanging on in there; I'm so proud of them. The organisation needs them; middled-aged people with life experience who aren't about to retire.

Hearing from ex-police officers, the training done in the past gave a far better grounding of the actual job; and more focus on discipline and physical fitness, not just running. It also involved refreshers, continued exams, and getting back to training school regularly.

Sergeants would be much more involved in a probationer's progress; and trainers would come from other forces which ensured some of the behaviour we saw play out would be avoided.

In the old days, probationers would also have more exposure to important elements of the job that we never did, such as port mortems, and visits to courts, to build an understanding of the bigger picture.

I understand now why people don't approve of the ADP. The programme simply wasn't set up to develop people effectively, and there were better ways to become a detective.

Before I left, after changing the ADP from a two-year, to two-and-a-half-year programme, it was then extended to a three-year programme.

In their wisdom to make these changes, it would have been sensible to consider those of us already on the path; check in with us, see how we're doing, do something to make sure we got a better experience, once they'd realised it wasn't working. They didn't.

I really hope the changes they've made are positive for new entrants; and I hope the level of support has massively improved.

I did notice, at the time of writing, they were still delivering false advertising, raising hopes of exciting roles early in your career.

It is still not made clear how long you spend doing the basic roles. The reality is you can get stuck doing a job you don't enjoy for a very long time, with no escape. Because that's the reality of resourcing in Oakshire Constabulary.

3. I had to work on my rest days

We're told not to, but my workload played on my mind, and piled up so fast in my first months, that it felt like there was no choice but to work on most of my rest days.

How other police officers choose to manage their workload is their business. It will be down to how they've been taught, or their personality, character, and attitude – we all do things differently.

I am who I am. I care too much. I am motivated and driven by working hard and doing a good job. There's no point doing it if you don't do it as well as you can.

With no one really keeping an eye on my progress, I didn't see any alternative. I didn't want to leave my Response team, who I admired so much, with extra work to do when I moved on to CCID.

I also didn't want to take it with me. That didn't make sense to me, it would dilute my CCID experience, and I know I'd just be getting more while there.

I just wanted to have a clean break, as I rotated from placement to placement, so thought that was how I had to manage my workload. But that's not how things work.

The culture, embedded by the pressure to avoid the cost of overtime, means there's a constant battle over whether your workload transfers with you to your next role. It's another game that is played, and one which sergeants constantly fight over, because people are forever changing roles.

I never did calculate how much of my time the King got for free. It must have been at least a shift's worth of money.

4. I had to work on my sick days

Apart from the time I had Covid in 2020, before vaccinations were introduced, I rarely took sick leave my entire career. Within a month of training school I got my first tension headache, because of the dysfunction in the classroom. I worked from home that day, trying to catch up on my learning.

A month later, I got Covid again, along with two other cohort colleagues, during PST. We were forced to be off sick, and away from the classroom for several days. I took the opportunity to spend the time catching up on my learning.

Again, when I had my Response meltdown, I had three days off sick. I worked every single day, trying to get on top of my workload.

And in CCID, the same thing happened, not one day of sick or bereavement leave went by, without me switching on my laptop, and working.

Let's be clear, however much they tell you not to, time off sick was the only way to get some control of my workload; and find time to teach myself the job.

5. I'm a person, not a number

There is little focus on the individual at Oakshire Constabulary. They don't look at us that way; at what we're good at, or what our needs are, before posting us to a particular team, or area of the organisation.

If they had, my team in CCID may not have been filled with trainees. If they had, everything could be different.

Unfortunately, everything is based simply on operational demands, without looking at the bigger picture; without looking at the people. Like society in general, the focus is on the economics, not the culture.

As a result, we individuals sacrifice everything, and the organisation doesn't budge. It's only when some individuals bend the rules, under the radar, that some sense can be applied, and little changes can be made, that make a huge difference.

6. Multiple line managers

When you're rotating between placements, your multiple line managers don't have a vested interest in you; no one else keeps a close eye on your progress.

Apart from irregular meetings with your Workplace Assessor, there's no consistent support. And they've got too much on their plates, without having to do the job of a line manager; or trying to encourage you not to leave, like mine constantly had to do.

Line management is an issue in all organisations I've worked for, but at Oakshire Constabulary it's layered with further complexity.

To become a sergeant, there are many hoops to jump through. Constables become acting sergeants through that journey and are allowed to lead teams. They are often absent, focused on, and developing their own careers.

Sadly, their training isn't equipping all of them to be good leaders or understand how best to manage or support their teams. All too often they are head down in their computers, ticking boxes for statistics.

Not everyone should be a line manager, and not everyone should be a sergeant. Just because there's a rank structure in an organisation, doesn't mean everyone should climb it.

7. I was a carer

And the organisation didn't support me when I asked for help.

8. IT wasn't fit for purpose

There's some basics that need to be fixed. Ensuring trainees have all the systems needed to do the job, applied to their laptops. Being given a list of those systems, what training is needed to use them, and where to access that training, would also help, enormously.

Finding out, ad hoc, as you need them, waiting ages to get them applied retrospectively, and then finding out you need time to train before you use them, is a waste of everyone's time.

I never heard back about the missing police emails. This is an issue that could be having a big impact on policing in Oakshire. This could make a big difference to the service provided to the public, and to victims.

I wonder how many people have lost faith in the police because of this issue alone.

9. I hate cameras in my face

Social media has so much to answer for, contributing to a wholly disrespectful society, where privacy is destroyed through an obsession to film and share everything.

People will never understand the invasion it is to be filmed, while trying to do your best to deal with difficult incidents; or being a victim in a vulnerable situation.

Publishing this content should be made illegal. Or everyone who thinks this is OK should have footage of them published that they don't want published and see how they feel.

Imagine sticking a camera in the face of a doctor trying to save someone's life? Or a teacher trying to teach a class. OR people behind the tills in any retail establishment.

Why is it ok to do this to police officers?

10. Society is in free-fall

Society in the UK is so broken, and I could sense an increase in the unrest brewing. At the time I started to write this book, riots were breaking out in the UK.

I was impressed by the response of the new Labour Government, and the justice system, to fast-track cases of rioters, and those inciting hatred, and get them convicted so quickly.

However, this is only possible where there is a strong focus, on a particular area of crime.

This immediate response to a dangerous evolving situation, will have been to the detriment of all the other cases those police officers, and the courts were working on at the time. The rest of their workload won't have gone away; and other investigations would have been on hold, impacting many individuals' lives.

11. People don't respect the police

I know there are bad apples in the police, I've met a few along the way. Some need help to change their behaviour. They are who they are because of their experiences, and their environments. Others are most definitely in the wrong job and need to be removed.

But there's not as many as the media makes out. And trust me, I've worked in so many organisations, I've seen bad apples in all of them. It's just the police are under so much more scrutiny than other organisations, and the media.

Society loves a negative police story. Social media has made this so much worse, so many opinions from people who don't know the full story.

I defy anyone, who has not done a shift as a police constable, to cope with the variety of incidents they have to deal with, in just one shift. The incidents happen when they happen, there's no control over when.

Depending on resourcing, in a single shift an officer could have to deal with all, or many of these:

- Being first on scene at a major RTC (road traffic collision). Having to look for bodies, and having no idea how many there are, or what state they will be in. Sometimes finding dead bodies, sometimes severely injured, and sometimes the relief that despite the mangled car they are trapped in, the occupants are still all in one piece, including a small child. And then having to manage the traffic, selfish people speeding past, or rubberneckers trying to film. Set up cones, create cordons, call the incident through for additional resources. All of this, at the same time.

Imagine your 10-hour shift starting like this? And, with no time to think, you're onto the next incident...

- Dealing with a fall-out in a family home (a domestic). Figuring out who is to blame, deciding who to remove from the property because someone must be, to avoid any risk. Figuring out if one person can go to another place, stay somewhere else overnight until things have calmed down. And probably drive them there. And if not, if it is appropriate to arrest and put an individual in custody overnight. Depriving them of their liberty. And using up additional police resources, as they will then need to be interviewed by a detective, an investigation and case created.

- Being first to hear the initial story from a rape victim, and ensuring the investigation doesn't collapse, because you didn't ensure every scrap of evidence is gathered.

- Being the officer that must help Social Services remove a child from an abusive home.

- Being out looking for a missing teenager; one that will be missing again next week. Knowing that their issues probably won't ever be resolved, and their lives are set to derail completely. In the system forever more. And engaging with the parents, who have given up trying to get the help they need, to navigate their own issues; let alone the inevitable issues their children suffer from.

- Dealing with a commercial burglary, or worse, a residential one; and the resulting fear of the victim, and their neighbours.

- Then finding the patience to explain to someone, that the threat to kill they've reported is unlikely to be anything more than someone mouthing off at them.

- And then you're sent to do a hospital guard, or deal with yet another RTC which you know was caused by bad driving. Someone driving too fast, selfishly, dangerously, not paying attention, using their mobile. So, not definitely not an 'accident'.

You're exhausted, and know you're going to be off late, again.

Please be kind to police officers. One day you could really need one, as people always discover on the worst days of their lives.

What I've learnt about myself

Response was where I had the biggest impact on people's lives, you're constantly problem solving, and that's what I love to do.

The job I applied to do was not for me: being a detective in the current climate, and with the current set of circumstances at Oakshire Constabulary.

I knew I loved learning, and how much I enjoy learning from others, in a trusted environment. But on this journey, I discovered just how much I need to learn by hearing from and observing others, being taught in a structured way, and doing the job at the same time.

After leaving, I asked myself several times if I bit off more than I could chew this time; was it a challenge too far, particularly at my age?

But I still believe it could have worked, if I'd had the right support; if providing support to trainees was something Oakshire Constabulary did consistently. The sink or swim approach is not acceptable; particularly if you want diversity, and life experience in a workforce.

I discovered that the person I am, and the organisation Oakshire Constabulary is, are not compatible; and this career was not going to do my health and wellbeing any good.

I was never going to be able to do the job as well as I wanted to do it; and stay fit and healthy, in body and mind.

I understand more about who I am, and what I need, to fulfil my desire to always do my best. And what compromises I am prepared to make, when I can't do my best.

I know for sure that my strong work ethic was ever present, it always will be, so allowing chronic stress to build was inevitable in that environment. I won't let this happen again, ever.

Police forces need to find ways to support people like me, there should be a place for all of us. But without the skills in place for managers to identify and nurture us, we will be few in numbers. Sadly, society, the vulnerable and victims, lose out.

***

Now I know it's time to challenge myself in ways that are a lot less stressful. I've put the work in during my working life; it's time to slow down. I've learned to go easier on myself.

Without constant, chronic stress in my life, my mind is now clear, I'm more creative, I've explored new ideas, new options for my working life, and embarked on them. Including writing this book.

I'm finding that I can learn and retain information like never before; and just how much I love writing and having headspace for the creativity that requires.

I know I need work that challenges me but doesn't cause me unnecessary stress; and I need to put my health and wellbeing first. I am finally doing that.

I've finally realised that I can just let most of life unravel in a more natural way.

And as a result, everything has been falling neatly into place for me. Some incredible new people, and ideas, have come into my life. I'm excited for the opportunities they have started to bring.

I intend to follow this guidance from Dr Elaine Aron, about highly sensitive people: You don't need to accept roles that will cause overwhelming stress and overstimulation. Others may thrive in those positions that would be detrimental to you. Working extended hours isn't necessary and may actually be counterproductive – shorter working periods might be more appropriate for your wellbeing. While you may not want to openly discuss this approach, maintaining your health and staying within your optimal stress levels is essential for being able to effectively support and help others.

I describe my policing journey as: "an utterly crazy idea, but one I have no regrets about."

It was an incredible journey that I am privileged to have gone on.

Leaving was a very hard decision, but one I will never regret; like the decision to join in the first place.

I hope my story can help others to feel less alone, and out of control.

And, like every other police officer who has written about the job, I hope someone listens, and makes changes for the better.

Afterword

W<small>HILE WRITING THIS BOOK</small>, His Majesty's Inspectorate of Constabulary and Fire & Rescue Services (HMICFRS) announced the results of a PEEL inspection of Oakshire Constabulary.

PEEL stands for police efficiency, effectiveness and legitimacy and HMICFRS independently assesses the UK's police forces and fire & rescue services – in the public interest.

The inspection looks at how well these organisations perform in nine areas of policing, rating each area outstanding, good, adequate, requires improvement or inadequate.

The assessment completed while I worked there rated the organisation adequate or below in all but one area.

The main reasons we do the job are the areas the organisation is worst at. I expect it's because of the layers and layers of bureaucracy, box ticking, duplication, inefficiency, and lack of training and support.

The Inspector told the population of Oakshire not to worry, he was sure things would get better.

Sadly, Robert Peel's original nine policing principles have been left by the wayside, replaced by constantly changing versions, at each of the UK's 45 territorial police forces and three special police forces.

And as a result, losing any strength of conviction, most solutions in modern day policing just end up having a negative impact on frontline police officers, those at the bottom of the pile, but who the public rely on, on their worst days.

One day, I sincerely hope that there will be enough positive, joined up change in the UK, that these stories aren't repeated.

In the meantime, let's focus on the incredible, awe-inspiring job our police officers do; and be grateful for the sacrifices they make.

Acknowledgements

THANK YOU TO EVERYONE who supported me, during my time as a police officer, and with this book, you know who you are.

Thank you to everyone who championed me or challenged me.

Thank you to everyone who tried to support me, I know you were doing your best. That's all we can do.

Thank you to all the victims, or rather survivors, that I had the privilege of supporting, and carrying out investigations on behalf of. And all the witnesses who supported those investigations. Thank you for putting your faith in me. Thank you for your feedback. It meant the world to me. I was new and I was learning; I worked my hardest and did my best for all of you.

To all the people underserved by society, I'm sorry that society has failed you, and continues to fail people like you. Caring for young children is undervalued in our society, as is supporting parents.

There's no such thing as a bad child; only children from challenging backgrounds. When children are labelled as 'bad' their lives become a self-fulfilling prophecy.

Thank you to the suspects that I interviewed, whose lives have been impacted by trauma, been underserved by society, or by those meant to love and care for you. To those of you whose crimes were against your perpetrators, or only impacted yourself. I understand it is hard when everything feels stacked against you, and I hope you can break the cycle. I know for some of you, going to prison is no way to learn a lesson. I know each time you come out, to nothing, or back to your perpetrators, you're a little more broken than before.

To the man with the Van Gogh tattoo, thank you for sharing your story with me in reception at midnight, as you waited for a lift home from my colleagues. I hope you have been able to return to a positive path. You've done it before; you can do it again.

To the paramedics I spent many hours with, you are awesome, and amongst the calmest people I've ever met.

To those of you unhappy at reading my story, because you don't agree, or you have identified yourself and don't see yourself in the best light, I hope one day your minds are open enough to learn. Ask more questions, judge and dictate less.

To those who took deliberate action to make life difficult for me or were simply not bothered enough to support me, you need to look inward, at yourself. If that's the kind of person you are, being a police officer, or a leader, isn't for you.

To anyone not prepared to grow or change, I have a simple message for you: be you, but do not hurt other people, or animals.

For those of you in need of support because this highlights issues in your life, if any of this book resonates with you, and you want to share your own stories, and frustrations to get it out of your system, please speak to someone.

Just starting to speak your story out loud is a brave and releasing thing to do. There are people out there that care and want to help. You just have to keep looking for them.

Please don't give up. You're not the only one.

Inspiration

Adam Kay

As I was working on this book, I rediscovered my love of reading. I finally had the time to quench my thirst for knowledge; especially in ways that help me grow.

I read Undoctored, by award-winning comedian, and writer Adam Kay; his memoir about life in the NHS. Our stories are remarkably similar.

Right at the end of Undoctored, Adam includes some words that are so powerful, that when I read them, first I cried, then I felt my whole body relax. Like a great friend, or therapist, his words made me recognise the impact of the decision I had made to leave policing.

I feel compelled to share it. Thank you, Adam.

"It's ok to change your mind. If you're living a life that doesn't speak to the real you, then you're allowed to press the reset button. You will feel the improvement, the people around you will notice it. No job in the world is worth destroying yourself over. It's ok to take a break, or step away altogether if that's the right thing to do. Only you know what's in your heart. You will sleep a lot better."

In the same way Adam talks to those responsible for recruiting doctors, I ask those responsible for training and promoting tomorrow's police officers:

1) Are you choosing the right people for the job?

2) Are you training them the right way?

Dr Rangan Chatterjee

I have so much respect and admiration for Dr Rangan Chatterjee and his work in the health and wellbeing space. I love his books and through them and his Feel Better, Live More podcast I've learnt so much about how to live well. Sleep is now my number one health priority.

My mind has been opened and sometimes blown away. I've made some big changes in my life because of the knowledge I've gained from him and his incredible guests, many of whose books I've also read. And without which I'd probably have carried on pushing myself in the wrong job, until I got sick, and died young, like my mum.

I started listing some of my favourite Dr Chatterjee podcasts, but the list got too long to include here!

Other books I'd recommend

Dr Gabor Maté's Myth of Normal, When the Body Says No, In the Realm of Hungry Ghosts, and Scattered Minds
Dr Gordon Neufeld & Gabor Maté's Hold On to Your Kids
Julia Samuel's Every Family Has A Story

Dr Elaine Aron's The Highly Sensitive Person
Charisse Cooke's The Attachment Solution
O. N. Ward's Husband, liar, sociopath
Chris van Tulleken's Ultra-Processed People
Eckhart Tolle's The Power of Now
Paul McGhee's Shut up, Move on

Quotations

There are millions out there, but these work for my story.
Buddhist nun and mindfulness movement pioneer, Pema Chodron: "Nothing ever goes away until it has taught us what we need to know."
Carl Jung: "The reason for evil in the world is that people are not able to tell their stories."
Joanne Rowling: "There are more important things in this world than being popular. That doesn't mean it's more important to me to be right. It means it's more important to me to do the right thing."

Useful websites and places to get help

https://refuge.org.uk/
https://www.womensaid.org.uk
https://www.nationaldahelpline.org.uk/
https://www.autism.org.uk/
https://www.adhdfoundation.org.uk/
https://adhduk.co.uk/
https://www.missingpeople.org.uk/
https://drchatterjee.com/

Making a silent 999 call

Calling 999 from a mobile: if you can't speak or answer questions, press 55 or tap when prompted and your call will be transferred to the police. The police will usually be able to find your location.

Call 999 from a landline: if you can't speak or answer questions and the operator can only hear background noise, they'll transfer your call to the police. If you replace the handset, the landline may remain connected for 45 seconds in case you pick it up again. Calling 999 from a landline automatically gives the police information about your location.